HE WHO DARES...

DEL BOY

HE WHO DARES...

MY GENUINE AUTOBIOGRAPHY

thePeckhamPress

3 5 7 9 10 8 6 4

Published in 2015 by Peckham Press,
a division of Trotters Independent Traders (New York, Paris, Peckham).

Ebury Press is an imprint of Ebury Publishing,
20 Vauxhall Bridge Road,
London SW1V 2SA

Ebury Press is part of the Penguin Random House group of companies
whose addresses can be found at global.penguinrandomhouse.com

Penguin
Random House
UK

Copyright © Shazam Productions Limited 2015

Shazam Productions Limited have asserted their right to be identified as the author
of this Work in accordance with the Copyright, Designs and Patents Act 1988

Only Fools and Horses was written and created by John Sullivan OBE for the BBC.
He Who Dares is produced and published by Ebury Press with the support and
involvement of the family of John Sullivan OBE, who sadly died in 2011.

Picture credits: © BBC and © Shazam Productions Limited

www.eburypublishing.co.uk

A CIP catalogue record for this book is available from the British Library

Hardback ISBN 9780091960032
Trade Paperback ISBN 9780091960049

Printed and bound in Great Britain by Clays Ltd, St Ives PLC

MIX
Paper from
responsible sources
FSC® C018179

Penguin Random House is committed to a sustainable future for our business, our readers
and our planet. This book is made from Forest Stewardship Council® certified paper.

AUTHOR'S NOTE

The following is a recreation of events and conversations as I remember them. In order to protect the privacy of certain individuals some of the names and other pieces of identifying information were changed… but then it got confusing so I thought, *Sod it* and put it all back the way it was.

For Mum

CONTENTS

ACKNOWLEDGEMENTS

I would like to thank my dearest, darling significant other, Raquel, the love of my life and mother to our son, Damien, who was, and still is, the best thing I have ever created. I would also like to give my heartfelt love and thanks to Rodney, Cassandra and Joan, and, of course, Mum, Grandad and Uncle Albert (God rest your soles). Thanks also goes to those others whom have helped make up the stitching in the rich tapestry that is my life to date: Trigger, Denzil, Boycie, Marlene, Mike, Jumbo, Albie (RIP), Reenie (RIP), Sid, Ron, Ronnie, Paddy, both Lennies, Abdul, Alan, Solly, Dr Becker (RIP), Alberto (RIP), Junie, Nat, Shazza, Amos, Pam, Joe, Mia, Nancy, Peter D, Paul B, Chas, John Boy, Dougie, Limpy, Dippy, Perry, Terry, Monkey, Chunky and Father O'Keith (RIP).

Finally, I would like to thank the Nag's Head public house and Star of Bengal restaurant, Peckham, for providing the necessary fuel and refreshments between writing sessions.

FOREWORD

It was with great pride, surprise and terror that I was asked to write this, the foreword to the autobiography of my older brother Derek 'Del Boy' Trotter. I thought long and hard about what I should and shouldn't say, and how I should and shouldn't say it. I phoned Del Boy and asked for his advice, and he told me to 'stop being a tart and just write the bloody thing'. Finally, after consulting with my wife, Cassandra, and a qualified solicitor*, I decided to go with a cautiously honest approach. So here goes.

I have known Del my entire life and I can say without any doubt whatsoever that he is, and always has been, a very unique person. As anyone who has ever met Del will confirm, it is impossible to do so without being deeply and indelibly affected in one way or another.

My earliest memories of Del are of him standing in front of a mirror (up until I was four I thought he was twins), and growing up he wasn't just a brother but also a father figure and hero to me on occasions.

In business Del has always tried his utmost, and with mixed results – I don't want to say too much about this particular area, only that I think it's important to remember that none of us are perfect.

It's probably also worth keeping in mind that, while Del does have many talents, the English language (or any other) isn't one of them – up until very recently he thought a semicolon was what Elvis died of.

Del and I haven't always seen eye to eye, and we are different in many ways (height, build, hair colour, hobbies, interests, artistic taste, business and fashion sense, temperament, and general worldview), but in another sense we are very similar. We share the same surname. We both like curry. I can't think of anything else right now, but I'm sure there's loads.

Needless to say, him having been such a strong guiding force in my life, I learned a lot of invaluable lessons from Del over the years, albeit mostly from his mistakes.

Finally, whatever anyone thinks about him, it can't be said that he isn't loyal or that he doesn't defend those he cares about to the hilt. His heart has always been in the right place, and while the jury may still be out on his brain, I love him and am most of the time proud to call him my brother.

Rodney Trotter
April 2015

* Rodney Trotter has not viewed any of the material contained herein and so does not and cannot verify or endorse said material nor be held responsible for its publication nor accountable for any legal actions that may or may not arise as a result.

INTRODUCTION

When the bird at Ebury Publishing got in touch and asked me if I'd ever considered writing my life story, I had to be honest and say yes, I have, many, many times. It's just, what with my having always been a man of action rather than words, I'd never found the time to sit down and make a really good go of it. But now that I'm semi-retired and enjoying my days of hard-earned rest sitting around staring at the carpet, I thought: *Yeah, why not? After all I've lived a rich and eventful life, why not share that with the world for a decent cut of the profits.* Lucy (I think that was her name, it was a while back now) was well pleased and couldn't thank me enough (but then I had laid on a bit of the old *apres moi, la deluge*, which in my experience is enough to soften up the toughest of birds), but I told her she'd have to discuss the matter with my financial advisor, and brother, Rodney, before I churned any words out. So I gave her his number and said bonjour for now (never make yourself look too keen). Rodney rang me five minutes later – so they must have had a pretty in-depth chat – and if Lucy had sounded excited, he sounded like he was having kittens! At first he'd thought it was his mate Mickey Pearce winding him up (Lucy does have an unnaturally deep voice for a bird).

Rodney then tried his best to put me off the idea (he's always doing that) but it was too late, I'd already found a Bic down the side of the armchair and was hunting about for a piece of paper. I didn't fully realise it at the time, but I'd been struck by the author bug. And from that day to this I've done pretty much nothing else but write: poems (well, limericks), short stories, longer stories, shopping lists, betting slips, I don't care, I just have this deep, burning need to express myself. And the really great thing, now that I'm not as lively on my feet as I used to be, is that I can do it all sitting on my arse.

When I told people I was writing a book some of 'em laughed. Fair enough I suppose, most people think Rodney's the main book-lover in the family (even though most of the material he ever read came in plain brown envelopes), but the truth is that I actually own a lot of books, double figures at least, and I've read and enjoyed a few of 'em. Classics too. A few years back I started reading that *To Kill a Mockingbird*. I didn't get to the bit where the bird got murdered, but what I did read was brilliant!

It's true that, as a writer, my style is more suited to the screen than books (I've had some blinding movie ideas, but more on that later), so before I got started proper, I got myself some books that I felt were similar to what I was aiming to achieve, the biographies and business guides of Lord Alec Sugar, Sir Richard Branston, all of that mob off the *Dragon's Den* etc. My other half helped too, getting me one of them chordroid jackets, you know, the ones with the leather patches on the elbow. Well, you've gotta feel the part, ain't you? Not that I'd ever wear it outside the flat, but I do find that slipping it on helps get me into the right frame of mind to bang out a bit of prose (and it comes in handy when you just wanna give your elbows a good lean on something). I also invested in one of those computer dictation things, where you speak and the computer listens and does the writing for you, sort of like a satnav for people who can't be arsed to type. There must have been something wrong with it though, 'cos I got one line out and it asked me what language I was speaking.

Lucy took a look at the first draft and asked me if I'd considered using a ghostwriter (and a dictionary, saucy mare), which I hadn't. Not that I've got anything against ghostwriters but, as I explained to her, this is my life story, not a horror story. Anyway, I took her up on the dictionary tip and went back and did a few rewrites. And this book you're reading now is the final result of my endeavours.

You probably don't realise it, but you are a very lucky person, 'cos not only have you made a very wise investment in a proper, pukka book (it's got footnotes, brackets, introverted commas, context, subtext, teletext, the lot!), but you are also quite literally holding my life in your hands. It's all there, the highs and the lows, the laughter and the tears, the sunshine and the rain, the… wide and the narrow, and so on and so forth. So pour yourself a drink if you're thirsty, if not, don't bother, and make yourself comfortable while I take you on the journey that is my life to date. It took me about seventy years going the long way, you'll manage it in a few hours.

Bonnet de douche
DT

CHAPTER 1

WHACKING BULLETS
WITH TRIGGER

I can't remember being born, I was too young at the time, but it took place on 10 December 1945, and most people in my area agreed it was the most exciting thing to have happened to Peckham since the blitz. With the end of the Second World War, my dad, Reg, didn't have to pretend to be an air raid warden any more and could get back to some proper lazing about. If nothing else, the owners of the houses on his patch could rest assured that their belongings were safe. Reg had got out of conscription due to 'back problems', but anyone who knew him knew that the only problem he had with his back was his addiction to lying on it.

Him and my mum, Joan, got married at Our Lady of the Divine Rosemary, Peckham. Father O'Keith performed the ceremony. I don't remember that either, but I'm sure he did a smashing job.

My earliest memories are of Mum looking down at me, a glowing vision, like Marilyn Munro with the sun behind her, and of her rocking me to sleep in her arms, singing a lullaby between puffs on a fag. At the time we were all living in a two-up two-down on Orchard Street.

I remember when I was about four or five, Mum had a job waitressing at a little cafe just round the corner from us, and most mornings I'd stop off there and she'd sneak out a little cake for me and some lard on toast for Reg. The place was filled with smoke and everything you touched was slippery with grease, you could see where drops of it had left trails on the walls. All you could hear was the clanging of pans and people coughing their guts up. I loved it!

They were rough times back then, but they were good times just the same. And you didn't have to worry about getting mugged or nothing. What with the local villains keeping watch over the manor, things like that just didn't happen. People in general were just a lot friendlier back then. They had to be or they'd get their heads kicked in. For me though, every day was like one big long adventure, which is why I hated it so much when I had to join Dockside Junior School.

From day one, school and I didn't see eye to eye. I got into so many fights I'd come home black and blue most days.

'He's been fighting again, Reg,' Mum said.

'Tell him to tell the teacher,' Reg said.

'The teacher knows,' I said, 'he's the one I've been fighting with!' That's the sort of place it was. On my very first day I got the cane. The English teacher asked me what always came at the end of a sentence and I said a parole date. Another time I had to stand up in class and count aloud to twenty. I got to ten then went into jack, queen, king... But that was all I knew back then. Education weren't that important in my house.

As a nipper, me and my mates would go exploring the local bomb sites. To us they were like giant playgrounds. One day we found a couple of bullets so we stuck 'em in a vice and gave 'em a whack with a hammer. My best mate at the time was a boy named Colin Ball. He looked like a horse, so he wound up getting the nickname Trigger (back then though, he was mostly known as either 'Colin' or 'Oi you'). Anyway, it was that day whacking the bullets with Trigger that I had what was to become the first of many brushes with death. See, one of the bullets ricocheted off a rock and came right back at me. I can still remember the ping and the whistle it made as it whizzed past, missing me by only a few inches. I was well lucky. Trigger was standing behind me at the time and somehow managed to knock the wind out of the bullet with his head. He was unconscious for a bit (at least I think he was, it was sometimes hard to tell with Trigger) and he had a bugger of a bruise on the side of his bonce, but it didn't seem to bother him too much.* It was lucky he got in the way really 'cos that bullet could have hit someone.

Some people thought that this incident went some way to explaining why Trigger ended up the way he was, but I'm not sure. He'd always been a bit odd – I used to catch him eating wood sometimes, and this was long before any head injuries that I knew of. Other times I'd catch him laughing at the telly. That don't sound too weird, but he'd do it when it weren't even on. To be fair, Trig hadn't exactly had the most brilliant start in life. His mum, Elsie, was known as being a bit of a goer. On his birth certificate, at the bit where you write the father's name, she'd put 'some soldiers'. Trigger didn't like to talk about it, just saying that his dad had died a couple of years before he was born. It was generally agreed though that his dad was Donald Turpin (brother of Mum's best mate, Reenie). It all happened by accident. The accident being a single Guinness and a shuffle in the dark by a pond. Elsie and Donald had been at the Peckham Rye fair and one thing led to another. When Elsie started showing, she claimed she'd been 'visited by an angel!', leading the rest of the Ball clan to

---

* I just realised this was probably more Trigger's brush with death than it was mine, but I witnessed it, so I can claim some of that brush.

start making plans for the arrival of a new messiah. But Donald had been heard bragging about how he'd lost his virginity on the night of the fair, giving full details of the time and place, and was therefore fingered as a much more likely suspect than the Archangel Gabriel. This was a great relief to the long list of suspects, which included the Christmas relief postman, Melvin the window cleaner, Reg Bleedin' Trotter and several soldiers from the Royal Artillery field-gun display team (who still remained Elsie's preferred choice judging by how she filled out the birth certificate).

When the baby was born, the family looked at it and tried to find one single feature they could recognise as a link to its father. Eventually they found it: its gormlessness.

Trigger was brought up by his grandparents, Arthur and Alice. Arthur was a road sweeper and was only too happy to pass on the legacy.

I quickly formed my own little gang. Along with Trigger there was Boycie, a decent enough lad even if he was as tight as Buck Rogers' spacesuit. Funny-looking too. When a child's born the midwife usually gives it a slap to get it breathing, in Boycie's case the midwife took one look at him and slapped his mum. Still, a bloke can't help how he looks, it's what's on the inside that counts. Although in Boycie's case the inside was a bit mixed up 'n all. You knew with Boycie that, when the chips were down and you needed someone to stand by you and cover your back, someone you could trust and rely on, it wouldn't be him. He couldn't help it, his old man was one of those dads you could never please. Whatever Boycie did he got an earful for it. He could have come home with a suitcase full of silver and his old man would've clipped him round the ear and asked why it weren't gold.

Then there was Jumbo Mills, a good mate with a heart of gold, even if he did rub people up the wrong way. He had a gob on him, which led to us having quite a few scraps, but I always won so I tolerated it.

Then there was Albie Littlewood. Thick as thieves, me and Albie were. Shame how things worked out.

There were a couple of others who came and went, Mickey Walker, better known as 'Fatty' (on account of how fat he was), and Kenny Harris, better known as 'Monkey' (on account of his ears and the fact that he started shaving when he was ten).

We used to have some right laughs. I remember one time me and Albie let down some tyres. You should have seen the palaver it caused. Everyone had to get off the bus.

Then another time Jumbo and me found our headmaster's bike and loosened all the nuts and bolts on it. We weren't there when the accident happened but it eventually fell apart when he was racing down a hill in Camberwell. We went and had a look at the hill the next day and you could actually see bits of his skin on the tarmac where he'd travelled the last twenty yards on his face. Not that that mattered too much in his case, he only had one ear to begin with. In fact, if anything, the crash improved his looks. And it weren't like he didn't deserve it either. Benson, his name was, and he was a right nutter. We nicknamed him 'Bendover' 'cos of the intense passion he had for wielding the cane. These days a bloke like that wouldn't be left in charge of a goldfish, but back then he was in charge of an entire school.

Some afternoons we used to bunk off over to the ponds and play pirates. Then the school snitch, Roy Slater, got wind of it and started following us. Apart from Bendover Benson, Slater was the biggest pain in the arse of my school years. The first time I met him was when I got stuck sitting next to him in form. He was always very prim and proper, the sort of kid who brought an apple in for the teacher. But beneath all that there was a viciousness about him. When he smiled at you, you got the impression he was wishing you was a daddy-long-legs and that he could pull your legs off one by one and watch you die slowly. I hated him from the word go and the feeling was mutual. He always seemed to be lurking about in the shadows looking for something he could get us into trouble with. We got our own back on him though when we invited him to join us at playing pirates. We'd been looking for someone to play the bloke that walked the plank, and he was perfect for the role. Not that I didn't try to be friendly to him. One time I even stood up for him. He'd got into a fight with Trigger over some itching powder when Fatty Walker decided to sit on him so they could get to his belly button. I stopped them. And how did he thank me? He caught me messing about with some bird down by the bike sheds and told the teacher. I mean, fair enough, it was his sister, but I didn't know that.

It weren't just me who couldn't stand him. Nobody could. Even his mum and dad. Course, it came as no surprise to us when he ended up joining the police force. It was his old man, Harry, I felt sorry for. It did him right in. He used to wake up at night screaming. What really sent him over the edge though was when Roy nicked him for driving with a faulty headlight. He'd only borrowed the bike to pop out and get a bit of rock and chips.

* * *

Back then it was just the three of us at home, me, Mum and Reg. There was my Grandad Ted and my Gran Vi, and sometimes there was my Great-Uncle George and Aunty Pat, but mostly it was just the three of us. We started seeing a lot more of Grandad once we got a television though (those stories about him and Trigger's nan, Alice, might have had something to do with it 'n all. Years later he insisted that it was all perfectly innocent, just a lonely man trying to help a lonely woman. Which sounds sweet until you realise Trigger's nan was lonely 'cos her husband was fighting in the war, and Grandad was lonely 'cos his wife had popped to the shops).

When war broke out he'd been too old for military service, so he was conscripted into the Home Guards instead. But even that was too close to the front line for Grandad, and after a fortnight he deserted. He was caught, obviously, but he pleaded not guilty on the grounds of temporary insanity and they let him off.

Like father like son, Edward Kitchener Trotter had never really held down a job. He'd been a painter and decorator for the council when he left school but got fired after a few days for wallpapering over a serving hatch. Then he'd got a bit of work as a lamplighter for the GLC, but what with the fact that electricity already existed, it didn't last long. Finally he decided to make it easier on everyone and retired at the age of forty-eight.

Laziness seemed to run in the family on my dad's side. Uncle George was big on kipping too, but then he had fought in a war.* Reg was lazy, but he at least had some hobbies outside the home, going to watch Millwall lose and getting legless down the pub being his favourites. You should have heard it at Christmas time after dinner, with the three of 'em together snoring away. Sometimes they actually harmonised, like a really knackered version of the Bee Gees. And what with the sound of Gran's knitting needles clacking away it was like having a mini orchestra right there in the front room. If you could endure it long enough you'd find yourself humming along. But yeah, Grandad loved nothing more than a good, long sit (and that ain't a typo). Still, he lived to a ripe old age and he never got any varicose veins.† I'd be tempted to say he was the black sheep of the family, only we didn't have one, we had a whole bleedin' herd!

---

* He claimed he had a bayonet duel with Hitler at the Somme.
† Tell a lie, there was that big one in his nose, but, as he said, that was stress-related.

My mum was a wonderful lady. Very refined. She was the first woman in Peckham to smoke menthol cigarettes, no word of a lie. She was very intelligent. I remember one time seeing her finish a crossword, and not one of them easy ones, this one had cryptical clues and everything. She knew her art too, and one time she even went to a museum up town and saw the DaVinci Cartoon. She said it was really funny but that it'll be even better once he colours it in.* I don't know what it was about Mum but she only had to smile and everything would become better. Problem was, being married to my old man, she never really had much to smile about.

I've got plenty of memories of my dad. No good ones though. See, he'd always had a temper on him and preferred to do his talking with his fists, but he reserved both for just Mum and me. Mum was definitely the biggest influence on my life and it was from her that I got my strong work ethic. Reg had a strong work ethic too, so long as it was other people doing the work. It was only really Mum and me who ever brought any money into the house.

When I was twelve Reg got me two paper rounds. He promised he'd get me a bike, but they must've all been chained up 'cos I never saw it. Mum held down two jobs, sometimes three, just to make sure there was food on the table. Apart from the odd bit of waitressing, she also worked part-time filing at the town hall, and as an usherette flogging ice creams at the Ritz cinema. Reg used to get her to bring him breakfast in bed every morning, full English if the housekeeping money would stand it. I remember watching her taking it up to him and then heading out to work. She'd get back a few hours later, clear it all up, then head out again to start her next job.

He once even had the nerve to moan that the house was going to pot when, according to him, he woke up with a baked bean stuck

---

* I haven't seen it yet, but it's on my to-do list.

to his forehead (like it was Mum's fault he ate like a two-year-old!). Mum weren't having none of it though.

'You've just woken up with the 'ump and wanna start a row,' she said.

'I'm telling you, there was a bean in the bed!' he insisted.

'All right, where is it?'

'I ain't got it on me, you daft cow.'

'Well, let's go upstairs and you show me where it is.' Mum weren't gonna let him get away with this one.

'Knowing 'im, he probably ate it,' I chipped in. I could never resist an opportunity to wind the miserable bastard up.

'You keep quiet,' he said, 'ain't you got any homework to do?'

'The dog had it,' I said.

'We ain't got a dog.' This was true, but like I said Grandad had started spending a lot more time at the house, so it was like having a dog. Anyway, Mum forced the bean issue and Reg finally admitted he had eaten it, and without the key piece of evidence his case collapsed. He did what he usually did in those situations and stormed off down the pub. That night I heard him come home, and it weren't long before the sounds of screaming, doors slamming and furniture breaking filled the house (it got so bad at one point it almost woke Grandad up). I'd had enough and decided to intervene. Downstairs I found Reg stumbling around spouting off about the state of the place, socks being pulled up, beans and what 'ave you. Then I saw Mum crying. If there was ever one thing in this world I couldn't take more than any other, it was seeing my mum cry. So I confronted the old man and told him exactly what I thought of him. He squared up to me, but I refused to back down. I stood my ground, met his glassy stare and held my breath (on account of his breath, which was going right in my face). Looking back on it I suppose I was a bit like the man with no name in one of them spaghetti Western stand-offs (just without the eye make-up and the dodgy dubbing). Finally Mum got between us, things calmed down a bit and, my point made, I went back to bed. Mum, bless her, she hated it when me and Reg got into one. Especially when the belt came out. 'Stop it!' she'd scream. 'Can't you see he's had enough?!'

'Well, *he* started it!' I'd shout back. I understand now though. I mean, nobody likes to see family members exchanging blows.

I made it up to Reg the next day, for Mum's sake, and offered to make him a bacon sandwich, which was his favourite. He accepted my offer with as much grace as he could muster, and he enjoyed the sandwich too. Trouble was, he must have copped an unfortunate rasher as he spent the rest of that day, all of that night and most of the following morning on the khazi. I remember knocking on the door at one point, just to check he was all right, but the reply I got weren't in any English I knew. (In fact the next time I heard something like it was when I went to see that Sigourney Weaver film, I forget what it was called now but it had an alien in it.) I just put it down to a spot of cabin fever and left him to sweat it out. When he finally did emerge he looked like a different man. To this day I often wonder if anyone else has ever lost the best part of two stone in just over twenty-four hours. He got over it eventually, although he never touched anything I cooked ever again. I don't know why he blamed me. I mean, it weren't as if I'd borrowed a bottle of Trigger's Grandad's colon stimulants and mixed the entire contents into the HP sauce or anything.

I just realised, I do have a good memory of my old man.

CHAPTER 2

NEW WORLDS

While Reg remained deeply and emotionally attached to his mattress, I took a different approach to life. From the word go I lived at full throttle. In late, out early, that was me, hungry to experience life and everything it could throw at me: football, fashion, motors, business, music… I couldn't get enough! Of course once I'd matured a bit, you know, around about six or seven, I started noticing the fairer sex, and I must admit I did have my fair share of birds over the course of my formulative years.

From Dockside Junior I moved on to Dockside Secondary Modern (later to become the Martin Luther King Comprehensive) and just my luck, Benson and Slater moved with me. It was there that my little gang gained Denzil Tulser. Him and his mum and dad had just moved down from Liverpool, so I took him under my wing. He was a good lad, Denzil, funny accent, but a diamond.

As you know, I'd never held school in the highest regard, and by this time I really couldn't be arsed with it at all. The only lesson I ever really exceeded at was chemistry, which came in handy when I hit on the idea of flogging my own fireworks. I got the idea watching an old episode of *Dragnet* where this gang had made moonshine liquor in their apartment. Being young and headstrong I didn't bother with all that periodical tables cobblers, I just used to sneak into the lab, raid the cupboards, mix stuff together and see what happened. I wore goggles though, so don't go getting the impression I was being irresponsible or nothing. And this brings me to what was my second brush with death. Denzil and I were in the lab doing detention. Nobody was bothering to supervise us, so I convinced Denzil he should do both our lines while I got busy with some experiments, you know, getting the old Bunsen burning, mixing up the zinc and the ethanol and the milk of magnesia and giving the test tubes a good shake. Everything was boiling away nicely when all of a sudden there was what I can only describe as a mini nuclear reaction. As luck would have it I'd just popped out to check the coast was clear, and like I said, I was wearing goggles, so I weren't injured. And although Denzil did take the main brunt of the blast, he was lucky in a way too 'cos he was hit by a flying desk, which shielded him from the worst of it. He was just in the wrong place at the wrong time. Still, after a few days' rest and a short period of quarantine, he was right as rain. And it weren't like his Afro didn't grow back.*

The school governors got together after that and threatened to expel me. Then they realised they already had expelled me a few months earlier, so they just told me to leave them alone. Not that I gave a monkey's either way. From the age of about twelve I'd already decided that school weren't going to be as useful as a paying job, so some days I'd bunk off and head down the market.

There was a bloke called Harry Dando who ran a fruit and veg stall on Rye Lane, and I'd help him shift the crates and keep the stock topped up. He didn't give me much to begin with (mainly 'cos he

---

* I just realised this was probably more Denzil's brush with death than it was mine, but as with the last one, I was there too, so same thing.

hadn't asked for my help) but in the end he would bung me a couple of bob here and there. After a bit he even let me mind the stall when he went off for a pint.

When Harry was quiet I'd do a bit on Bernie Turner's fish stall. It weren't nice work shuffling cod about, but it was more pennies in my pocket. After a while though, this weren't enough for me, so Jumbo and I decided to go into business together. We had no problems getting our hands on stock – Denzil's old man worked as a security guard down at the docks, so he was perfectly placed as the go-between for several marketing opportunities.

After a little nocturnal negotiation with some American sailors we had a regular pipeline of vinyl records coming in, Del Shannon, Buddy Holly, Brenda Lee, whatever we could get. Most of 'em hadn't even been released in the UK yet so there was a big market. I'll admit, it weren't legal in the strictest possible sense (as in, according to the actual law) but we weren't harming nobody. These days kids nick all their music anyway, at least we was paying for it. So we set ourselves up down the market, selling 'em out of an old suitcase.

Using my new reputation as music mogul I managed to blag a double date with Glenda and Pam, two girls from school. I dragged Boycie along so that whichever of the two weren't up for it would have someone to talk to. I've always been considerate with women that way.

We went round Glenda's house 'cos her parents were away. Her nan was asleep upstairs but that wasn't a problem as long as we kept the noise down.

So, we got ourselves comfy on the sofa and waited for the inevitable.

Glenda and Pam were into all that beatnik jazz cobblers, wobbly trumpets and drummers that sounded like they was falling over their kit. So me and Boycie were sat there while this miserable bloke on the record player wailed on about something or other. When he weren't wailing he was blowing a harmonica.

'Have you ever listened to Lead Belly before?' Glenda asked us.

'Oh yeah,' I told her, knowing full well the way to a girl's heart, 'love him. Who's this?'

'This *is* Lead Belly,' she said, the pair of 'em laughing at us while sipping their Chianti.

'Why's he sound so miserable all the time?' Boycie asked.

'He used to be a slave,' said Glenda.

'So was Spartacus,' I laughed, 'but he didn't go around playing his harmonica all day.'

Apparently that comment made both of us 'squares' and I realised I was gonna have to pull out the big guns.

I asked to use the toilet, which was upstairs (posh birds these two) but Glenda didn't want to risk me waking her nan up so she told me to use the kitchen sink instead (maybe not so posh).

Stood on tiptoes, glad to be out of the blast range of Lead Belly and his problems for a bit, I thought of a joke to break the ice.

I stuck my head back in. 'Got any toilet paper?' I asked.

Apparently this weren't as funny as I'd thought, as they both started screaming and waving their arms around. Before you know it, the nan's up and doing her nut, and Boycie and me are back out in the cold.

Some girls have no sense of humour.

Calling it a night, we both headed off home.

It was even more crowded than normal in the house 'cos Reg had brought back a few mates from the pub. They were drinking a few beers and listening to him murder an Adam Faith tune. Clayton Cooper (Reenie's boyfriend) was there, but the other two blokes were new to me. They were smartly dressed and hovering at the edge of the room like they didn't really belong. One was a heavyset bloke called Gerald

Kelly, aka Jelly. The other was a tall feller with a pencil moustache. His name was Freddie Robdal, aka Freddie the Frog. He'd just been let out of Dartmoor where he was doing a stretch for blowing up a few safes and, little did I know then, he was going to have a big impact on the lives of the Trotters.

Thanks to Denzil's old man giving us the nod again, Jumbo and I were able to branch out into carpet laying. We got a load of top-quality, hundred per cent natural, nylon carpet that was straight from New York (and was supposed to be going straight back there as someone with less of a discerning eye than us had decided it weren't up to scratch).

We offered to fit a whole house for a fiver. I did our house first, so it could act as a showroom for our skills. Fair dos, the static was a bit of a 'mare, but it gave your hair plenty of body, and as long as you were careful turning on a light switch, the most you felt was a little jolt.

Mind you, if I'd known Mum had put in an application for us to move to a brand-new flat on the New Worlds Estate I wouldn't have bothered. The head of planning at the council made it clear she was unlikely to get approved though, 'cos they were giving priority to growing families.

Showing off the carpet worked a treat. We sold the lot and ended up fitting almost every house in the street.

It was a good time for us Trotters. Mum was promoted at the Ritz, becoming the assistant manager just in time for the safe to get robbed. Not her fault of course but it knocked her back a bit.

Even Reg managed to earn a few quid when his new mate Freddie wanted his place decorating and, not knowing any better, asked Reg to do it.

Don, the landlord at our local, the Nag's Head, had organised a coach trip to Margate. It was the first of our 'Jolly Boys Outings' (we'd end up having them for years) and most of us signed up for it. For some people, sitting on a coach to the seaside for hours, surrounded by beer-drinking, fag-smoking, loud-singing blokes would be a nightmare, but we loved it. The only people on board who didn't join in were Freddie and Jelly. They just sat there behind their sunglasses looking like a pair of crooks (which, of course, is exactly what they was). Oh, and Roy Slater didn't have much fun either.

I don't know why Slater even booked to go. He didn't like us and we didn't like him. All he did was prowl up and down the aisle, looking for reasons to moan.

Around that time, Albie and Jumbo had started taking Purple Hearts. Some of you may not remember them but they were around a lot back then, little blue amphetamine triangles that were prescribed as antidepressants. I thought they was idiots for taking them but, mates or not, they wouldn't listen to me.

When Slater spotted Albie unwrapping a pile of these things he immediately pounced.

'Are they drugs?' he asked.

'Course not,' said Jumbo. 'They're breath fresheners, you know, in case we bump into any girls.'

Slater's piggy little eyes lit up at that. 'Good idea!' he said, and he swallowed a few.

By the time we hit the first pub, Slater was off his head, dancing around the place like he was on fire, staring at his hands and going on about how big they were, right up until he passed out and spent the rest of the day on the floor.

What we didn't know at the time was that, while in town, Freddy and Jelly had taken the opportunity to knock off a jeweller's. We'd only find that out later, but it explained why they went from sitting in the corner looking like a pair of undertakers to getting the rounds in and celebrating like the Queen had dropped triplets.

On the subject of which: shortly after, Mum announced she was pregnant. I was stunned, and, I'll admit, not best pleased. Nothing against Mum, but with the way Reg was I just couldn't believe she would have let him... well, you know. Reg was more shocked than anyone as he couldn't even remember when the deed had took place.

Still, it turned us into the sort of growing family the council were looking for and, before you knew it, the Trotters were moving up in the world. Literally.

Goodbye Orchard Street, hello Sir Walter Raleigh House.

When you get used to something you can fall out of love with it. After years of living in Nelson Mandela House (as Sir Walter Raleigh House later became known), the flat became just a box in the air you had to climb to when the lifts were knackered (and they usually were), but when we first saw it we was blown away. It smelled of fresh paint and concrete dust, a brilliant, new smell that seemed so luxurious. The immaculate kitchen (before Grandad had a chance to get at it), the empty boxes of the bedrooms, the massive lounge and that view... looking out over south London like you were the king of your own concrete castle. It even came with its own allotment, just a few minutes down the road. Best of all though, you could chuck things at people down below and they never knew who it was.

I decided I had to do something, a gift for Mum that would make it even more special. She'd always been sad that we hadn't been on the phone at our old place. With the money she brought in, there hadn't been enough spare. So I went out and bought the brightest, shiniest, most reddest phone I could find and set it up next to the sofa. She was made up. Course, she'd have been even more pleased if we could've afforded to have it connected, but I could only do so much.

Three months after moving in, the baby was born. Born in this very flat in fact, with the midwife hovering over Mum and good old Reenie puffing away on a fag in the corner.

Rodney Charlton Trotter. Poor sod. It was Mum's idea. Reg had named me so she wanted to choose Rodney's name. She loved the movies, you see, always had. Like for so many of us, the cinema was where she went to dream of anywhere but her own life. So she went for Rod Taylor ('cos he'd just been in H. G. Wells' *The Time Machine*, so was a bit cultural). You're probably thinking Charlton came from Charlton Heston – most people do – but it was actually 'cos Mum was a big fan of Charlton Athletic.

It was nearly Christmas and, as a special gift, the officers of the Metropolitan Police force decided to give Freddie Robdal and Jelly Kelly a trip to the Isle of Wight, all expenses paid at Her Majesty's Pleasure, after an eyewitness claimed he'd seen them breaking into the jeweller's in Margate. Thanks to Slater, the police were also giving me and Jumbo a bit of grief. We'd bumped into him at the market while flogging the American records. He seemed in a good mood for a change, flicking through the stock and laughing about how we probably hadn't bothered those busy people at Customs & Excise with our little venture.

'What are you doing with yourself these days then?' Jumbo asked him. 'Still at school?'

'No,' he said, unbuttoning the heavy coat he was wearing to reveal a policeman's uniform. 'I'm a police cadet these days.'

That was us dragged in to the station.

The desk sergeant seemed as pissed off about it as we were, 'cos it really weren't the crime of the century and they had more important things to deal with. So we tried to prove they were ours by showing him the receipts Jumbo had knocked up.

'This is interesting,' the sergeant said, reading one, 'Sun Records. Elvis cut his first record there. They've been around a bit.'

'Oh yeah,' Jumbo agreed, 'ages.'

'Yeah,' the copper agreed, 'you'd think in all that time they'd have learned to spell the city they're in.'

'Idiot,' I whispered to Jumbo, 'I told you Memffis had two "f"s.'

CHAPTER 3

RUNNING RINGS

I'd been hanging about down at Alberto Balsam's car showroom. Boycie had got a job there, washing the cars and learning the trade (and he'd learn it well, he'd buy that garage off Alberto one day) so I used to pop in every now and then to see how he was getting on, but mainly to eye up the scooters and wonder whether I had enough coming in to get myself one on HP. I liked Alberto, he was worth listening to. You had to take a lot of what he said with a large pinch of salt (like that he was a trained bullfighter), but he did come out with the occasional gem. Alberto being Alberto, we usually ended up talking about women, and I'll never forget one piece of advice he gave me on how to get somewhere with the birds.

'You see, Derek,' he said, 'boys and girls are different. The girl she want to get married and have babies. But before the church and the wedding and the fighting is engagement. The girl, she doesn't want to lose her fiancé boy 'cos then there is no wedding, no babies... so she want to keep him happy. And how she going to keep him happy? The jiggy jiggy.' He winked at me and somewhere in Barcelona a bull crossed its legs. 'You know what I'm saying? Is a give and is a take,

Derek. Back home in Spain we have a saying. When the ring go on, something else come off!'

Now obviously, in the cold light of day, this was a terrible, crass, narrow-minded and sexist thing to say about women. But just in case he had a point I went out the next day and bought myself four engagement rings. At school I'd known a kid called Abdul whose dad owned the Bermondsey Wholesale Jewellery Emporium, and it was doing a big line in fake jewellery. Rich sorts were putting the real things in their bank vaults and getting glass copies to wear, so I got myself four pukka-looking rings for a quid.

Now all I had to do was decide who I wanted to give one to.

There was this lovely girl called Amita, and she was definitely on the list. I took her out for a coffee, just to test the water, and soon found myself one ring down.

Then there was Glenda. I bumped into her at the bus stop and we got chatting. About her parents mainly, they were proper smart, always going on holiday and cooking foreign food (like spaghetti, which was unheard of back then unless it came in a tin). It sounded lovely so I asked if I could come round for dinner.

'I can't just drag you round,' she said, 'what am I going to say to them? They don't know you. I don't really know you!'

Which was exactly the problem I was trying to fix.

'We could start courting,' I suggested.

'Why?' she asked. 'I've always hated you.'

'That's when we was younger,' I said, 'we're more grown up now. Wanna get engaged?' I showed the ring and her eyes went sort of dreamy.

'All right then,' she said.

'Cushty!'

Good old Alberto, the man was a genius!

Back at the flat things were getting complicated 'cos Gran was staying around to help look after little Rodney. Between her and Grandad and Mum and Reg, an argument was never far away. It felt like ever since we'd come to the new flat, Mum's moods had got worse. Sometimes you'd hear her in the bedroom, crying her eyes out, and I was desperate to think of some way we could cheer her up. I say 'we', I mean 'me' of course, Reg couldn't have cheered her up if he tried. One night he announced he'd had some brilliant news 'cos one of his contacts had offered him a job.

'It's only cleaning,' he said, 'but it's ten bob a day, three days a week.'

For a moment Mum was genuinely relieved.

'That's brilliant, Reg!' she said.

'I knew you'd be happy,' he replied, 'I told him you'll start next week.'

Turns out his contact was Freddie Robdal, who was out on bail.

As it happened, working for Freddie three days a week seemed to do the trick. Her mood lifted and she was much more like her old self.

Meanwhile, I was finding that being engaged to two girls at the same time weren't all it was cracked up to be. While I was round Glenda's house having Cock Oh Van with her family, Amita was at the flat, introducing herself to *my* family. Luckily, Glenda's parents took an instant dislike to me. They'd been banging on about how much they liked France so I tried a few phrases on them. Next thing I know I'm being escorted out the door. All I'd said was 'J'adore un soixante-neuf', which I'd been told meant 'I am enjoying this dinner'. I suspect they were just intimidated. They'd been trying to show off and I came rolling in and upstaged them, some people just can't take that.

Thankfully, it meant I was now down to a far more manageable number of fiancées. It was even lower come New Year's Eve when Amita twigged what I was up to. Sad thing was, in the last couple of weeks I'd realised I really liked her. Alberto hadn't told me what I was supposed to do about that, had he?

I wouldn't be lovesick for long though, because shortly after that I met Barbara. I'll be honest here and admit that Albie saw her first but, at that age, you don't worry about that sort of thing much, do you? I clapped eyes on her and decided that what she really needed was a large dose of Derek Trotter in her life. I invited her out for a cup of coffee and she told me about her love of art, which was a brilliant coincidence because I'd recently decided that I was going to make a really artistic movie. It was called *Dracula On the Moon*. It was about these astronauts up on the moon, then Dracula turns up and, before you know it, it's all kicking off up there. Barbara's old man was an undertaker and stinking rich, and she was convinced he'd put up the capital so I could get it made! They lived on Kings Avenue and she told me her mum weren't allowed out to work 'cos her dad didn't think that sort of thing was right. I was honest and told her mine was all for it.

I really liked Barbara, but the choker was, having just finished her exams, her dad had paid for her to go on a trip around art galleries in Europe, so the deep and meaningful romance we'd begun over a pair of frothy coffees was gonna have to go on hold for a few weeks. I could wait though, I was a changed man.

Besides, I had plenty to be getting on with. Word about my movie had spread. Even Mr Rayner, the manager at the Ritz cinema, had heard about it and he reckoned it could be the movie of the year. He was a strange one old Rayner. He was always damp and panting, like a tubby dog after a run, and he apparently took a very 'hands on' approach to uniform inspections. One night he got in an accident. He'd said he'd fallen off his bike, but nobody believed him. I mean, how do you fall off your bike and not do any damage except for breaking every single finger and thumb on your hands? I reckoned someone might have taught him a lesson, and with hindsight, I reckon I know who.

Freddie Robdal got himself pulled again while having a drink in the Nag's Head. Reg was full of it, 'cos they'd arrested him for murder! By the time it came to him being charged it had somehow turned into a couple of petty driving offences. The old bill around here always were a bit over-ambitious.

While all this was happening I was far more interested in my new scooter. I'd finally taken the plunge after Alberto had done me a decent deal on HP. It was a Lambretta, a beautiful chromium-plated snarling hornet. When I rode down the street, twin contrails of exhaust would spurt out of the back and I thought I could probably take off. Always one to give advice, Alberto let me have a few more tips when I picked it up:

'The most important thing,' he said, 'is to get the momma to like you. Take some nice flower, say some nice thing, like: "Oh I see where Barbara get her good looks from." Then the momma say to Barbara, "He's a nice boy, I like him." Then Barbara think, "OK, I let him squeeze my titties."'

He was a proper Casanova that Alberto.

Barbara came back and I got myself all suited up to take her out for a meal. I'd booked a posh restaurant up West, and on my way to pick her up I bought some flowers to give to her mum. I rang the doorbell and was muscling up to compliment her looks when the door was opened by a woman that looked like she could curdle milk just by grinning at it.

'May I say…' I started, 'that now I know where Barbara gets her…' It was no good, some lies will never sail. 'These are for you!' I said, handing her the flowers. 'Is Barbara in?'

'Yeah,' she said, staring at the flowers. Then she looked over her shoulder and shouted: 'Mrs Bird? I've hoovered the hall. There's some weird kid at the door to see your Barbara.'

I'd only gone and chatted up the bleedin' charlady.

Thankfully when Barbara's mum turned up she weren't quite as terrifying so I tried the good looks line again and got a shy giggle for my efforts. She invited me in and introduced me to Barbara's dad. He was a strange bloke, but maybe you need to be if you bury people for a living. He told me to call him Bernard and offered me a sherry so I decided it was going well. There was a bit of a misunderstanding though when he told me he'd heard my dad was a doctor.

'Doctor?' I laughed. 'Nah… he's a *docker*. Well he was. Once. They gave him the old heave-ho for nicking stuff.' *Best to be upfront about these things*, I thought. I've learned better since.

'Make sure she's not back too late!' he called as me and Barbara left. 'She's got to be in bed by twelve.'

'She will be, Bernie!' I laughed. 'Otherwise I'll bring her right back.'

Just a bit of the old banter, though by the look on his face I'd slightly misjudged my audience. I popped Barbara on the back of the Lambretta and off we went to Leicester Square. I'd booked one of those Golden Egg places, they've all gone now but there used to be a few of them dotted about. They were all bright colours and funny-shaped menus. Looking back on them now, they seem a bit plastic, like a lairy Happy Eater. At the time though, we were used to gloomy restaurants, all dark wood and lace, so they were a breath of fresh air. I certainly thought it would do the trick with Barbara.

'What you ordering?' I asked her.

'Mushroom omelette,' she said.

'You sure you don't want a nice steak?' I offered. Even back then I believed you should always offer a girl a steak dinner. It showed you meant business.

'I haven't eaten meat for eighteen months.' She smiled.

'Well, tonight's your lucky night, girl, 'cos I'm loaded.'

'I mean I'm vegetarian. Not a single piece of meat will ever enter my body.'

Not the sort of thing a young man likes to hear on a first date. And it went downhill from there. I'd ordered plaice and some dozy twonk had chucked a lemon on it.

'Sorry, pal,' I told the waiter, 'I don't want to get you in trouble but someone's dropped a bit of lemon on my meal.'

'That's garnish,' he said.

'That's lemon,' I corrected him.

'He means it's supposed to be there,' said Barbara, getting all embarrassed, 'you squeeze it on your fish!'

'Squeeze it on my fish?' I'd never heard something so weird. 'What about my chips? Don't suppose you've got a tangerine handy?'

I was young and naïve. These days I'm always having lemon with my fish. Can't whack it. Back then though, according to Barbara…

'You're so gauche! I've never been so embarrassed in all my life.'

'You should look in the mirror then,' I told her, 'you won't believe what riding on the back of my scooter has done to your hair.'

It *was* a bit of a sight.

'That's it!' she said. 'Take me home right now!'

There was only one way of pulling this date back from the brink of death.

'Don't be like that,' I said, offering her one of my rings, 'fancy getting engaged?'

It was like time rolled back and everything I'd done wrong vanished to be replaced with a warm silence and a lovely night out.

A few days later, me, Mum and Reg were invited to an engagement party over at the Birds' house (they called it The Aviary, which Bernard thought made him as funny as Tommy Cooper). Obviously I was worried about Reg being there. If there was one likely suspect for blowing the whole thing, it was him. He drank half a bottle of Bernard's Johnnie Walker and kept *nearly* putting his foot in it. I saw Bernard sneer a few times but I couldn't hold that against him, anyone that recognised Reg Trotter as a wrong'un was a wise man in my book.

But while the night certainly did go tits up, it weren't Reg that was to blame. It was Barbara's mum. She was a mixed-up sort (married to Bernard, who wouldn't have been?), a simmering, repressed, middle-aged wife who got by on sherry and fantasy. Her husband was a cold, weird, burier of men. Beryl was a woman of passion. The problem was, she chose to fling it at me. I was in the kitchen, mixing a couple of drinks when she came in, staring at me the way a starving python stares at a chubby mouse.

'Turned into quite a nice engagement party, hasn't it?' I said, as she closed in on me. 'You make a lovely sausage roll!'

She unpinned her hair, took her glasses and jacket off and fixed me with a stare.

'Give me your hand,' she said.

'What are you doing?' I asked, getting a bit worried.

'Give me your hand,' she insisted.

I did, and the next thing I know it's got one of her boobs in it.

'Give me your other hand.' I could see where this was going. Now I had hold of the full set. 'Erm…' I said, 'Mrs Bird…?' I couldn't say anything else 'cos she started kissing me so hard my teeth panicked.

Which is when Bernard walked in, closely followed by Barbara, closely followed by Mum and Reg. Awkward ain't the word.

'Is it so surprising I might actually like to be kissed or touched?' said Beryl, looking at Barbara. 'You don't know how lucky you are.'

'Lucky?' Barbara shouted. 'To have a mother who rapes my fiancé?'

'Come on now,' I said, trying to get things back on an even keel. 'It were only a bit of… you know…'

'Let's just go back in the living room and talk about it,' said Mum, always the politician.

'Yeah,' said Reg, 'let's go and have another drink.'

Beryl was having none of it. This was years' worth of bottled-up feelings, the cork about to pop. And it did.

'I watch you,' she said to Barbara, 'in your miniskirts and your high heels. I hear you playing your records. I feel you dancing. I'm pleased to see you enjoying yourself, because I never had your enjoyment.'

'Oh,' moaned Barbara, 'not the war again, it's *so* boring.'

'Oh no, it was much worse than the war. I got married!' she replied, tossing her head at Bernard. 'The blitz was fun compared to him! I've spent the last twenty years trapped in this house. The Aviary? To me it's a cage! Do you know what I do when you're all out?' she asked. 'I put on Barbara's clothes, play her records and dance.'

'You pretend to be me?' Barbara asked, all disgusted.

'I just wanted a sip of your wine,' said Beryl, 'be fair, you selfish cow, after all, you drained my vineyard dry years ago…'

'I think you need to see a doctor,' suggested Bernard.

'I just need another drink,' Beryl said, walking out.

Bernard had one last go at putting his foot down. 'I absolutely forbid you to…'

'Oh fuck off, darling!' Beryl shouted on her way back to the sherry bottle.

So that was that, another engagement off.

Reg couldn't stop laughing on the way home but Mum's face… she looked heartbroken. I tried to tell her it would be all right. After all, there were plenty more fish in the sea, weren't there? But when we got back to the flat she just shut herself away in the bedroom and started to cry.

'Women, eh?' said Reg. 'Off their heads, all of 'em.'

CHAPTER 4

DARK DAYS

Plenty more fish in the sea. Yeah. I did a lot of fishing over the next few years.

I went out with a girl I met at a betting shop in Lewisham Grove for about a month. Her dad was a tattooist, and she had one on her thigh of a heart with a dagger going through it. She was going out with someone else at the time but I didn't judge her for it, after all so was I. I took her home to meet the family and the next thing I know she's hiding from me. I went to the betting shop one day and the governor said she weren't in, but I knew she was 'cos I'd spotted her crash helmet on the counter. I found her on the roof. She said she was sunbathing but that didn't seem likely, not on a sloping roof while wearing stilettos.

I got the message and moved on.

It was the sixties so, in a year or so, after the fights in Brighton, being a mod was like being Public Enemy Number One, but there weren't much of that really. Most of the time it was just dancing, drinking and shaking off the working week.

And it was girls. I'd met this bird called Linda and she was electric. Just the smell of her, the perfume on her neck, the lacquer on her hair and that slightly chemical aroma of recently dry-cleaned clothes. She smelled new, which I liked, in that first dance kind of way, before the gin and fags and crisps could smudge it (which I also liked). Smell's always been important to me. So much of what I remember from back then is the smell. Mum smelled of spring and fruit, and not just one, *all* of 'em, a whole orchard. To this day I can't eat a fruit salad without getting tearful. Gran smelled of cake (until she became ill that year, then she just smelled of hospitals and goodbyes). Even Grandad was upset at that, for all he'd moaned about her.

But right then, all I could smell was Linda, and she smelled exciting.

I could feel an engagement coming on.

She lived in Croydon, which was good, 'cos it meant there weren't much chance of bumping into her in the off-licence when I was with one of my other birds. 'Never fall in love twice in the same borough', that was my motto back then. It didn't last of course, they never did. As much as I always thought they were 'the real thing', there was always more Lindas.

At some point amongst the engagements I officially left school. It would have passed me by completely if it hadn't been for them posting my O-level results, after all, I hadn't been there for years. See, I'd always been more interested in what was happening in the real world, the sights, the sounds, the smells, mooching about the markets and the docks, watching how it all operated, picking up the tricks of the trade. A piece of paper with a few letters stamped on it, given to me by some miserable old mush I'd never see again, well, that was no use to me at all. And that's why I didn't bother doing my exams. So you can imagine my surprise when I came home one afternoon and found everyone celebrating the straight 'A's I'd received. It only took a few minutes for someone to twig that the 'A' stood for 'Absent' and things took a sharp turn for the worse.

I'd known Mum would be disappointed, she always had big dreams for me. However much I tried to explain to her that dreams didn't need certificates, I knew she'd take it badly. It weren't the exam results that really broke that night though, it was the fight.

'I ain't surprised,' Reg said, 'I always knew you were a waste of space.'

Well, I weren't gonna let that lie, was I?

'Maybe if you'd been more of a man and looked after the family, I wouldn't have had to go out and try and earn some money!' I said.

Which was when he punched me.

It was hardly the first time, but it was the first for a good few years. As I said before, Reg may have had a violent streak but he also had a solid sense of self-preservation. He never punched anyone he thought might punch him back harder. Which is what I did.

I'm not ashamed. Maybe I should be but, thinking about it now, how it felt to give him a taste of his own medicine... It felt good. There, I'll admit it. It felt bloody brilliant. Every single one of Mum's tears, every black eye she'd tried to hide behind her big, showy sunglasses, I gave him a beating for each and every one of 'em. Mum was crying, Grandad was shouting for me to stop, but he'd had it coming.

Reg spent a couple of days in hospital.

I spent a couple of days in Brighton.

I couldn't hang around the flat after that, I couldn't even look Mum in the eyes.

I rang her the next morning, just so she'd know where I was. We had a bit of a cry down the phone and I knew I couldn't stay away long. The longer I did, the harder it would be to ever go back. And as much as I wondered what real freedom would feel like, to just get on my scooter and see where it led me, I couldn't leave Mum and Rodney.

So I went home and said I was sorry. I even apologised to Reg. But when I looked in his eyes I saw something had changed there. I knew then he wouldn't hit me again. But I also knew he wouldn't hit Mum again either.

⁂

That summer, Freddie Robdal and Jelly Kelly blew their last safe. Unfortunately for them, they were right next to it at the time. It was a little sub-post office in Plumstead, nothing special. They'd wired it up and then, nobody knows why, Freddie went and sat on the detonator and – BOOM – they were sent first class to the pearly gates.

Of course, everyone was talking about it, it was the best bit of gossip Peckham had had for years. Reg kept on about how he knew them, how Mum had worked for Freddie for years and how he was a close friend of the family. But Mum… Mum didn't want to talk about it at all. In fact she stopped talking about a lot of things after that. Which brings me to a period that was very much the winter of misconsent of my life. Things at home had been more strained than ever. Mum was hitting the bottle hard, going out at all hours, staying out too sometimes. To begin with, the fights between her and Reg were worse than ever, but then they just stopped. Reg, like always, never started a fight he couldn't win, and this one was beyond him. Mum would do what she wanted and nobody was going to stop her.

It took its toll. You can only hammer away at something for so long until it starts to give. She looked worn out, like the life had been sucked out of her.

Then one morning she just wouldn't get out of bed. Course, Reg did what he always did when the going got rough and made himself scarce. Grandad, bless him, stayed around to help out with Rodney, but in the end we decided it was best he took him back to Gran's. I called our local GP, Dr Becker. He came over right away, took a look at Mum and called for an ambulance. While we waited he took me to one side and told me to sit down. I knew he was gonna tell me something horrible, but when he said *that* word… well, the impact it had on me he might as well have smashed a chair over my head. Him and Mum had known for some time. She'd obviously been hiding it from everyone. Typical Mum. Never wanted anyone to worry. I went with her to the hospital and spent the night kipping in reception. I called Grandad and told him, and within the hour him and Rodney turned up. No Reg, he was obviously out gallivanting, but it was probably for the best he weren't there 'cos I would've caused a scene.

<hr />

Mum recovered that time, but we all knew she didn't have long. And I vowed then never to leave her side, even when she went into the hospice. We talked about… well, everything. I bought her presents and surrounded her bed with daffodils, her favourite flower, anything to see that smile.

She died on a freezing cold March morning, and I was holding her hand right to the end.

We did our best to carry on as normal, but who were we kidding? We weren't normal in the first place. The only thing that had been holding us together was Mum. The old man ignored me. I ignored him back. Then one day I came home and he was gone. He'd taken pretty much everything of value in the flat, which admittedly wasn't much, but still. There was no note, no nothing. Grandad kept saying he'd be back soon, not wanting to admit his own son could be so spineless, but he knew really, just like I did. By that point I was too numb inside to get angry. *Good riddance*, I thought. We didn't need him anyway. Rodney and me would be all right on our own.

Shortly after losing Mum, and then Reg, we lost Gran too. And so two became three again, just this time it was me, Rodney and Grandad. Course, I was gonna be the only breadwinner.

Always on the lookout for Slater, Albie and I started hawking stuff door to door. He didn't have the patter but he had his pretty-boy looks. It didn't matter what he was flogging, when the housewives saw him on the doorstep the purse strings loosened, along with everything else. I can't say I was fulfilling my lifelong dreams, but the rent had to be paid and I was making it work. Grandad would look after Rodney in the day, which basically meant sticking a rusk in his gob and plonking him down in front of the telly. Not that he minded though, he loved his rusks. So did Rodney.

Reenie helped out too. She took Rodney shopping with her once down Woolworths. When she got home she found he'd been picking things up off the shelves and shoving them in his pushchair. She had three bottles of scent, a packet of Weights and a Helen Shapiro record. The next day she took him up Selfridges.

I didn't see as much of some of my mates for a bit around this time, but they were all busy in their own ways too. Boycie was doing more and more hours at Alberto's. He'd moved up in the world from just swinging a sponge and bucket, and was even handling a few sales. Denzil was loved up, he'd met some bird in a betting shop in Lewisham Grove, and when they weren't hiding out in his bedroom he'd started training for a heavy goods licence. Trigger was... well, Trigger was Trigger, he just kept getting taller and started carrying a broom. But while I did my best to hold things together and steer HMS Trotter into calmer seas, I soon discovered that the storm weren't quite over yet.

I'd started dating this bird named June Snell, lovely girl, big and bouncy, but she had a nice personality too. For our first date I took her to see *The Ape Woman*, which I thought was gonna be a female version of *King Kong* but turned out to be some foreign rubbish about a bloke who falls in love with a hairy bird. Anyway, after a brief fling with some sort he'd met in Lewisham Grove, Albie got together with June's best friend Deidre, and we started double dating. Albie was still enjoying his 'happy' pills, but I never needed anything like that to have a good time. The way I saw it, I *was* the good time.

Things had been going all right for a bit, June and I were engaged, Rodney was coming along a treat with his alphabet, Grandad had discovered breath mints, and I'd began to smile again and think that things might turn out OK. Then tragedy struck. Albie'd been on his way to the Nag's Head one night, taken a shortcut over the railway track, and fallen onto the live rail. So in the space of a few months I'd lost my mum, my dad, my gran and my best mate. On top of that, Junie then decided she'd had enough of me, gave me the heave-ho and moved out of the area. Then it was Reenie's turn to say bonjour to Peckham. By this point I thought I must have picked up a curse. I understood Reenie leaving though, Mum had been her best mate, and life here just weren't the same. She'd packed in her relationship with Clayton (apparently she'd caught him having a fling with some bird he'd met in a betting shop) and what she wanted now was a fresh start, so she decided to move down to the Hampshire coast where she still had family. I'd miss having her help with Rodney of course, but I didn't blame her. I promised I'd keep in touch and waved her off as she got ready for a new beginning in a place that didn't reek of bad memories. Part of me wished I could have gone with her.

<hr />

I decided to give it a break with the birds and focus my attention on Rodney. A few weeks later I got engaged to Rosalynn who worked at the local creamery (a place where they make cream). She was a smashing sort. She had this big beauty spot just above her top lip. Well, she called it a beauty spot, it was actually just some sort of growth that she painted brown. It looked nice though. From a distance.

One night I took her out to a Greek restaurant that had opened up on the high street, and she had a violent allergic reaction to the taramasalata. I went with her in the ambulance, held her hand and tried to keep her calm, thinking the curse had struck again. I'd never seen anything like it. Her tongue blew up so bad it looked like she had a bit of liver hanging out of her mouth. By the time we got to the hospital her head had gone the same way. She looked like a cross between Boy George and the Elephant Man. I thought the experience would bring us closer, but it just weren't quite the same after that.

Anyway, where was I? Right. Things had been going well. Rosalynn and I were planning the wedding and the Trotters had never eaten so much cream. I was worried about Rodney though. Naturally, he was pining for Mum and it was tearing me apart seeing it, so I promised him that if he waited around by the phone he'd soon be getting a call from heaven (yeah, I know, but I'd had a few). I got Grandad in on it and popped over to Rosalynn's to tell her she had a very important phone call to make. She had a really nice telephone voice, proper well spoken, but with a couple of cotton wool buds shoved in her cheeks and a tea towel over the receiver, she could have easily passed for Mum. She weren't too keen on the idea, but I'd promised to take her to see the Kinks, so she agreed to do it. So there's little Rodney, hanging round the phone all the next day, wetting himself 'cos he didn't want to leave it for a second, and no call comes. The next afternoon he's back by the phone, and still nothing's happening. So I popped back over to see Rosalynn only to discover she's come down with a bad case of laryngitis. Poor cow could hardly talk. I felt relieved, not that she had laryngitis, it's just by that point I'd gone off the whole idea. That's when she told me not to worry, 'cos she'd already got her friend Bridget to take care of it. This wouldn't have been too bad, only I'd met her friend Bridget, and she was very, *very* Irish. I shot back home as fast as I could, but I was too late. Poor Rodney was more confused than ever. He'd been expecting a call from Mum, and instead he got some Irish sort giving him 'it's your mammy and I'm calling from heaven, so I am.' When Grandad asked him who he was on the phone to, he said it was Mimi calling from Devon, so that was Grandad confused 'n all.

❦

We plodded on.

Grandad decided it was time for some fresh air and started pottering about on the allotment. Well, he set up a deckchair next to the shed and sat there with a Guinness in his hand staring at the mulch. Apart from the odd carbuncle he never grew anything. I tried to explain to him that you had to plant something first, but he didn't have time for all that. It gave me an idea though.

Christmas was rolling around, and I decided to get into the spirit of things by turning the shed into a grotto. Nothing too fancy, a bit of tinsel, a few sprigs of holly, that sort of thing. Then I got a Father Christmas outfit for Grandad and a little elf costume for Rodney. If I'd known where to find a snow machine I probably would have hired one, but we had to make do with Grandad's dandruff. I posted up fliers all over the manor: 'Meet the real Father Christmas at his winter wonderland grotto'. I was even offering a free photo for the lucky sprogs so they could have a keepsake of the experience to treasure for eternity.

I admit now, it weren't the best idea I'd ever had, but the rent was calling and I had to do something. For the first couple of days we just hung about in the shed to get out of the rain. Rodney had had a funny turn in his eye and was coming down with a cold, so I did my best to make him giggle and forget where he was. Eventually a few mums and their sprogs started to show up. I gave it all the patter to get the nippers excited and knock the mums bandy, but once inside the grotto the smiles dropped. A couple of 'em legged it as soon as I opened the shed door. I don't blame them. I think I oversold it a bit. When you're expecting a snow-covered meadow and a jolly, rosy-cheeked Saint Nick in a cosy den, and you end up with a flooded allotment and some half-cut old geezer coughing his guts up in a shed, you're bound to be a bit disappointed. And Grandad kept getting his lines wrong (he only had to say 'Ho, ho, bleedin' ho!'). Rodney didn't help either. I mean, there's nothing cute about an elf with a squint sitting on a crate of Guinness blowing bubbles out of its nose, is there? There was a funny smell in that shed, too. Eggy. So most of the photos I ended up developing were of mums and their kids either looking frightened or in mid-heave.

My next big idea was a lot better. The World Cup was just around the corner, England was hosting it, football fever was rife and only a total wally brain could've failed to cash in on it. I got a contact I'd made at a plastics factory to knock me up a load of seven-inch figurines of England's star player, Jimmy Greaves. He did a bloody good job too. They were so lifelike it was scary. And I mean that literally, Rodney wouldn't even look at them. All we had to do then was sit back and wait for the right moment to pounce, and the readies would start rolling in. That's what I thought anyway. Course, Greavsie got himself injured in the group stage, didn't he? So by the time the tournament started he weren't even in the first team. It was a double blow! Still, I was sure that, with some last-minute modifications, we could save the day. So Grandad and I set to work painting Greavsie's barnet orange and soon we had a load of seven-inch figurines of Alan Ball. At least that's what I told people. The reality was that, even though we'd set out to touch up each and every figure with meticulous detail, we ended up with a load of seven-inch figurines of Jimmy Greaves that looked like they'd been dunked in a bucket of orange paint...'cos that's what they were. Well, I'd bought 850 of the sodding things, and after about the twentieth one we were bound to relax and get a bit sloppy. I think I sold one to Trigger, but that was it. Not that I cared by the end of the tournament 'cos England won and I was too busy doing cartwheels down the street!

CHAPTER 5

EELS ON WHEELS

It was the late sixties and London was the hub of all things cool and fashionable. It was a magical time of E-Type Jaguars, Concorde, the boil in the bag curry and what must be the greatest invention of the last two thousand years: the miniskirt! It was a time to be noticed, for being bold and making a statement. So me and Jumbo set up a fish stall outside the Nag's Head. 'Eels on Wheels' we called it. I admit I didn't go a bundle on it at first, but Jumbo could be very persuasive when he wanted to be, plus he knew where we could get a regular supply of dirt-cheap fish. It turned out to be a decent earner for a while. We used to knock out all sorts, home-made fish fingers, jellied eels, cockles, all the sort of slimy, wriggling stuff a bloke wants after a few pints. Jumbo handled the food while I worked the spiel. He didn't mind taking a back seat, he'd hooked up with some bird who worked in a betting shop in Lewisham Grove and was happy to stand there, daydreaming about her while lopping the heads off haddock. We were gonna build an empire. Every pub in south London would have had one of our stalls outside it. What knackered it was the way television started to personalise fish. That smart-arse shark, Flipper, Squiddly Diddly the drumming octopus,

Michael Fish. People started feeling guilty about tucking in to anything with fins. The health inspector's report didn't help either, of course.

By that time I was finding it hard to focus on whelks and winkles anyway. My mind was on Pauline Harris. I met her one night while I was cruising the manor on the Lambretta. In a way the scooter was the last link I had with my carefree youth. I'd kept it in good nick. I had to, I was still bloody paying for it (Alberto's terms might have been affordable but the loan agreement was so long he'd be putting it in his will), but it weren't quite the blazing metal beast it had been.

Since I'd started looking after Rodney more I'd had to knock the Brighton trips on the head anyway, so when The Who sang about 'My Generation' I was already feeling like I was slipping away from it. By the time they were telling us the story of Tommy I was listening to it in the front room ironing Rodney's school shorts. I'd still take the scooter out in the evenings though, once Rodney had gone to bed, celebrate a day of wheeling and dealing by giving it a roar through the streets. That's where I met Pauline, sat on the back of another bloke's GS. We'd been riding along next to each other and she'd been laughing and giving me the eye. I tipped her a wink as we pulled up at a red light, and by the time it went green she was on the back of my bike. I didn't feel sorry for the poor sod she'd casually dumped, I was so full of myself, her arms gripping my waist, that blonde hair of hers whipping behind us like a racing flag, I didn't give him a thought. I did later of course, 'cos by then it was me.

But for that first week it was the most excitement I'd ever had (and I'd had a fair bit). I'll be honest, everything else went to the wall for a while, business, family. I had tunnel vision and at the centre of it was Pauline. Would you be surprised if I told you we got engaged that week? Course you wouldn't.

'Do you love me, Del?' she'd ask, then laugh as if my answer was the funniest thing in the world. But there was always a touch of the old *fem fatal* about Pauline. She was the mods' pin-up girl, and 'cos she knew how popular she was, she played on it. Sometimes it was like she was deliberately trying to make me jealous. Up to then I'd never been the jealous type, but when I caught her outside the chippy smooching with Bobby Finch, I saw red. Bobby was one of the other top mod boys at the time. We weren't mates, and he was a bit of a flash git, but we'd never had any problems. Right then though, watching him with his hands all over my bird, I wanted to kill him. I would have too if I hadn't had a bag of prawns getting warmer by the minute on the back of the Lambretta.

Bobby and I eventually decided to have a straightener over on the recreation ground. Everyone was there, all my mob, all his mob, it was like something out of *West Side Story*, just without the music and the soppy dancing. It was a close-run thing, and I'd give Bobby his due, but the sneaky bastard wore a ring and split the side of my face open. I've still got the scar to this day. In the end though, he looked a lot worse than me. We shook hands afterwards (that's what you did back then) and that was it, everything straightened out. Problem was Pauline had already moved onto some other mush by then, a big lump who was a semi-pro boxer, and, well, while she was special, she weren't *that* special. She eventually got back with Bobby. They ended up getting engaged and moved abroad.

Soon it was Jumbo's turn to decide that his future didn't lie in Peckham. With the council putting the clamp on Eels on Wheels, he decided to emigrate to Australia. Like I said, we had fought a lot, but I was still going to miss him. It was costing him all he had to get over there and I couldn't let him turn up in Oz brassic, so I gave him my last two hundred quid and told him to make it last. I could always make more.

The rest of the old gang were all moving on in their own way. Monkey Harris was buying and selling like me, Denzil had got his heavy goods licence and was driving a lorry up and down the country, Trigger had got his road sweeping licence and was pushing a broom up and down the high street.

Boycie? He'd moved away 'n all... to HM Wandsworth. It was nothing major: perjury, embezzlement, conspiring to pervert the course of justice, fraudulent conversion of traveller's cheques and attempting to bribe the mayor of Lambeth. We've all done it at some time or another, ain't we? Some people might think that Alberto would regret giving Boycie the opportunities he had in the showroom, I reckon he realised he'd found the heir to his throne. When Boycie got out, Alberto announced he was retiring* and sold the garage to him. Boyce Motors was born, and from that day on no wallet in Peckham was safe. Boycie didn't let his bit of a stretch hold him back either, he was minted within a couple of years and it looked like nothing could go wrong for him. Then he married Marlene Lane. Not that there was anything wrong with Marlene of course, absolutely not, all the boys loved Marlene. He'd met her in a betting shop in Lewisham Grove. That's where she worked.

I'd got engaged to a bird named Trudy. She was a bit of a dog, granted, but I'd matured a bit by then and was seeing past the looks. She didn't even mind Rodney being about. Well, she didn't moan, and that was worth its weight in gold at the time. To celebrate our engagement I splashed out on a romantic weekend away at a little

---

* He went to Gibraltar to live out his considerable nest egg eyeing up female tourists and throwing ice cubes at monkeys.

caravan park in Sheerness. Rodney had been after a pet so I'd bought him a mouse (it was a small flat, what do you expect, a Great Dane?). But a couple of days before me and Trudy left for Sheerness, he lost it. I'd done my best to convince him it would be all right, even though I was pretty sure the cat that lived by the bins was probably eating better than us that night. The mouse hadn't been eaten though, it had taken one look at the crappy little shoebox Rodney kept it in and decided it could do better.

So there's me and Trudy in the caravan, getting ready to go out on the town, she's standing in front of the mirror making some final adjustments to her wig, when Speedy bleedin' Gonzales pops his head out of it. She screamed so loud it made *me* scream. We had a blazing row and while we were fighting a storm broke outside. The rain was lashing on the caravan as she started throwing stuff (at me or Speedy, I couldn't really tell, I think he'd burrowed into the fold-up bed to get a bit of peace and quiet). Finally, it seemed even God had had enough and the caravan was hit by lightning. Trudy screamed again, which made me scream again (and I'm sure I heard Speedy let out a little squeak), and she bolted out the door. The last I saw of her she was running across a field. All she had on was a polo neck

⟡

I did my best by Rodney, but it weren't easy. I tried to make sure he weren't deprived of the things I'd missed out on. I took him on holiday once a year (well, we went hopping in Kent, but it got us out of the flat and we earned a few quid). I made sure he did his homework and got it in on time. I even helped him with the difficult stuff (I remember once when I was struggling with my homework I'd asked Reg what a cubic foot was. He said he didn't know and then tried to have a week off work with it).

Course, having Rodney about made things a bit awkward when it came to my love life. To begin with I was upfront with the birds I met, but a lot of them didn't want to know once they'd met Rodney. I think they just thought the whole set-up was a bit weird (which it was). Either that or they thought Rodney was a bit weird (which he was). There was one bird though, Leslie, who didn't seem to mind. She'd even sit with Rodney and play trains with him. I found it quite endearing at first, but then they started getting into arguments about whose train was whose, who was hogging the track, that sort of thing. A couple of times they both ended up in tears. It was a bit odd, but I thought she was just highly strung. It took a while longer to discover that she really weren't the full shilling.

I'd been seeing her for about a month by that time, we were already engaged and I was even thinking of asking her to move in, when we got into a row over a bag of chips and she stabbed me. I had a six-inch gash in my shoulder! I won't lie, I started having some niggling doubts about our future together after that. The final straw came though when I discovered that her stepdad was old bill. Well, you've gotta draw a line somewhere, ain't you?

I changed my approach with birds after that and stopped telling 'em about Rodney and Grandad altogether. Obviously, they still wanted to come back to Chez Derek (well, you don't get the full Del Boy experience if you don't), but as much as I tried to make excuses, sometimes things got a bit urgent and there was no way out. I'd developed a strategy of only bringing a bird back to the flat when it was very late at night, so that Rodney and Grandad would be asleep and out of the way. My line of thinking was that it'd be a quick 'in-out, Bob's your uncle, give you a bell in the week' type operation. Nobody would be any the wiser. Well, it sounded easy in theory but in practice it was bloody hard work! Just imagine it: you've met some game sort who's all over you like a scab, you come through the front door, she's nibbling your ear and whispering sweet nothings, you come into the front room, articles of clothing already flying off in all directions, hands too busy to bother with the light switch, you're halfway across the floor, inching closer and closer to the boudoir, and she treads on a Tonka Truck and goes arse over tit! And that was nothing compared to the time I had to explain away the Huckleberry Hound pyjamas draped over the hallway radiator. Add to that the ever-real and present danger that she might pop to the kitchen to get a drink and bump into a semi-conscious Grandad coming out of the bog, and you can see what a minefield it was. I ended up developing a way of taking care of 'business' keeping one eye on what I was doing while the other scanned the perimeter for incoming threats. It didn't 'alf give you an 'eadache. Course, as I matured I stopped caring so much, but back then I weren't much more than a kid myself. And of course it weren't Rodney's fault. It weren't no one's fault. It was just... well, *Chapelle Ardente* as they say in the Basque region.

CHAPTER 6

FLY ME TO THE MOON

I honestly thought there was more chance of Boycie buying a round than there was of man walking on the moon. Not that I weren't excited by the prospect. And jealous. Yeah, I envied those astronauts, blasting off up into the unknown, bringing the eagle in to land where nobody had ever been before. It was tense, unpredictable, on the edge of your seat stuff (the closest I was getting to feeling like that was sitting down to one of Grandad's Christmas dinners). Rodney was excited too. He'd been learning all about it at school and wouldn't stop asking questions.

'What is the moon, Del?' he'd ask.

'It's a big rock in space, innit?' I'd tell him.

'Who discovered it?' he'd ask.

'I dunno, some bloke called Moon, I s'pose.' The stupid things he used to ask, bless him. I didn't mind though, it was important that he learned. He loved his science back then, did Rodney. I got him a telescope for his tenth birthday so he could have a look at all the planets up close. He got bored with them after a day or two and started having a look at the bird in the flat opposite up close instead. Boys will be boys, eh? Then one day Grandad decided to find out what the surface of the sun looked like and lost half a retina, so I got rid of it after that.

On the night Buzz Armstrong was set to get out and walk on the moon, I let Rodney stay up and watch. Grandad was there too, but the excitement became too much for him and he fell asleep. Finally, the hatch opened and Buzz popped out, mumbling something about a giant leap, and that was it. He just had a mooch about, really slowly, collecting samples and rocks and what 'ave you. There was no aliens, no buildings, no nothing. Just an empty, desolate wasteland.

A few days later I got a letter from the school saying the headmistress wanted to see me in her office. Right moody old mare she was, face like a bloodhound in a wind tunnel. She explained that Rodney and his mate Mickey Pearce had been caught trying to sell 'moon-rocks' in the playground. Well, I don't know what she was telling me for, it weren't like I gave him the idea or nothing. She said she was worried about Rodney and how 'certain external influences were affecting his behaviour'. *Probably your face,* I thought. I weren't daft though, I knew what she was getting at, so later that day I told Rodney to stop hanging around with Mickey Pearce. He was always a wrong'un that boy. To be honest though, I felt relieved. Finally Rodney was showing a bit of initiative.

A lot of people moan about the 1970s. To many it's sort of like the ugly bridesmaid of the decades. You know, it's horrible and you'd rather it weren't there, but it is and there's no way round it. The way I see it, if the sixties was the big shiny balloon that just kept getting bigger and shinier, the seventies was what it looked like when it burst all over the wall. Maybe that's a bit harsh. All that happened really was things got bigger and droopier in some places (collars, sideburns, Grandad), and tighter in others (the economy, trousers, Boycie). But it weren't all bad. Wine entered its heyday with the arrival of Blue

Nun, the prawn cocktail became yet another weapon in my arsenal of ways to knock birds bandy, and we got a colour television, which was pretty much all Grandad had ever wanted. In fact he loved his colour telly so much that by the end of the decade he had three of 'em. That doesn't sound so strange now, in a time when a lot of households have four or five tellies, but Grandad had them all in the same room and watched them all at the same time.

It was during this period that Rodney entered his ugly duckling phase, you know, he became all gangly and awkward looking.* He just wouldn't stop getting taller. I'd buy him a new pair of trousers for school and by the end of the week they looked more like Bermuda shorts. I keep telling him it will all be over soon, but there's no sign as yet. Rodney had carried on at school and was doing his GCEs by now, with a bit of help from me. I was so proud when he came home and told us he'd passed two. Fair dos, he failed the other eight, but I ain't a miracle worker, am I? I thought then that he was on the verge of breaking the Trotter mould and would go on to become a success in his own right. But puberty had already kicked in and it was all downhill from there.

He became right mopey and serious too. He was always either thinking or reading or writing. I worried about him, I really did. I tried to get him to come down the pubs with me, but he wouldn't have it. I tried to get him interested in sport, thinking a bit of exercise and fresh air would do the trick, but he never even touched the snooker cue I got him for his birthday. Instead he hung around the flat like a moody spider, writing in his diary and drawing bowls of fruit and things.

Anyway, as inflation inflated and the country went to pot, the opportunities inflated and, for a while at least, so did my pot. I really

---

* You should have seen him on a spacehopper.

came into my own down the market, streamlining my sales technique, fine-tuning the patter. The punters loved me, especially the females. Well, I was in the prime of my life, weren't I? Looking back on it now, I probably looked like a right wally, but at the time I was a walking turn-on (not my words, but those of several different sorts on several different occasions back then). My hair was thick and luxurious, all I had to do was give it a flick in the right direction and the birds would get all fluttery and giggly. I wore platforms on my platforms and had a strut that made John Travolta look like Douglas Bader.

I'd realised the importance and power of clothes from a young age. I must have picked it up from Mum. She always made an effort and turned heads. I remember she used to wear a fur coat in the winter time, genuine simulated beaver it was. I definitely didn't get it from Reg or Grandad. The only fur they wore was growing out of their ears. Of course, as a mod, being well turned out was important, and I always tried to sport the latest Ben Sherman and the smartest Crombie. The seventies was a time to be daring and experimental. I know it probably looked daft, but I weren't the only one at it, and I weren't the worst either. Trigger took to wearing sheer nylon shirts. It wouldn't have been too bad, but combined with the hobnail boots and the broom, it just looked off. And that's nothing compared to Denzil, whose Afro got so big he had trouble getting through doors. And then there was Boycie, who looked more like an extra from *Planet of the Apes* with each passing year.

I had to hand it to him though, as big a prat as he could be, he'd really done well for himself. In a few short years he'd risen to become the undisputed king of second-hand cars in the Peckham, Lewisham and Camberwell districts. The problem was he made sure everyone knew it, and then reminded them repeatedly just to be safe. He started really lording it over the manor, driving around in a brand-new Ford Cortina one day, a brand-new Rover 2000 the next, flaunting his moustache and flashing his wad like he was Billy-Big-Bananas. What I wouldn't have given to have had my own Ford Cortina. Still, I managed to get the next best thing when he did me a deal on a cracking little Hillman Minx. It was pond green with a teabag-brown trim (well, it was by the time I got it), only sixteen years old, cost me fifteen quid! It was one of a kind that motor. Course, it had its flaws, but then they all do, don't they? It weren't the most powerful of cars, so slopes were a big no-no, and apparently the heater and windscreen wipers had given up the ghost back in 1958, so it was always best to check the weather forecast before setting off for anywhere too far away. And while it did have four doors, only two of 'em opened. I didn't care though, it was a workhorse, and as long as you planned your journey well in advance, and you didn't mind extreme temperatures or getting your clothes a bit creased, it usually got you from A to B.

⁂

By 1977 Trigger had teamed up with Monkey Harris doing a bit of buying and selling. God knows what Monkey was thinking – putting Trigger on your team was like putting a piranha in your bath – but they managed to get by. They were doing a lovely little line in hot-pants, which were all the rage with the birds back then (probably a few of the geezers too, but none that I knew of), 'cos they were tight and, you know, they accentuised that whole... area. I had a gander at a couple of samples and they weren't bad, covered in zips and little silver sequins and things. So I did a deal and ended up taking a hundred and fifty pairs off their hands. The problem, as I later discovered, was that, unlike the samples I'd seen, they were all XXXL hot-pants, which defeated the whole object really. Not meaning to be rude about the plus-sized woman (I love a bit of meat as much as the next man) but these things would have looked baggy on Barry White. And as much as I tried my best to flog 'em, most of the bigger girls I chatted with were trying to get rid of their arses, not make them sparkle. So I got Mrs Murphy from the estate – a whizz when it came to a bit of sewing – to make some adjustments to a few pairs and then tried to flog 'em as beach towels. That didn't work either.

I soon had other things on my mind. The time had arrived to celebrate the Queen's twenty-fifth year on the throne, and all across the land big parades and street parties were being arranged, so I decided to chuck my hat into the ring and get involved in the estate's celebrations. I'd already clocked the plans for the do over on the Bob Marley Estate, and there was no way I was gonna let them upstage us, so I gathered all the heads of the flats (Nelson Mandela House, Zimbabwe House, Desmond Tutu House, etc.) and laid out my vision for *our* party. I say 'party', but what I had in mind was more of a sort of mini World's Fair. Anyway, I pulled out all the stops, drew on all my contacts and got the job done.

Come the big day the precinct was packed. We had a coconut shy, an ice-cream van, a jellied eel stall, and we even got a brazier fired up so that Mrs Obuku (who'd recently moved into the flat beneath us) could knock up two dozen or so litres of her famous goat stew. We had a fancy-dress competition for the nippers (first prize: fifty pairs of hot-pants!). I wanted Rodney to go as a Beefeater and he got in a right strop about it. I talked him round in the end, but looking back now I can see his point, I mean, he was seventeen at the time. Still, you've got to enter the spirit of things, ain't you? But the brick on the top of the chimney was the petting zoo I arranged to be set up over by the pram sheds, you know, a few rabbits, a donkey, a couple of them ugly-looking llama things. Course, everyone had to add a little donation to the pot and there was a small admission fee, but it weren't like I was getting any backing from the council or nothing, so fair's fair.

It was all going well, the precinct awash with union jacks, everyone enjoying the grub and the booze we'd laid on, when disaster struck. Well, 'disaster' was what the press later called it (that and something about 'mindless carnage', I can't remember exactly), but it just got a bit out of hand, that's all. See, this geezer from the council turned up asking whether we had a licence for all the animals. I told him we did, which weren't strictly true, 'cos we didn't, but he wouldn't have it. He was just looking for a fight, and in the end, that's what he got. I don't know who threw the first punch, it weren't me, but the bloke ended up going for a burton right through the jellied eel stall. Things would have been fine – after all a party ain't a party till someone gets knocked out – but then someone got the old bill involved, and before you could say 'God Save the Queen', we had a battle on our hands. The plod called in reinforcements, so the residents called in theirs. The plod brought in their horses, so the residents brought in theirs, and what had begun as a lovely day of neighbours coming together to share and enjoy a common bond ended in a full-scale riot. You should've seen it: the brazier, stew 'n all, got knocked over, there was smoke and truncheons and screams everywhere, coconuts and jellied eels and massive hot-pants flying through the air, rabbits hopping about and humping each other all over the place. The poor old donkey collapsed from the stress of it all. I remember scarpering to the flat, sitting on our balcony, watching the madness below (sipping a Campari and cherryade to steady the nerves), and thinking to myself, *That's what hell most probably looks like*. But what did the authorities expect? Everyone had had a skinful, and I reckon that goat stew helped stoke the passions 'n all. It got cleared up in the end anyway, the donkey made a full recovery, and I'm sure Her Maj understood. Looking back now, I can see it was just another example of the kind of heady, Mardi Gras atmosphere I tend to generate.

I decided it was best to keep my head down for a while. I'd already had a run-in with a local magistrate over my trader's licence (in that he wouldn't let me have one), so I took to a bit of low-level ducking and diving where and when I could, just about making ends meet. What I really fancied was a holiday. Concorde had well and truly taken off by then, zipping people to and fro across the Atlantic at the speed of light. I could just picture myself up there in the clouds, mingling with the glittering well-to-do over a bottle or two of Don Perrig Non. I knew then that that was the sort of Mal de Mart lifestyle I was cut out for, and that I'd live it just as soon as I became a millionaire.

So we bundled into the Minx and headed south for a few days in Bognor. We had an all right time in the end, but stone me, Grandad didn't 'alf moan. First he was too hot, so I had to pull over so Rodney could get out and wedge the window open for him (and I didn't like stopping the Minx once I'd got it going 'cos it had a tendency to *stay* stopped). Then he was too cold, so I had to stop again. Then him and Rodney got into a row over which one was Bodie and which one was Doyle in the bleedin' *Professionals*! I would have turned back if I'd have thought the car could've handled it. We finally got to our chalet and Grandad was off again 'cos there was no telly and he was missing the season finale of *Wonder Woman*. We didn't do much, just sat about, eating fish 'n chips and talking about the old days. We talked about the new ones too, especially where Rodney was concerned. And that's when he told us of his plans to go to art college. If I'm honest, I weren't best pleased. I'd always wanted him to be someone, you know? I pictured him one day having his own Ford Capri. Not that there weren't money to be made in art, it's just most of them artists, the good ones at least, only made it big after they were brown bread, and what's the point in that? A lot of 'em went mad too. Van Coff for example, brilliant painter (my favourite), but mad as a box of frogs! Cut his own ear off! I didn't want to see my kid brother ending up penniless minus a lughole. But Rodney had always been quite headstrong once he set his mind on something (looking back now, I reckon he might have had a touch of that OCDC), so I couldn't persuade him otherwise.

Despite my doubts, the day he left home to start his new adventures at Basingstoke Art College, I felt proud, and I knew I'd miss him. I also felt a warm satisfaction deep inside that I'd kept my promise to Mum and done right by him. However bumpy the road ahead was gonna be, with all the lessons I'd instilled in him over the years, I knew he'd be all right.

CHAPTER 7

I HAD A DREAM

The little dipstick got caught smoking a reefer with some Chinese tart! On top of the college booting him out, he'd been given a court appearance for possession of cannabis. It was an absolute travesty! He'd only gone to her room to borrow some charcoal, and even then he'd only had one bloody puff! I was all set to represent him, I wrote to our local MP and went round the markets and pubs drumming up support for his plight. I even got some T-shirts done. I was ready and willing to take his case to the highest court in the land if it meant justice was served. Meanwhile, that little plonker went and pleaded guilty by post! He got an eighteen-month suspended sentence and a three-hundred-quid fine.

It hit him quite badly. Well, it would, wouldn't it? He put a brave face on it, saying he'd refuse to let this one little slip-up define his life, and he tried, bless 'im. He applied for a few jobs but no one would take him, what with his record. Actually that's not strictly true, he did have a real shot at becoming a milkman, but he failed the entry exam. This was a real shame 'cos Rodney had always loved his dairy. Then he did a bit of volunteer work manning the phones at the Samaritans. He was good too. Nobody ever phoned him back. After a week or so he packed it in and took to just lying about the flat, almost like he felt too ashamed to go out. I tried to talk to him and find out what was going on in his head, and one night I almost broke through.

'I feel like a leper,' he said.

'What, one of those little Irish troll things?' I asked. But then he just clammed up again and went off to his room. In the end it was like he became a piece of the furniture. It was almost like having two Grandads in the flat. I did what I could to get him out, even giving him my old scooter. It cheered him up for a bit, then one day he was giving Grandad a backie down to the shops when he hit a pothole and they went for a burton. Luckily Grandad landed on top of Rodney so he weren't injured. Rodney weren't either, except for his pride. Course, he blamed the scooter, but I knew that thing like the back of my hand and there was nothing wrong with it.

'The steering's really unresponsive,' he moaned.

'It is now you've crashed it!' I told him.

I took a look at it, gave it a squirt of oil and a few whacks, and he gave it another go. Then he got pulled over by a copper and fined for not wearing a crash helmet. I found the copper and tried to smooth things over, explaining that Rodney had already had a crash and his head was fine, but it didn't help.

One day I went into his room and found a disturbing magazine. This in itself weren't out of the ordinary, his bedroom was full of disturbing magazines, but this one was all about guns. I got really worried then. I told Grandad and he suggested getting Mickey Pearce round to talk to him.

'Grandad,' I said, 'we're trying to help him, not push him over the edge!'

A few nights later, we'd just finished tea, and Rodney came out with it:

'I'm gonna join the army.'

Course, it took me by surprise. If I hadn't been sitting I'd have had to sat.

'The Salvation Army?' I asked.

'No, Del,' he said, 'the *army* army.'

I could see the seriousness in his face, so I knew I had to tread carefully. 'Don't be a twonk, Rodney, they wouldn't take you,' I said.

'Why not? I'm young and healthy, and on top of that I care and want to make a difference.'

I must admit, a part of me admired him for showing a bit of drive and determination, but I couldn't have it, could I? He just weren't soldier material. If a bumblebee buzzed past his head he threw a paddy. Plus I couldn't be sure he'd stopped growing. He was already a bit of a beanpole, add another few inches and you could just imagine the trouble he'd have keeping his head down in the parapets. Enemy snipers would have a field day with his bonce popping up and down all over the place. And it weren't just him I was worried about. I mean, you couldn't give Rodney Trotter a gun. He'd end up shooting someone! War zones are stressful enough places without sending a Rodney in.

'But soldiers go to war,' I told him. He just looked at me like I was a moron or something.

'You're the one who keeps on telling me to get out more.'

'Yeah, to help me shift some of my gear or join me at the Nag's Head for a swift half,' I said, 'not to become a soldier of fortune and go and get your head blown off in a jungle!'

'Grandad was in the army,' he said.

'Exactly!' And look at him!' I looked to Grandad, hoping for a bit of backup, but he was just sitting there, heavily involved in his tellies.

'Grandad,' I said, 'have you heard this?'

'Hold on, Del Boy,' he replied, not taking his eye off the screens for one second, 'I can feel an important twist coming up and I don't wanna miss it.'

Stone me! He was only watching *Worzel* bleedin' *Gummidge*!

'Del's right,' he finally croaked, 'I never liked it in the army. Take it from me Rodney, as someone who's been there and done it, you don't wanna end up becoming a broken, haunted shell of a man.'

'Bloody hell, Grandad, you only spent a fortnight in the Home Guard.'

Rodney did have a point. People had weekends at Butlins that were more harrowing than Grandad's tour of duty.

Rodney then tried to explain that joining the army weren't that bad, and he thought the routine and structure of army life would be good for him.

'I've gotta do something, Del.'

'I told you,' I said, 'come and help me.'

'But I don't want to be a box-lugger!' he moaned. 'I didn't get two GCEs to spend my days poncing about in markets!'

Well, that hurt. It really did. It was a bloody liberty too!

'You make me die, Rodney,' I told him. 'I don't hear you complaining when you're eating the food and drinking the drinks and enjoying the warmth my "poncing about" brings you!'

I could see the point had hit home.

'Look, Del,' he said, his voice softening, 'you keep telling me I should toughen up and become a man.'

'Yeah, a man,' I said, 'not a *dead* man!'

'I thought you'd be proud of me,' he said.

'Rodders, there are loads of things you can do to make me proud of you, but Mum would turn in her grave if she could hear you talking about throwing your life away like this.'

'No she wouldn't, Del,' he said, getting up from the table, 'you've gotta have a life before you can throw it away.' And with that he went off to his room.

I kept playing it over in my mind. I knew deep down that Rodney had a point. I'd had enough of things too by then. All my old mates had moved on in their lives. Most of them were already married and settling down, doing all the normal things that normal married people do, buying homes, starting families, getting divorced, etc. Then there was me. But Rodney couldn't understand that I was just worried about him. He was depressed. The whole country was. Everywhere you turned there was strikes and riots and doom and gloom.

I needed cheering up, so the next day I went down to the cemetery. My old contact at the plastics factory had only recently come through with the new headstone I'd ordered for Mum. I'd had a bit of an 'eadache getting the proper planning permission for it, but it was a beautiful headstone.* It had all angels and cherubs and things on it. No rubbish either, genuine fibreglass. Anyway, I spent an hour or so there, chatting with Mum and cleaning the pigeon shit off the cherubs, and then I headed off back home.

That night I had a dream. I was floating over a meadow full of yellow flowers. There was a massive rainbow stretching off into the distance, a shimmering yellow glow at the end of it. Then I heard a voice whispering to me, but I couldn't make out what it was saying. Whatever it was, it said it again, but it was still very faint. It said it a third time, but I still couldn't make out the words. By this point it was really starting to get on my tits. 'Speak up!' I shouted. 'I can't hear a bloody word you're saying!' The voice began to get even quieter.

---

* The only bit of trouble we ever had with it was when some vandals broke into the cemetery one night and painted it aluminous yellow! Took me bloody months to scrub it all off!

'Stop whispering!' I shouted, and the next thing I knew Grandad was standing over me, poking me in the shoulder (this weren't in the dream, I'd woken up). Grandad told me I'd been calling out 'Stop whispering' over and over again in my sleep. I couldn't get back to kip after that, wondering what it all meant. Was someone or something trying to give me a message? Could it have been Mum? Could it have been God? Could it have had something to do with the lamb madras and three banana daiquiris I'd stopped off to have on the way back from the cemetery?

It was a couple of weeks later when I decided to make the change. I realised I needed to stop going about business half-cocked and start making a disconcerted effort to become the success I knew I was destined to be. It was the beginning of the eighties. I needed a new image, a new face (for the business, there was nothing wrong with my actual face), a new beginning. And I needed to be mobile. So, first things first, I went out to find myself a proper set of reliable wheels.*

Trouble was all the proper sets of reliable wheels I looked at were a bit out of my price range. I went over to see Boycie, the go-to man for specialist (i.e. cheap) vehicles, but even he drew a blank. My plan was to entice Rodney to get on board, so I needed something with at least two seats. Boycie, being the sarky git he is, suggested a rickshaw. With the money I had to spend he weren't far off the mark.

I didn't want to let it stress me out, so I decided to bide my time a bit and popped down the auction to see a mate about another mate… and there it was, parked round the back under a dirty old grease-stained sheet. Some of the people at the auction were taking the piss out of it, but I knew it was the perfect motor for me. I hadn't seen many three-wheel vans around at the time (or since, now I think of

* The return trip from Bognor killed the Minx.

it), but while the others mocked, I saw through that deceptive layer of ugliness to the unique, beautiful swan that it was to become. And it *was* unique, just like me. It had two seats *and* there was plenty of room in the back for boxes and crates and Grandad. It was yellow, which I saw as a bonus, I mean, the whole point was to get noticed, and nothing gets noticed like a yellow three-wheel van gets noticed. I was ready and willing to get into a bidding war. As it turned out, mine was the *only* bid.

With the transport sorted, I then had to come up with a name for this new venture. I wanted us to be seen as being a genuine, pukka company. I weren't looking for anything too fancy, just something to let the punters know who we were and what we were about. I originally came up with 'Trotters Wares And Trade', but it was a bit dull. What really put me off though was when I noticed the initials (see, you've gotta be very careful to check all the minor little details in this game or you could end up making yourself look a right plonker). Then it struck me. Something simple yet startling, something that summed us up perfectly.

'Trotters Independent Traders' was born.

It weren't until about a month later when it all fell into place. The dream I'd had. The yellow flowers. Mum's favourite, daffodils. And the voice and my crying out 'Stop whispering' in my sleep. Mum had been telling me to be bold, to think big and make a noise about it. And that's what I decided to do. That time the following year, we'd be millionaires!

Rodney had wanted a dream, and I delivered it to him.

He shrugged his shoulders and said, 'Yeah, all right.'

CHAPTER 8

THIS TIME NEXT YEAR...

The key to success when you're a man of business is following your gut. You look at some gear and know whether it'll sell or not. You look at your pitch and know if it's the right spot. It's an animal instinct, like when a lion looks at a pack of gazettes and knows deep down which one it has the best chance of giving a right good chew. That's me: the lion of business, keeping the flies off and getting the charcoal lit on the barbecue for another piece of deer steak. I'm not perfect of course, sometimes even I make the wrong decision. I'll give you an example: the day I made Rodney my financial advisor.

Right off the bat he started trying to mess my system up by introducing things like order and morals into the equation. He even started keeping receipts! Then he started whinging that I was cheating him somehow. Well, it hurt. I explained to him that as brothers everything between us was split straight down the middle, 60/40, and then he gave me a lecture on the bleedin' government. I couldn't believe it. Here I was paying him a wage to advise me financially and all I was getting was a load of verbal. Still, it didn't go too badly, in the first week he only set me back two hundred quid.

I'd decided that it was time for Trotters Independent Traders to expand. Flogging at the market was all well and good but I wanted to build empires! I wanted to start moving into a wide range of bespoke, high-end retail opportunities. Class goods aimed at an exclusive clientele. So I bought a second-hand Cortina off Boycie. Vintage automobiles would be the first of Trotters Independent Traders' new commercial ventures.

I'd seen worse cars. I owned one. But with a bit of TLC and a lot of wax I reckoned we could make ourselves a killing. In fact, Rodney nearly did exactly that driving it back to the estate. Apparently the brakes were a bit soft, but then so was he, so it's hard to say where the blame really lay.

It had its faults (windows, gearbox, brakes, exhaust pipe, upholstery and engine), but it was at least a challenge, and there's nothing Derek Trotter likes more than a challenge. So I set my refurbishment team on the task and, after a day of moaning, he'd got it scrubbed up a treat.

Priced at a highly competitive figure, it wasn't long before it was snapped up by a connoisseur of vintage vehicles. It wasn't long before he crashed it either, but I can't be blamed for that, he was Australian, he was probably driving upside down or something.

I must admit it took the wind out of my sails a bit.

Then I struck lucky during a high-powered business meeting down the Nag's Head. That's the other important rule about business, know an opportunity when you're looking at one and grab it. So, when I heard a very important local business leader, Crinkle-Cut Billings, moaning about how hard it was to hire a nightwatchman for the local bus depot, I knew I could help. Business ain't just about taking, sometimes you have to put yourself out a bit too, you have to be generous and think of others. So I bought him 'alf a mild and told him Rodney would be there by six o'clock the following evening. Even better, I didn't do the deal for cash, I did a trade! He got a security guard, a man with extensive military experience (Rodders had been soppy for Action Men when he was a kid. I say Action Men, they were actually knock-off Barbies I'd painted beards on, but he loved 'em, even if they were a bit confusing). In return I got the use of a double-decker bus for my next brilliant plan: Trotters Ethnic Tours.

If I had to pick the best of the brilliant ideas I've had over the years I couldn't. I've had too many. Don't get me wrong, I'm not being vain (although I've probably got every right to be), it's just I'm the kind of bloke who has several industry-revolutionising ideas before he's finished his Weetabix. If I'd only had the time and the financial backing I could have changed the world. Trotters Ethnic Tours was definitely a corker though, way ahead of its time, that's the reason it didn't work. Well, that and the fact I trusted Grandad to do something properly. You look at holidays nowadays and they're all about adventure, getting your flip-flops lost in mud pits or breaking your guts open on deep-fried grasshoppers (if you wanna challenge your guts then pop down the Star of Bengal and try one of their specials, that'll keep your holes busy for forty-eight hours). Not that I was being as adventurous as all that, I just wanted to show people the alternative London. Your average tourist was fed up with all that Houses of Parliament, Buck House and National Galleries guff. Once you've seen one Rubens, you've seen 'em all, ain't you? I was going to offer them the romantic places they'd only heard of in fairy tales, like the Lea Valley Viaduct, the glow of Lower Edmonton at dusk, the excitement of a walkabout in Croydon.

Of course, my new financial advisor was slow to see the potential, even having a pop at my brilliant new leaflets.

'What's all this squiggly stuff and the Chinese?' he asked. I explained to him that the squiggly stuff was Arabic and that the Chinese was actually Japanese. It's a well-known fact that ninety per cent of all foreign tourists come from abroad, and we weren't gonna get anywhere if we didn't try and speak their lingo. Mind you, if Rodney was hard to convince, Grandad was worse, the saucy old goat actually bet me fifty quid that nobody would turn up. Course, I took him up on it 'cos I knew I was onto a winner. And I was. But you just can't rely on people, can you?

I'd planned a whole day of exciting events, taking the punters to see the house where Sherlock Holmes was born, the cemetery where Jack the Ripper was buried, the summit of Mount Pleasant... What I ended up doing was standing on a bus all day with a pair of divs, 'cos instead of handing all the leaflets out to hotels and B&Bs like he was supposed to, Grandad went and dumped the lot down the rubbish chute. What a way to win a bet, eh?

As tempting as it was to put Grandad where he'd put the leaflets, I soon had more important things on my mind after I bumped into an old flame in the Nag's Head. I say old flame, she was more like a volcano.

If you remember (skip back if you don't and pay attention in future), the last I'd heard of Pauline Harris she'd married Bobby Finch and gone off abroad. Well, turns out she'd moved back into the area and Bobby had taken up a little place (about six foot square) in a cemetery on Blackshaw Road. Not that it had held Pauline back.

'After Bobby died I went to San Francisco,' she told me. 'I got a job as an air hostess, it's a good salary, uniform, free travel.'

'It's in your blood, innit?' I told her. ''Cos your mum was a bus conductress.'

She laughed at that (always knocked a girl bandy with my wit, that and a splash of Yves Saint Dior, I was unstoppable).

'You never married yourself?' she asked.

'I never fancied myself,' (see above), 'to be honest I never met a girl that I cared enough about.' Which wasn't quite true, but a little white lie never hurt anyone…

Maybe it was the blackcurrant and Pernod I was drinking, but my feelings for Pauline were coming back thick and fast.

'Well,' I said, 'there was one.'

There was something in the air, there always was in the Nag's Head, the carpet was dirtier than a wino's beard, but this was something else, something magical. Then Rodney turned up and Pauline and I fell back to earth sharpish.

He weren't best pleased. He'd only been a kid at the time but he remembered enough to have decided Pauline was more trouble than she was worth. But then what did he know? He'd never experienced that magical pull that exists between a man and a woman, he was still twanging bra straps and hoping for the best. Grandad didn't help either, chipping in with his opinion on the matter, but the last time he'd had a romantic thought the Queen was in Pampers.

I tried explaining to them both that things were different. Back then, Pauline and I had just been kids. Now, we were emotionally mature adults who approached life with a calm, sensitive attitude that suited our age. And if the two of 'em didn't like it they could just shut up 'cos I weren't listening anyway.

So, Pauline and I made another go of it. It was a bit weird to begin with, the last romantic dinner we'd had was from a roadside van and covered in fried onions. I did right by her this time, treating her to a steak and a bottle of that classy wine that used to come in a basket. I wanted her to be in no doubt whatsoever that I'd matured into a man of taste and distinction. I took her to the pictures to see *The Cannonball Run* (nothing sets the romantic mood more than Burt Reynolds in a fast car). And it worked 'cos we were engaged by the end of the week.

Of course, the news went down with Rodney and Grandad about as well as a pork pie in a mosque. They thought I was moving too fast, which was cobblers as I'd left it at least forty-eight hours before popping the question. Then I told them the really good news: Pauline was moving in!

Looking back, I can see why they weren't exactly doing the conga, but at the time it hurt. Rodney stormed out and Grandad said nothing, just sat and stared at his tellies, which I know is what he always did, but this time he did it in a way that made it very clear he weren't happy.

As I say, looking back, I get it. We had a nice thing going at the flat. Well, not nice, but we all rubbed together fine, you know, three blokes getting by. Bringing Pauline into the mix with all the things that are important to women, like hygiene, air fresheners, food that's cooked in something other than a frying pan ... well, it was bound to cause ructions.

Pauline didn't help matters. Things were fine in the bedroom, but on the rare occasions we stepped outside of it (mostly so I could catch my breath and slurp a Lucozade) fights would kick off. I gave her the housekeeping money but she didn't pick up much food for Grandad and Rodney. She also hid Grandad's teeth 'cos the noise of him sucking on 'em had been driving her up the wall. I could understand that of course, but still, you don't nick a bloke's teeth. Next she started talking about buying a place of our own (well, *her* own, she suggested it was all done in her name) and then it was, 'Oh, by the way, Del, have you ever thought about getting life insurance?'

Course, Rodney and Grandad had a field day with that, and before you could say 'black widow' they'd decided Pauline was out to bump me off, adding another name to the list of ex- – both in the marital and breathing sense – husbands. I laughed it off, but when Trigger rang to say he'd heard the old bill were looking into Bobby Finch's death 'cos he'd apparently died of food poisoning… well, I'd be lying if I said I didn't start doubting the peas on my plate.

That was enough for Rodney and Grandad who announced they were going to stay with an Aunt Rose down in Clacton. *Good riddance to the pair of paranoid wallies*, I thought. Then I changed my mind and went with 'em.

I later found out that Grandad had put Trigger up to the phone call but, tell the truth, I didn't have it in me to be angry about it. You can't go back, you know? I'd loved Pauline once upon a time but it weren't the same (and even if her food weren't killing me her libido soon would have).

We had a lovely few days in Clacton with Aunt Rose. Actually, it turned out it wasn't Aunt Rose (she'd moved years earlier), but by the time we discovered this we'd already had a bath each and eaten this old girl's shepherd's pie, so it was a bit awkward. She didn't seem to mind though, it gave her a break from her embroidery, and I bunged her a few quid for her trouble. Everyone's a winner.

By the time we got back Pauline had made herself scarce, leaving a heartfelt letter (addressed to 'That No-Good, Lying, Two-Faced Creepo') thanking me for the fun times we'd had. She also left us a phone that had been speaking to the American talking clock for the last four days. Expensive, but I reckon I got off lightly in the long run.

CHAPTER 9

LOVE REALLY,
REALLY HURTS

Soon it was Rodney's love life that was causing us problems. Life was so much easier when he only fancied people from a distance, mooning after girls behind tills or on the other side of a beer tap. It was easier still when they were on the pages of his 'specialist art magazines', the only thing you had to worry about then was slipping on one when you went in his room (which anyone with any sense tried to avoid, it was all BO and pot, as if Bob Marley had been in there and farted). He'd had girlfriends between all the ogling of course, but something about Rodney always put them off. His personality probably. But then I discovered he was kinky. To be fair, it weren't too bad on the face of it. He had what was medically termed 'a predilection for women in uniforms'. But I soon realised it was much worse than that, and Rodney had a secret that threatened to shame the entire family. Don't get me wrong, I've never been adverse to a bit of sexual experimentation, and a bird's a bird whatever she's wearing, but Rodney couldn't have been a normal pervert and got the hots for air stewardesses or nurses (even lollipop ladies would have been forgivable). No, Rodney had a thing for *policewomen*. It still affects me now just writing these words. I just burped up some of last night's mutton tikka.

Now, I've nothing against policewomen, as long as they've got nothing against me (and they ain't, whatever they say, it's bound to just have been a simple misunderstanding), but to hear Rodney go on about the uniform, the shoes, the handcuffs… well, it's just not right, is it?

On a personal note, and for the record, I have never knowingly bought or handled any illegal items (including but not limited to: electrical goods, officeware, clothing, toys, kitchen implements, furniture, building materials, scrap metal, designer watches and assorted jewellery, heavy plant machinery, livestock, home entertainment items, sports equipment, fine art or unicycles). But you can never be too sure of your sources in this game, it's full of crooks.

Rodney fancying policewomen was one thing, I could *almost* live with that, but going on a date with one was something else.

It all began when I'd hooked up with a couple of birds down the Nag's Head, a mother and her daughter, and thought I'd do young Rodney a favour by making a double date of it. It weren't all charity on my part, if he kept the mother busy then it meant I had more time with the daughter.

Of course, Rodney, who never met a gift horse whose gob he didn't want to stare gormlessly into, went and got the right hump. True, Valerie had a bit of a cough on her, but she loved her Rothmans and she couldn't help it if they made her chesty. Besides, a couple of port and lemons soon cleared her out. But no, Rodney whinged all the way and, just when I thought the night couldn't get any worse, we ended up in the middle of a right barney in a club over New Cross. It was Tommy Razzle's fault. He'd partnered up with Monkey Harris in a business putting in false ceilings. They'd been working over in

Saudi Arabia and Tommy swore blind he'd seen a salt beef bar in Jeddah, but Monkey Harris was having none of it and, before you knew it, there was more furniture flying through the air than at a January sale at DFS. This club was used to a bit of alcohol-inspired refurbishment, but this got so bad someone called for the manager, and once everyone realised he'd climbed out of a window somebody else called the old bill. Five minutes later and Juliet Bravo's younger sister turned up. Well, Rodney immediately started running around like he'd been deputised, trying to impress her. I tell you, when she put Tommy in a chokehold, Rodney nearly fainted with excitement.

If that's where it had stayed, with him dribbling after her from a distance, it would have been fine, but he suddenly got a rush of blood to his head and asked her out on a date. And she said yes!

Course, I dealt with the matter with calmness and sensitivity, but calling him a pervo and threatening to disown him made no difference. Grandad was beside himself too, obviously, being one of the old school.

'What are the neighbours gonna say?' he asked. 'Why's he doing this to us?'

I explained the scientific reasoning behind the problem. "Cos he's kinky, ain't he? He's got what leading psychiatrists call "a thing" about policewomen's uniforms.'

'Well, if that's all he wants, can't we club together and buy him one?'

'He don't want to wear it!' I said. 'He may be perverted but he ain't dangerous!'

They ended up having a pop at one another, with Grandad accusing Rodney of putting a slur on the family name (which was a bit rich coming from him, I'll admit). Rodney then went a step too far by saying that nothing short of molesting chickens could put a slur on the Trotter name.

'It's a good job your mum died when she did,' said Grandad, taking his ball home in the way only he could, ''cos hearing that would have killed her.'

So Rodney went out on his date and I settled in for the night with Grandad. I couldn't relax though, thinking about how Rodney was growing up and becoming his own man. I would have felt proud if it hadn't been that he was turning into a massive tit in the process. It was a sobering thought, and I said as much to Grandad.

'I've had a lot of sobering thoughts in my time,' he said, flicking through his tellies, 'it were them what started me drinking.'

He had a point, so I poured myself a large one and hoped for the best. Not much good it did me though, as a few hours later Rodney returned... with date in tow!

Like I said before (in a completely frank and legally admissible manner), I have never knowingly dealt in stolen goods, but sometimes things can slip through the net – especially when you're as trusting as I am – so I had a bit of a conniption when we heard her at the door. I mean, you can only hide so much in a few seconds, can't you?

As it turned out, my suspicions were right. Rodney's date ended with his bird promising she'd be back in twenty-four hours with a team of colleagues and a search warrant so they could go through the flat with a fine-tooth comb.

Well, I'd been saying for a while the place could've done with a spring clean, and the job was much easier once we'd stripped it bare.

Rodney being Rodney, it weren't long before he'd forgotten all about his WPC and, after a brief flirtation with a skinny bird at the dry-cleaners, he'd moved on to his next obsession. Her name was Irene Mackay and she fell for him thanks to a nice line in lingerie he had on him. He weren't wearing it – just to be clear – he was selling it door to door. He let her have the lion's share, paying it off on the weekly to give him an excuse to keep popping round (he was a div but he weren't completely stupid).

Grandad and I had seen the signs of course, watching him lolling about the place with that glazed look in his eyes, nicking a few splashes of my aftershave, so we knew he was on the prowl again, but we didn't know how hard he'd fallen.

'I think I'm in love,' he confided one night, seeking to sup a drop from his big brother's pool of knowledge and expertise in this most delicate of areas. I was always touched by these moments when he opened up to me and laid his feelings out on the table, knowing that a man of my sophistication would handle the situation with care and consideration. It was flattering. Anyway, once me and Grandad had finished laughing, I pointed out that he was always falling in love with one little girl or another and not to let it go to his head.

'Irene is not a little girl,' he said. 'She's forty.'

Now, I don't want to cause offence, but on this occasion even Grandad admitted he would have thought twice. I know people say that life begins at forty, but so does sciatica.

The biggest problem though was her *husband*.

'He don't live with her,' Rodney insisted. 'He's away.'

'Where?' asked Grandad.

'Parkhurst,' Rodney told him.

I seem to remember doing a bit of shouting at that point. When I'd calmed down I asked him what Mr Mackay was in for.

'You know, this and that.'

'Like what?' I asked, knowing smoke when it's being puffed up my posterior.

'Wounding with intent, GBH and attempted murder.'

'Got a bit of a temper, has he?' I could see Rodney had really fallen on his feet with this one.

'That's why Irene's had such an unhappy life with him,' he said, 'he used to beat her up. She's moved over here from the East End to get away from him.'

'Get away from him?' I said. 'He's on the Isle of bloody Wight!'

'Yeah, but that's the problem,' Rodney said. 'He's being released soon. Do you think I should go and see him, tell him about me and Irene, man to man?'

You know I said Rodney wasn't completely stupid? I was wrong. There were times when he made Trigger look like Stephen Dawkings. I pointed out to him that the merits of his plan depended entirely on how much he enjoyed having knees in the middle of his legs, and he stormed off (he marched out of the flat in a huff about five times a day as a rule, it was his main bit of exercise) spouting the usual 'I'm a grown man and I'll live my own life' cobblers.

I thought about looking into the price of private medical insurance, but knowing Rodney as I did, I decided he'd either be given the heave-ho within the week or he'd go off her. Either way, he'd be well clear before Tommy Mackay came sniffing around.

It didn't quite work out that way. While Tommy Mackay counted down the days to release, Rodney and Irene got closer.

So I did what any older brother worth his salt would have done and stuck my oar in. Well, you've gotta look out for family, ain't you?

I popped round to see Irene, took her out for a drink and gently discussed the subject of Rodney. Basically, I told her that if she had any feelings for him she'd steer well clear. Me being a bit of a charmer, especially with a cocktail in my hand, she saw my point.

Of course, when she gave Rodney the push he weren't in a good way, but I'd rather his eyes were puffy from crying than from having had Tommy Mackay's toecaps shoved in 'em.

I should have known that wouldn't be the end of it though. We bumped into Irene's son, Marcus, and he only went and told Rodney I'd talked to Irene. So, obviously, Rodders went and got the hump (again!). Best laid plans and all that…

The night was young as far as bad luck was concerned. After a few light refreshments at the Nag's Head, I was doing a bit of business knocking out some camel-hair overcoats, when who should I bump into? I'll give you a clue: he didn't have much of a suntan. Yeah, Tommy Bleedin' Mackay. Him and a mate pulled me into an alleyway to have a quiet word about a little problem named Rodney Trotter. Problem was, they thought I was Rodney.

I could have put 'em straight of course, but where would that have left Rodney? Like I said, you've gotta look out for family, whether they want you to or not. Well, I weren't in the best of moods anyway since, thanks to Tommy, I'd just ruined a brand-new coat (and if there's one thing you don't interfere with besides a bloke's bird or his family, it's his clothes), so I told him he'd got the right man and that I'd be happy to discuss the matter at some length. I came away with some cuts and bruises (my face looked like the inside of a Fray Bentos pie by the time it was all over), but I gave as good as I got, and Tommy learned the error of his ways: I left him unconscious next to some bins. His mate legged it.

It took me half an hour to get back around the corner to the pub, with legs that would only bend in the wrong direction and a head that felt twice as big as it had five minutes earlier. Later, I'd turn the bath pink trying to get myself scrubbed up. Still, Tommy Mackay weren't all that, and while I'd rather have explained it to him without going down the fractured ribs route, I was confident Irene wouldn't be hearing from him again.

Rodney was back at the Nag's Head by then. I'd already decided I'd give him some old pony about falling down the stairs (I didn't want him worrying), I just wanted him to know that the path was clear for him and Irene. Course, once he'd recognised his handsome older brother underneath all the purple swelling, he was concerned... for about a minute. His main concern though was telling me all about a new bird he'd met at a roller disco. Zoe her name was.

'Irene was just infatuation,' he said, 'but this is love!'

He introduced her but my vision was fading by that point so I can't really say what she was like. Just before they left he called back to me.

'I'd get that head looked at if I was you.'

Truest bloody words he'd ever spoken!

Above and right: Joan Mavis Trotter, Mum, circa early 1960s.

Grandad Ted, circa 1959.

Reg Trotter, circa 1962.

Watcha bruv!
Rodney Charlton
Trotter, aged 3½.

Orchard Street, Peckham, circa 1959.

Fifteen minutes from the West End, fifteen minutes
from the motorway, and fifteen minutes from the ground.
Chez Derek, AKA Nelson Mandela House, Peckham.

Colin 'Trigger' Ball, circa 1961.

Same look, different suit. Trigger circa 1988.

The Driscoll Brothers, Danny (right) and Tony.

One-time 'Detective Inspector', Roy Slater, AKA 'Slater the Slag', AKA 'Bullshit of the Yard'.

Freddie 'The Frog' Robdal, circa 1961.

A chromium-plated snarling hornet. My old Lambretta, pictured here before Rodney crashed it.

Admittedly not the best looking motor, but a workhorse that never let me down. The Hillman Minx, circa 1977. A few weeks after this photo was taken the Minx died on a return trip from Bognor.

I didn't find the van. We found each other – a bit like in that film *Seabiscuit* where Spiderman and Seabiscuit find each other.

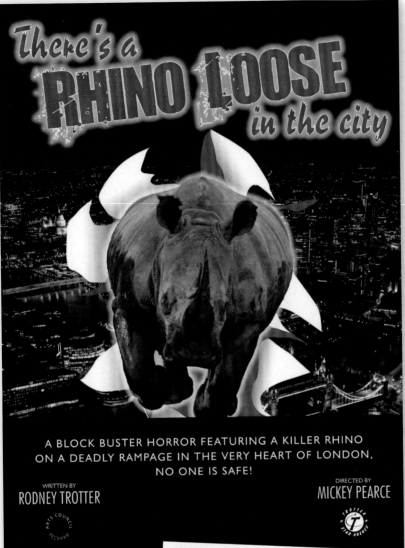

There's a **RHINO LOOSE** *in the city*

A BLOCK BUSTER HORROR FEATURING A KILLER RHINO
ON A DEADLY RAMPAGE IN THE VERY HEART OF LONDON,
NO ONE IS SAFE!

WRITTEN BY
RODNEY TROTTER

DIRECTED BY
MICKEY PEARCE

It could have been
the next *Jaws*. *There's
a Rhino Loose in the
City*. One of my bestest
movie ideas to date.

I could have been
the Freddie Laker
of the highways.

Trotters Independent Trading's original A-team:
me, Rodney and Grandad, circa early 1980s.

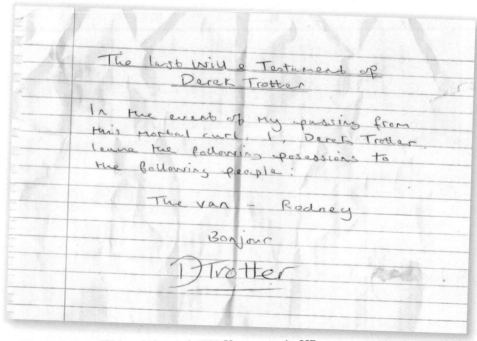

The last Will & Testament of
Derek Trotter

In the event of my passing from
this mortal curl, I, Derek Trotter,
leave the following posessions to
the following people:

The van — Rodney

Bonjour

D Trotter

Desperate times. Written in hospital, 1989. You can see the HP sauce
stains from the bacon sandwich Rodney smuggled in for me.

We lost Grandad and found Uncle Albert. Pictured here on the Jolly Boys Outing to Margate, 1989.

A fiery end to an otherwise brilliant day out. The coach that took us to Margate mysteriously explodes.

The gang.

The name's Trotter… Del Trotter. From a young age I was aware of the important statement the right clothes can make. Like the peacock displaying his plumage, when I walked into a room all the lady peacocks knew I meant business.

CHAPTER 10

EL DEL

It'd been raining so hard even the ducks were sheltering in bus stops. I don't mind a bit of wet, but with a consignment of Mexican sun hats to shift, it was really starting to get on my nerves. It's no fun being stood in the rain for hours trying to flog the unfloggable, a bloke could catch a death. So I sent Rodney out, and he nearly did.

I'd been chatting to a mate of mine, Alex, down the pub. He ran a little travel agents on the high street and had been struggling to get the punters in, so I came up with a belter of an idea: if he put it around that he was going to offer his next customer a holiday to anywhere of their choice at a knock-down rate – say eighty per cent off – he'd have herds of punters through his door hoping to get lucky. Course, he knew it made sense. I like to help other people out if I can, when you've a mind for business as sharp as mine it would be a crime to keep it all to yourself. Besides, I was dying for a holiday and at that price I'd have been an idiot not to raid the piggy bank.

But where to go? With a once-in-a-lifetime opportunity like that I didn't want to blow it on just any old package. This was our chance to see one of the jewels of the world, to soak up new culture and expand our horizons on glistening foreign shores. We needed to get away from the usual tourist spots and try something fresh, something with a bit of class. So, a week in Benidorm it was.

I dashed back to the flat to tell Rodney. I knew he needed something to lift his spirits and the news of our forthcoming dose of sun and sangria did just the trick. Then Grandad announced how much he was looking forward to coming and Rodney's spirits took a swift nosedive. Mine too if I'm honest, I hadn't thought to book Grandad a ticket.

'I've always wanted to go to Benidorm,' he said, 'where is it?'

'Spain,' I told him, racking my brain to come up with an excuse as to why he shouldn't come. I know it sounds mean but you never met him. I was picturing eager foreign sorts on tap, dancing the night away in paradise, but paradise just wouldn't be paradise with Grandad sat moaning in it.

'Spain?' he said. 'I've been to Spain before.'

'Well, you wouldn't wanna go again, would you?' I said. 'It'll be the same old thing.'

'I ain't never been to Benidorm though,' he said, 'it'll be a nice break.'

He shuffled off into the kitchen to do something 'orrible to some food, and I was left with Rodney, trying to figure out how we could put him off from going.

'Tell him the food will upset his stomach,' Rodney suggested. But that wouldn't work. Grandad had a stomach like a rubbish skip.

'What about the change of climate then?' Rodney asked. 'Remember the last holiday we had, he was moaning about it all week. We'd only gone to Bognor!'

He had a point, but there was no way around it. However we dressed it up, it would break the old git's heart if we said he'd have to stay at home. So I got on the blower to Alex and got him to book an extra seat on the flight and shove another bed in our room. We'd just have to hope it was hot enough to keep the windows open.

Three weeks later and we were off to Luton Airport.

From the word go Grandad complained. He complained about the early start, the queue to check in, the breakfast at the airport (which was rich, considering, but by that point he was so enjoying having a moan he couldn't stop). Thankfully he fell asleep on the plane, which was a relief for us, but not so much for the bloke he ended up slumped over.

Arriving at the hotel, I noticed it didn't look quite like it did in the brochure. But apart from the exterior, the interior, the staff, the room, and our window looking out over a scrap-metal yard, it was all right.

That evening, we ate in the hotel. Grandad wanted to find some 'proper English grub' but I told him he should expand his horizons. He never was one for exotic food. I showed him a bottle of Thousand Island dressing once and he broke out in a cold sweat. Tell the truth though, Spanish chicken 'n chips ain't that different to English ones.

Rodney kept going on about how we should take the opportunity to experience a bit of culture, so, after Grandad had shuffled back to the room for the night, we went out on the town and took in a show. It weren't bad, it was some Spanish bloke doing a Roy Orbison impression. A bit later, and with a few more San Miguels down his gullet, Rodney got brave and took to the dance floor. If you've never seen Rodney dancing, count yourself blessed. It was, and always has been, a painful sight.* The best that can be said of it is that he don't do it all that often. But sitting there watching him writhing around to some sweaty fat bloke singing 'Preety Woman', well, it made me feel a bit Tom Dick. So, before the chicken 'n chips could make an abrupt

---

* Think Billy Elliot with worms.

comeback, I did a quick shimmy onto the dance floor and escorted Rodney to the nearest exit. He weren't best pleased.

'I'm just letting myself go a bit,' he said when we got outside.

'I'm all for having fun, Rodders,' I explained, 'but we don't have to make spectacles of ourselves.'

'Spectacles!' he said. 'I'm not the one wearing bright white shoes and enough jewellery to make Liz Taylor jealous!'

At this point he was sailing dangerously close to getting a clip round the lughole, but it was our first night and I didn't want to ruin the overall holiday experience (Grandad would take care of that). Rodney had always been a sensitive lad so I chose my words carefully.

'You looked like a right tit out there, Rodney, that's all,' I said.

'Well, those people over at the bar waving and cheering me on obviously didn't think I looked like a tit,' he said.

'They weren't cheering you on Rodney, they were calling for the bouncer to step in and do something.'

'How do you know, you don't speak Spanish.'

'*Moules à la crème*,' I replied, putting right his error.

Later on back in the hotel bar, he said he'd been going for the *Saturday Night Fever* effect. I told him that was all well and good but there's a very fine line between *Saturday Night Fever* and typhoid fever. In the end I think he understood I was just looking out for him. I mean, what are big brothers for?

Aiming for a high-class joint, the following night we took up position at El Sid's Sports Pub and did our best to prove irresistible to the local talent. Rodney tried, but the only attention he got was from some old Spanish bird called Maria who thought he was ill. After we'd convinced her to stop shoving cold, wet serviettes on his forehead, we got chatting to a pair of English sorts. Obviously, I was out to impress, so I told a few little white lies, explaining that we were two business traders stopping over for the night while our jet was refuelled in Alicante (always give yourself a time limit otherwise you might get stuck with 'em all holiday). The charm offensive worked and they ended up coming back with us to our hotel. As you know, I've always been able to stun birds with my words, but the best patter in the world couldn't keep the night afloat once we'd opened the door to our room and they were faced with the sight of Grandad sprawled on his mattress. We were hit by a wall of smell that I can only describe as being cabbagey. And what with the snoring and the false teeth sitting in a glass on the bedside table, any romantic prospects the evening may have had were shattered. They turned on their heels and hotfooted it out of there,* leaving Rodney and me no choice but to put a pillow over our heads and try and get some shut-eye.

The next morning, rather than mope about how the evening had worked out, Rodney and I decided to make the best of it and got ourselves on the beach to soak up some sun. Grandad had been paddling for a bit, staring out to sea, then he announced he was going back to the hotel room for a fiesta. *Best place for him*, I thought. I'd brought him along, if he was determined to have a crap time then there weren't much I could do about it, was there?

A bit later, while Rodney went up to check on Grandad, I got chatting to a French sort by the pool. I'd been giving her a bit of the old *defense de fumier* and I could tell that she was putty in my hands. I was about to move in to accept her surrender when Rodney rushed up to tell me Grandad had been arrested!

---

* A couple of days later I spotted the pair of runaways across the street while I was on my way to the chemist to get Grandad something for his guts. I waved and called but they dived into some bushes and didn't come out.

We shot over to the local police station but they didn't know nothing about him and we ended up chasing all over town trying to find where they'd shoved the old sod.

Eventually we found him sitting in a cell block a bit like one of them ones in *Tenko*, you know, all dirty bricks and rats making the most of the shade. Señor Old Bill weren't much help, being all vague and Spanish. Finally, we got in to see Grandad. *OK*, I thought, *at least he'll know what happened.* Except, of course, he didn't.

'I was just crossing the road to the hotel,' he told us, 'when this police car came screeching up. It nearly run me over. Next thing I know, I was banged up in here! They ain't even charged me with nothing!'

Rodney and I weren't having that, he must have done *something*.

'Well,' he admitted, 'there was a little incident. It didn't happen today though…'

'Now we're getting somewhere,' I said. 'When did it happen?'

'1936.'

I can't say patience is my greatest feature but I have my moments. Just then, for example. At no point did I give Grandad a whack round the head with his state-provided bedpan.

'In 1936 I was deported from Spain and all her territories and dominions,' he went on.

This was the sort of thing you'd hope he might have mentioned earlier, say before I'd put my hand in my pocket and ponied up the price of his bloody airfare. I asked him why.

'I was up to no good, weren't I?'

'Well, I didn't think they deported you for doing sodding missionary work!' I said. 'So what happened in 1936?'

'The Spanish Civil War, that's what. The family was living in Peabody Buildings, Peckham Rye. They were hard times, no money, no food, no future. Millions of unemployed on the dole. One day, me and my mate Nobby Clarke decided we'd had enough so we ran off to join the Foreign Legion.'

'The Foreign Legion?' asked Rodney. 'You don't mean the British Legion?'

'Na, the French Foreign Legion, you know, camels and forts. So we hitchhiked to Southampton.'

'That's where their headquarters were, was it?' I asked.

'No! That's where we stowed away on a tramp steamer, hidden under the tarpaulin. The voyage was terrible. Us Trotters ain't never made good sailors.' Which was true enough, as I'd find out for myself in the years to come. 'Nobby was all right on the water though. I think it came from the time when he was a caretaker at a seamen's mission in Grimsby.'

'I don't want to worry you,' I told him, 'but our plane leaves in three days, so can we get to the bit about Spain?'

'I'm just coming to it, ain't I? So, when the ship finally docked, guess where we were?'

'Spain!' Rodney and I shouted.

'No,' he said, 'Tangiers. That's where the Foreign Legion had one of their main bases. So, we jumped ship and made our way to the barracks. When we got there we couldn't believe our eyes, they were the biggest band of cut-throats, villains and murderers you could ever hope to see! They were the scum of the earth!'

'So you didn't join, then?' asked Rodney.

'We tried, but they wouldn't have us. That left Nobby and me in right lumber. We had no money, nowhere to sleep and we was thousands of miles from home. Then we had a bit of luck, we bumped into an Arab who offered us a job. He said he'd pay us to take his motor launch over to the Spanish coast and deliver... well, a cargo.'

'What sort of cargo?' I asked him. I had a horrible feeling curling up in my guts.

'Guns,' he said.

'Guns!' Rodney was beside himself. 'You were gun-running in the middle of a civil war?'

'Best time to do it, Rodney,' Grandad explained. 'Supply and demand. But we weren't doing it purely for financial gain. We both felt a deep commitment to a political cause.'

'Which side were you selling to?' I asked him.

'Whichever had the most money.'

I couldn't believe it! I had no idea he had even half a head for business.

'So,' he continued, 'it was after the seventh trip when it happened. There was government troops lying in wait for us. They arrested us and took us to a little prison outside a town called Tarifa. They took Nobby away and tortured him. Oh it was awful… all you could hear were his screams, echoing through the night. But no matter what they did to him he wouldn't talk. Then it were my turn…'

'They tortured you?' Rodney said.

'No, but they would've done if I hadn't told them everything I knew! A couple of days later, these government geezers arrived with our deportation papers and… well, that's about it, really.'

'Are you sure?' I asked him. 'You haven't forgotten any minor details? Like how you popped over to Hong Kong and became an opium peddler, or how you got a Saturday job in the white slave trade?'

'Nah… I just came back to Peckham and put my name on the housing list.'

At point, the guard came back and I decided to try and talk our way out of the situation. I took him to one side and laid a bit of patter on him, plus a sizeable donation to the charity of his choice (I was sure she'd be grateful). Course, he let me do that before explaining that they'd only picked the silly old duffer up on a jaywalking charge and he was free to go. Five minutes later we were back on the street, one berk up and several hundred pesetas down.

At least the last few days of the holiday weren't too bad. Grandad didn't even moan about having to sleep in the bathroom.

CHAPTER 11

LAWNMOWER ENGINES

Every now and then Rodney would go through a self-reliant phase.

He'd spent a couple of weeks as head of the tenants' association, and I'd had great hopes for him. The day he entered office the drums began to bang. All night long you could hear 'em, beating out a message of hope to the four corners of our mighty estate. You could almost hear the chant, 'Bwana Rodney, he come daylight.' He had the opportunity to make the town hall tremble, to bring about a hurricane of social unrest in order to give the people what they deserved. In the end he filed a complaint about Grandad's shopping trolley being nicked from the pram sheds. He didn't even get the sodding lifts fixed. Still, it had obviously gone to his head as he suddenly announced his plans to break away from Trotters Independent Traders and set up his own business. Apparently he'd spent the last couple of weeks reviewing his life and come to the conclusion that he was going nowhere and never would unless he started making his own decisions in life. So he was going it alone… with Mickey Pearce. To be fair, this amounted to going it alone, as Mickey Pearce had all the intelligence, charm and business sense of a bucket of chutney. Grandad knew it too.

'He'd rob his own grandmother, he would,' he said.

'That was never proved,' Rodney said. 'Mickey's quite an astute businessman, and he's putting capital into the venture.'

'Putting money in, is he?' I asked, honestly surprised.

'Well, he will as soon as his giro cheque arrives.'

That sounded more like it. 'And what about you then?' I asked.

'I've got money, Del,' he said, which, I'll admit, was a bit of a shock as I'd recently caught him rummaging in hedgerows for returnable bottles. 'I've got my half of the partnership.'

This was a bloody liberty, but I realised it was the perfect opportunity to teach him an important lesson in independence. On her deathbed, Mum had made me promise that I'd teach Rodney how to stand on his own two feet. 'Let him be his own man, Del,' she'd said, 'let him find his way in this world.' Which had turned out to be a difficult promise to keep, given what I had to work with.

'All right,' I said, taking out our current capital and peeling a chunk off for him, 'if that's the way you want it. But you'll have to understand one thing. Going it alone means exactly what it says. From now on you pay your own way in the world, you pay your own way in the pubs, and you pay your own way in this flat. You make a mistake, you *stick* by that mistake. All right?'

'Fine,' he said, snatching the notes off me. 'Bloody 'ell!' he moaned. 'All them years of working and all I get is this?'

'Yeah well, profits are down.' I weren't going to give him a fortune to throw away, was I? 'Besides, I had to buy some stock off Alfie Flowers yesterday so most of the capital's tied up.' This was half true, Alfie had caught me a bit non compos mentis down the One-Eleven club the night before and swung me for a load of gear that I was now lumbered with.

'This'll have to do then, won't it?' he said, shoving it in his pocket. 'I'll see you down the auction tomorrow.'

As much as the ingratitude felt like a dagger to my heart, I'd quite like to have had Rodney prove me wrong. For one thing it would have meant one less person to look after, but also 'cos he's my brother and I wanted him to make something of himself. Not that I weren't a bit torn. I mean, there's nothing more annoying than placing a bet and seeing the other bloke win, is there?

I needn't have worried.

Next morning down the auction I saw Rodney and Mickey eyeing up the goods. Mickey was in his usual pinstripe, thin tie and trilby. He thought he looked like one of the Specials, but he looked more like a spiv butcher in negative.

'Hello, young Michael,' I said to him. 'What you after?'

'Cut-glass goblets,' he admitted, not being the sort of bloke to keep his cards close to his chest, or even in his hand.

'No we ain't!' Rodney interrupted. 'We're just gonna see what comes up.'

There weren't much on offer. The auctioneer had opened with a load of smoke-damaged fire alarms which hadn't exactly seen the bids come flooding in.

'Well, listen,' I told 'em, 'the one you want to watch out for is Lot 37. It's nothing but a load of old scrap iron. Save your money.'

I left them arguing the toss and went off to have a bid on the cut-glass goblets they'd been after. Funny, they didn't make a single bid for 'em. Instead, they went for Lot 37. But that's Rodney for you, always overthinking things. I found them outside afterwards, staring at the pile of junk they'd blown their cash on.

'This stuff is a load of old rubbish!' Rodney moaned.

'I did try to warn you,' I told him.

'What are they?' Mickey asked.

'Those, Mickey,' I told him, 'are lawnmower engines.'

'Lawnmower engines?' Rodney weren't impressed.

'Yeah,' I said, 'but they ain't *ordinary* lawnmower engines.'

'No?' I could see by the greedy look growing in his eyes that a little bit of hope had returned to him.

'No,' I said, 'they're *broken* lawnmower engines.'

He crumpled then.

'Er… Del,' he said, 'we're gonna have problems getting them home, we came here on the green line. I don't suppose we could put some in the back of the van, could we?'

'Back of my van?' I laughed. 'You must be joking, I've only just cleared 'em out of it. That was the rubbish Alfie Flowers stitched me up with,' I explained. 'I never thought I'd sell it, but you know what I always say, "he who dares wins"! I actually made a tidy little profit on it.' I just wished I'd had my Polaroid on me. You should have seen their faces.

<hr>

Over the next week I had a blinding time. I'd picked up a load of woollen tea cosies that just weren't shifting, but I'd got Mrs Murphy to sew the holes up, then I took 'em down the youth centre and flogged the lot as hats to some West Indian kids. The cut-glass goblets had gone straight out, earning a nice profit, and I was feeling on top of the world come the weekend.

Rodney? Not so much. He was still trying to work out what to do with those knackered engines. Apparently, they'd stored them in Mickey's mum's garden shed and one night someone had broken in and nicked a couple. The following night they broke in again and put 'em back.

To make matters worse, Mickey had been off work for a few days. According to Rodney he was out of town finalising some major deal with an important investor. Judging by the postcard Mickey's mum showed me, the important investor must have been the Swedish bird he'd copped off with on a last-minute break to Spain. I felt for Rodney, but if there's one business lesson worth learning, it's not to leave Mickey Pearce in charge of the dosh. So there he was, out of cash, loitering around the flat writing out I.O.Us and still trying to pretend he was the second coming of Richard Branston. I respected his optimism, but that alone don't put food on the table, does it?

Being the kind brother I am, I decided to help out a bit. I was down the Star of Bengal enjoying a ruby when a business associate and pal, Towser, came in.

''Ere, Towser,' I said, 'sit down a minute, I want you to do me a favour. You know those broken lawnmower engines that dozy twonk Rodney got himself lumbered with?'

'Yeah.' Towser had been laughing as hard as the rest of us.

'I want you to buy 'em off him.'

'Do me a favour, Del. Alfie Flowers offered me those a month ago, I don't want nothing to do with 'em.'

'It's all right, you don't have to spend any money.' I handed him a bunch of notes. 'There's two hundred quid. I want you to offer him that.'

'Two hundred? But they're not worth a score as scrap!'

'I know that, but Rodney's had a bad week and I want him to think he's made a good profit.'

'Why don't you just give him the money?'

'Because it'll seem like charity.'

'And he'd be too proud to take it?'

'No, he'd snap it up like a shot, but I want him to think he's been successful. I want him to think he's proved me wrong. Now, don't let him know where the money's come from, just say you've got a contact in the GLC parks department and they can't get enough lawnmower engines or something.'

'All right, Del.'

I bunged him twenty quid for his trouble and advised him to take the engines straight back to Alfie Flowers once he'd bought 'em (Alfie could have 'em for free for all I cared). Y'see, with my plan, Rodney would gain a bit of confidence, realise he'd be better off being my partner again, and then I'd get my money back when he bought back in. Everyone's a winner.

I'd underestimated the stupidity of Rodney Bleedin' Trotter.

I met him down the pub the next day and, as predicted, his mood was on the up. I gave him a ribbing about the engines and, course, he came straight back at me.

'For your information, Derek, this morning I successfully negotiated the sale of those engines to Towser.'

'You're kidding me!' I said.

'Good business sense, see? I knew all the time that if I held on long enough I'd get a good price.'

'Well,' I told him, 'I admire your courage. Mickey Pearce will be pleased when he gets back from his holiday, won't he?'

'Don't talk to me about Mickey Pearce,' he said. 'I've liquidated our partnership. I was thinking... well, you know...'

'We go back to how we was? You and me together?'

'Yeah! You and me, Del, eh? And now I've got experience of buying and selling.'

'That could be invaluable, Rodney,' I told him, somehow managing to keep a straight face. 'All right then, let's pool our resources. How much did you get for those lawnmower engines?'

'One hundred and sixty-five quid,' he said.

'Is that all?' Saucy git!

'It's not bad, Del,' he said. 'I mean those engines are only worth about a score scrap value.'

'All right,' I said, 'cos I could hardly argue without blowing the whole thing. 'Hand it over then.'

'I ain't got it,' he said. 'I've got something even better.'

'Oh yeah?'

'Yeah,' he said, 'I went straight down to Alfie Flowers's yard and bought a load more of those lawnmower engines – he had another load delivered this morning!'

CHAPTER 12

IT WAS ONLY
A CHOPPER

With Rodney back in the fold, things went back to normal, and it was around about this time that Trotters Independent Traders started to make a name for itself in the painting and decorating game. I'd always had an eye for a quality interior (in a purely manly sense, you understand), and what with Grandad's brief stint painting for the council and Rodney's GCE in art, it was only natural that we'd try our hand.

It was nothing massive, mind you (not that it couldn't have been), we did a couple of local jobs – the kitchen of a Chinese takeaway and the front room of my old mate Denzil's flat. But despite the craftsmanship and attention to detail being to perfectionist standard, and some mostly satisfied customers, the venture never took off as I'd hoped it would. There's a couple of very good reasons for this. One was Denzil's missus, Corinne. She was a right moody mare at the best of times, but by this time she really had it in for yours truly. It was all a big misunderstanding. See, I'd been in charge of the catering for hers and Denzil's wedding. Cooking has never been my strong suit

(I can knock together a decent egg 'n chips or a sausage sandwich no problem, but I'm certainly no Heston Fearnley-Bloominstall). I weren't keen on the idea, but Denzil insisted. I don't know what it was with Denzil, but he's always had a way of wrapping me right round his little finger. I gave it my best shot though. I brought Rodney on board, well, I needed someone to carry the grub to and from the van, and we had a lovely menu lined up: lobster vol-au-vents, beef and anchovy savouries, Philadelphia truffles, the lot! But the night before the big day our fridge packed up and all the food went manky. Even the wedding cake went for a burton. Well, there weren't much I could do at such short notice, so I improvised. It was still a lovely wedding, and I think, despite everything, the grub went down a treat. I mean, who don't like a nice bit of pie 'n mash and a slice of jam sponge? Never one to focus on the positives, Corinne had to go and get all nit-picky about it. They're divorced now, but it didn't take a Sally Morgan to see that the marriage was doomed from the off.

There were also cosmetological reasons for why the venture didn't take off. When it came to walls back then, most people were going for the same old tones: Duck Egg Blue, Apple White, Dawn Pink, etc. And that's fair enough, but being the natural born innovator that I am, I decided that Trotters Independent Traders would open people's eyes to new possibilities in the wall colour stakes, like Battleship Grey and British Rail Yellow for example. Like with so many of my ideas, people just weren't ready for it, and the whole thing ended up being, well, *San Fairy Ann*, as the French would say.

Not that I let it hold me back though. I'd been having dinner with Boycie in Mario's fish restaurant and between me, him and Mario we'd done a bit of business. I'd take the family down to Boycie's holiday cottage in Cornwall, take a bit of kit and tackle with us and see if we couldn't net a few decent salmon. We were gonna split the profit three ways. Of course, it was all above board, you know me, I'd never do anything illegal. All we had to do was bung the gamekeeper twenty-five quid and he'd show us the best place to stick our hooks. So, I got all the gear, bundled Rodney and Grandad into the van, and we headed south for a nice little break that should've also seen a few sovs come our way. We were about twenty minutes from the cottage, it was pitch black, the rain was lashing down, when all of a sudden we get flagged down by a local copper.

'You haven't given a lift to anyone in the last half hour, have you?' he asked. 'Only we've had word that a patient's escaped from the local hospital.'

'Escaped?' Rodney said. 'What you got out here, National Health stalags?'

'It's an institute for the criminally insane,' the copper explained. 'See, the storm brought some power cables down, blacked out the entire area. It even put the institute's security system out of action. So this patient took his chance and made off across the moors. For all I know he could be watching us right now.'

Which cheered us all right up.

'What was he in there for?' I asked.

'Ten years ago, this very night, he killed a party of weekend fishermen. You may have seen it on TV? They called him the Axe Murderer.'

Well, I must have been out that night 'cos it didn't ring any bells.

'Don't stop for anyone, no matter what the circumstances,' the copper said. 'And if you see or hear anything suspicious, phone the police immediately, your lives may depend on it.'

With that, PC Vincent Price gave us a grin and wished us a lovely weekend.

Course, Rodney went into full tart mode and wanted to turn the van around and go home.

'We can't go on,' he said, 'there's a crazed axe murderer out there somewhere!'

'I know that,' I told him, 'but we'll be locked up safe and sound in Boycie's cottage.' Well, we English don't get put off our holidays that easily, do we? You can't let a little thing like a crazed axe murderer on the loose ruin a weekend away.

'Besides, there's three of us.' I looked at Rodney, then at Grandad, then changed my mind. 'Don't worry,' I sighed, 'I'll look after you.'

It took some finding in the storm, but finally we pulled up at Boycie's place. It weren't quite what I'd pictured. Knowing Boycie, I thought it would have been a bit ostentatious, but it was a dingy little gaff at the end of a dirt track, with an outdoor lav and a leaky roof. Still, any roof was better than none, so we piled in. The electrics were down, but with the help of a box of matches and some candles, we fixed ourselves up with the basic necessities: a bottle of Scotch and some meat paste sandwiches.

Rodney and Grandad were being a pair of girls, panicking every time there was a bit of thunder, swearing they'd seen things moving out in the trees (fancy that in the middle of a force nine typhoon!).

Then Rodney found a small axe in a sideboard and threw a paddy.

'It's only a chopper!' I said.

'It's an axe!'

'Same thing.'

'No it ain't, Del,' he said. 'The police ain't looking for an escaped *chopper* murderer.'

'Listen, you two,' I said, 'he ain't gonna hang around here, is he? He'll have made himself scarce the minute he escaped.'

'Yeah,' Rodney said, 'he's probably halfway to London by now.'

'Right,' I agreed, 'he's probably looking for somewhere empty to hide out up there.'

'I hope he don't find our flat,' said Grandad.

I eventually calmed them down, and we cracked open a Monopoly set and settled down for the night. Everything was going fine till Rodney threw his dolly out of the pram 'cos the game weren't going his way. Outside the storm was getting worse. Rodney took a look out of the window and immediately had kittens when, according to him, he saw some bloke looking in at him. 'Del,' he said, 'there's somebody at the window.'

I went to take a look but it was all clear.

'What did he look like?' Grandad asked.

'Horrible,' said Rodney. 'He had these evil eyes and this grotesque, evil face.'

'Maybe it was a reflection?' I suggested.

'That was no reflection, Del,' he said. 'I swear to God, he... 'ere, what do you mean a "reflection"?'

'Well, you know, your imagination sometimes tricks you into believing you saw something that isn't really there.'

'Del,' he said, getting stroppy, 'I saw the rain running down his forehead. I saw the blood vessels in the whites of his eyes. I saw the hairs coming out of his nostrils!'

'Maybe it was the shadows in the trees,' suggested Grandad.

Suddenly, there was a loud knock at the door and a voice shouted out, 'Is anyone there?'

'I think there's someone at the door,' Grandad said.

'No,' Rodney replied, 'it's probably just the shadows in the trees, innit?'

'Who's there?' I shouted.

'The name's Robson,' the voice replied, 'I'm chief of security at the institution.'

'Thank God for that,' said Rodney, opening the door, trusting idiot that he is.

Robson was a big bloke, six foot and small change, dressed in a long black coat and a peaked cap. 'Appalling weather,' he said, reaching for his wallet, 'if you want to see some identification there's everything there from my driver's licence to my blood donor's card.'

'That's all right, Chief,' I said. 'So you haven't caught him yet?'

'I'm afraid not,' he said. 'We've extended the search with the entire police forces of three counties out looking for him. I don't suppose you've seen anything?'

'Only a face at the window,' said Grandad.

'Face at the window?'

'I was only three inches away from him,' Rodney explained. 'He was about fifty and he had this gaunt, hungry expression and his eyes were like a wild animal's.'

The Chief nodded. 'You're quite sure it wasn't a reflection?'

'Look!' Rodney said. 'It weren't a reflection, all right?'

'I have to ask,' said the Chief, 'because at times like these people's imaginations run amok. We've had two hundred sightings this evening alone. What colour was his hair?'

'Grey?' said Rodney.

'Sounds like my man. No doubt he saw me coming and made a run for it, he's probably a long way away by now.'

'So,' I said, bursting to get to the important details, 'do you think it's safe for me to go outside to use the khazi?'

'Perfectly safe, I'm sure.'

Despite the reassurance, I admit I weren't looking forward to it, but sometimes a man's gotta do what a man's gotta do, and there was no way this particular man was doing it in one of the saucepans we were using to catch the leaks from the roof.

So I popped outside.

I took an umbrella, but by the time I got to the toilet and sat down to take care of business, I was soaked anyway. It was very dark in there, and as business got under way, I remember thinking to myself, *Bloody hell, I hope this is the toilet.*

Job done, I opened the door and came face to face with some mush looming up at me out of the rain. Well, you can imagine the shock, my old april went from nought to sixty in two seconds flat. I mean, I'd come up against my fair share of nutters in the past (I'd been engaged to a couple), but up to that point I'd never had to deal with one immediately on exiting a toilet in a hurricane. A lot of blokes claim they don't know the meaning of the word 'fear' (Trigger being one, but then he means it literally so that don't count), not me though. Fear and I go back a long way. I have felt it, and still do, as much as the next right-minded man or woman. But as someone famous (it was either Winston Churchill or Rocky Balboa) once said, '*Being brave ain't about not being punched, it's about being punched but continuing to come back to get punched over and over again*'. Actually, reading that back I realise it's probably not the greatest quote. Maybe I didn't get it a hundred per cent accurate, but you get the gist of it.

Anyway, there I was standing face to face with this hulking, snarling axe murderer, but before the danger could fully register, I found myself sending a short, sharp uppercut to his solar plexus. Naturally, he bent over double, wheezing as he went, providing me with the perfect opportunity to deliver the *coup de tarte*: a karate chop to the back of his neck. He went down like a sack of King Edward's. I called out to Rodney to bring some rope, but at that point it didn't really matter. The bloke might have been mad, but he'd have to have been bloody stupid to get up from that.

I'd be lying if I said I weren't pleased with how I'd handled the situation, but not in a boastful, big-headed way. That just ain't my style. And while I did fill the others in with a blow-by-blow account of how I'd apprehended the man three entire police forces couldn't, I left out the fact that I'd managed to do it all with a brolly in one hand.

As Rodney, Grandad and the Chief tied the geezer up and bundled him into the back of the van, I sat and took stock. The bloke was an axe murderer, granted, but truth be told I felt sorry for the poor cock. Who knows what torment drove him to do what he did? Still, once Rodney and Grandad had driven the fruitcake off to the nearest police station, the Chief and I decided to finish off Boycie's Scotch to celebrate, and I felt right as rain in no time.

Honestly, I thought we should have all gone to the station together, but the Chief insisted he had to write out his report immediately, and as I was the one what had apprehended the murderer, he needed me there. But as we got on with the report, I couldn't help but notice he was acting a bit weird, staring out the window at the moon, pacing up and down, looming up behind me whenever I turned my back. Something was up, and I weren't completely surprised when Rodney called to tell me what it was.

'You won't believe this,' he said, 'but the bloke you knocked out ain't the murderer, he's the gamekeeper.'

I'd noticed that the Chief had picked up the little axe we'd found earlier and was weighing it up in his hands.

'Apparently,' Rodney continued, 'Chief Robson was knocked out by the lunatic when he escaped. He took his uniform and wallet and everything!'

I watched as the man we'd *thought* was Chief Robson started rubbing the edge of his thumb across the blade of the axe.

'Triffic, Rodders,' I said, 'well, you hurry back, won't you?'

I put the phone down, forced a grin and turned to face the axe man.

'Rodney just wanted to let us know they'd got there all right,' I said.

'Good,' he said, looking at me the way a cat looks at a mouse just before it rips its head off. 'Tell me… do you like fish?'

'Fish? Yeah,' I said, 'bit of salt and vinegar, lovely.'

'I only like *living* fish,' he said, his hackles shooting up, 'I only like fish that swim in rivers and seas. I hate anybody that kills them.'

'Me too,' I agreed. 'Bastards, ain't they? Killing all the lovely fishies.'

'But I saw fishing rods in your van!'

'Nothing to do with me,' I said, 'that's Grandad's and Rodney's stuff. I keep telling 'em not to hurt the fish.'

'Good.' He seemed happy with that and lowered his axe for a moment. 'Do you like snooker?'

'Snooker?'

'Yes,' he said (actually it was more of a yell). 'Do you like snooker?'

I weren't getting caught out twice. 'Do you?'

'I love snooker.'

'So do I!' I told him. 'Brilliant, innit?'

'Shall we play a game?'

I tried to think of a way around that one, snooker not being the sort of game you just had a spur of the moment crack at.

'All right,' I said, 'tell you what, I think I saw a snooker table in the shed at the bottom of the garden, I'll just pop out and check.'

I made towards the front door but he stepped in to block me. 'No need, we can use this one here,' he said, pointing at sod all.

I decided to take a gamble.

'All right then. Tell you what though. Why don't I put that axe somewhere safe, eh? I mean, you won't be able to hold your cue properly with that in your hand, will you?'

He stared at me for a few tense moments. Then he relaxed. 'I suppose you're right.'

He handed it over and I stashed it away in one of our bags, quick as you like. When I turned round he was stood right behind me, holding out his fists as if offering me something.

'Which cue would you like?' he asked.

I reached for one but he pulled his hand back so I went for the other.

'Good,' he said, holding up the imaginary cue he'd kept. 'This one's my favourite.'

'You can see it's a good'un,' I agreed.

'I'm not very good at snooker,' he said, 'I always lose.'

'I've a feeling you're gonna win this one,' I said.

'I hope not! My father used to force me to win at everything. But people challenge winners, you feel open to attack!'

I knew exactly what he meant.

'Losers are anonymous,' he continued. 'No one wants to challenge a loser. I *really* like losing.'

I decided to take another gamble.

'Well,' I said, 'what do you say we make the game a bit more interesting? How about a tenner a frame?'

'All right,' he agreed, pulling his wallet out.

I was up forty quid by the time the police came crashing through the windows.

CHAPTER 13

SORRY, GRAN

After our little brush with death (I told you, I've had loads), I decided to branch out and get involved in the antiques game. I've always known a fair bit about it, never missed an episode of *Antiques Roadshow*, and had built a fair collection of old pieces myself: couple of Rembrandt watercolours (I thought they were Rembrandt anyway, it was hard to read the signature), a genuine Da Vinci sculpture in the original fibreglass, and a sofa that must have been knocking on a century.

I'd picked up what I was sure was a Queen Anne cabinet at one of the auctions and got Rodney and Grandad to help me get it up to the flat. Grandad was his usual helpful self, moaning all the way up the stairs 'cos the kids had knackered the lifts again. You'd think, as a trained painter, he'd have some appreciation of the arts, but slopping a bit of gloss around for the council fifty years ago hadn't given him an eye for treasures. Rodney, with his GCE in art, should also have been knocked bandy by it, but all he could do was moan.

'It's got woodworm,' he said. 'Look at all them little holes.'

'Maybe Queen Anne played darts,' I told him. 'Besides, you don't know nothing about antiques. Dealers often put holes in stuff to give them a "distressed" look.'

'Distressed?' he said. 'This thing looks panic-stricken.'

Fair enough, it had seen better days, but that's what an antique's all about, innit? You want it to look as if it's been around the block a bit. That's why you have to be very careful about restoring every precious year of life they hold, to maintain their authentic appeal. I was considering letting the British Museum take a look at it once I'd given it a going over with some UHU and a squirt of Pledge.

In the end I decided to turn it over quickly so I whacked an ad in the local classifieds: 'Queen Anne cabinet. Genuine antique, good as new. Lovely condition throughout, a snip at £145.'

It weren't long before a collector came knocking at the door. Her name was Miranda and, I must say, she was quite a woman. She exuded class, the sound of her voice, the way she moved, the way she carried herself. She had a smashing pair on her 'n all.

To begin with she weren't interested in the cabinet. She'd been working as a dealer for most of her life and had picked up a few more tricks than me when it came to recognising the real McCoy. It was inspiring to watch her work though, the way her practised eye covered the whole piece, noting tiny details, like the type of veneer used, the shade of the wood... the word 'Fyffes' printed on the inside panel suggesting that it had probably been made out of banana boxes. She also clocked a painting on the wall of the flat that drew her interest. I didn't rate it much, but Gran had been given it by an art dealer she used to char for, and it had been hanging in the flat for decades. Anyway, Miranda's mood took a more positive turn and she suggested we went into business together over the cabinet. She'd take it over to her place and restore it then we'd sell it on and split the profits. It was an interesting proposition, so I dragged Rodney into the kitchen for a quick conference meeting.

'Well,' he said, 'if you want my opinion, I don't think we should let that cabinet out of our sight.'

I clarified our position. 'That cabinet is definitely going to her shop to be tarted up and sold for a ridiculously high profit, end of discussion.'

'Well, there's nothing like talking things through,' he said. 'If you weren't interested in my opinion what did you drag me in here for?'

''Cos I want your advice,' I said. 'I think she fancies me.'

'Leave it out, Del, she's an intelligent woman.'

I shouldn't have asked. What did Rodney know about women anyway? Miranda had a Mercedes. Most of his dates arrived by skateboard.

'If you're that interested,' he said, 'why don't you just give her a sign of your mutual attraction?'

He was right of course, I had to let her know how I felt. Let the unwritten language of love do the talking, plant a subtle, almost subliminal signal into the conversation that would make my feelings clear. So I walked back in, gave her a smack on the bum and asked if she fancied a curry. Of course she said yes.

The Star of Bengal let us down a bit, mainly due to some very rubbery chicken tikka. Miranda was chewing one bit for so long I was half expecting her to start blowing bubbles. Still, my charm saw me through and it weren't a bad old night, even if we did both suffer a touch of Gandhi's revenge the following morning.

After a swig of Pepto-Bismol, I headed over to her shop, a real pukka establishment, the sort of place royals go when they're in the market for a new sideboard. I was thinking I'd really fallen on my feet, especially when she agreed to go out on a second date. Realising I had a woman used to the finer things in life, I decided to book a table for two at a place I reserved exclusively for only the most special of ladies. I told Miranda to put her finest evening dress on, did myself up in full black tie, and we headed out for a no expenses spared evening at a Berni Inn. The drive to the restaurant didn't go as smoothly as I'd hoped. She hit her head getting into the van and hit it again getting out, and we broke down twice on Peckham High Road, but once we arrived all that was forgotten. You should've seen the looks we got when we walked in (anyone would have thought Berni himself had turned up). All those eyes on her made Miranda go a bit quiet. She was obviously a bit stunned by the whole experience, and that was before the grub had even arrived. But I'd seen it all before. You know, they say the way to a man's heart is through his stomach, but with my experience I'd argue the same can be said for a woman's heart. Take it from me, slapping a plate of chicken Gordon Blue and breaded mushrooms in front of a bird can make her see stars. Follow it up with a Berni Special Meringue Fountain and you're laughing. Those were the days, eh?

Anyway, I took her back to the flat and treated her to a tequila sunset (well, a gin sunset, we were fresh out of tequila). I could tell she liked it as she sipped it, staring at Gran's painting. She was obviously a connoisseur of drinks as well as antiques.

'Do you like Cézanne?' she asked.

'Oh yeah,' I said, 'bit of ice and lemonade, lovely.'

'I do love that painting,' she said. 'Your grandmother must have had very good taste.'

'Not really,' I told her, 'she married my grandfather.'

'Do you like the painting?' she asked.

'I hate it,' I said, being honest. 'Can't wait to get rid of it.'

'Oh don't ever throw it away. It would look so nice in my flat. I'd hang it just above my bed. Can you picture it? Oh, you can't… I've just remembered, you haven't seen my bedroom… yet.'

At this point I was thinking the ball was in the back of the net. I was heading over to the record player to whack my Richard Clayderman

LP on when she announced she needed to be heading off as she had an early start.

'Mummy and Daddy are bound to ring me first thing to wish me happy returns, you know what parents are like.'

'No,' I said, 'I haven't had any for ages. Did you say it was your birthday?'

'Surely I told you?'

She hadn't, I was sure she hadn't, but, if I'm honest, I was still thinking about her bed.

'Oh you haven't bought me a present?' She laughed. 'You really shouldn't have. It's very sweet of you.'

And with that it was a peck on the cheek and a dash for the door. She'd strung me up perfectly.

I wrapped up the painting and whipped it around her flat, leaving it where she'd find it with the morning post. She'd have a nice surprise when she got *out* of bed and, with a bit of luck and a following wind, I'd have a nice surprise when I got *into* bed that night.

Grandad kicked up a fuss when he noticed the painting was missing.

'Your gran brought that painting into this house,' he said.

'I know, and she left it to me,' I told him. 'One night, when she weren't feeling well she said, "Del, when I die that painting's yours."'

'I don't remember that,' he said.

'Well, you were out. There were witnesses though. Mum and Rodney. You remember, don't you, Rodney?'

'I can't say I do, Del.' Typical Rodney.

'You must remember, you were over there in the corner with Mum, having your nappy changed.'

I was in no mood for it, so I headed over to Miranda's shop, stopping to pick up a bunch of flowers on the way. The shop was closed for the fumigators (a sudden outbreak of woodworm), but Harry, one of the restorers, said Miranda was down at Huddleston's auction rooms so I made my way over, just in time to see Gran's painting turn up as one of the lots. Apparently it was by some old dauber called Joshua Blythe and bidding was starting at seven grand.

Part of me weren't surprised that Miranda had stitched me up, after all business is business, and you didn't get to have a bank balance like hers without having a bit of ice in the blood.

'Let's get one thing perfectly clear,' she told me, 'that painting is now mine. It's been legally registered in my name. Mummy and Daddy have even signed an affidavit to swear that it's been in our family for generations.'

Which was lucky, as things turned out, 'cos it soon came to light that the painting was stolen. I mean, I can't believe my gran would have done such a thing, but there you go. Just think, all those years it had been hanging on my wall where it could have led to my collar being felt, thankfully it was now out of my hands and into Miranda's. I believe she ended up doing a bit of bird actually, especially once they found a few other little treasures in her shop that she'd got hold of by slippery means. I never did see her bedroom wall. I could picture her new one though, there were bars on the windows.

<hr />

While I was still recovering from having been fleeced by Miranda, who should turn up but Roy Bleedin' Slater! Or, I should say, *Detective Inspector* Roy Bleedin' Slater. I knew he'd been doing well, rising through the ranks, over West London way. It was an 'orrible world he moved in, everywhere he went the risk of a sound kicking was never far away. But that's how the police force was back in them days. There was none of this human rights stuff, which was just as well for Slater 'cos he'd never been fully human. He'd built a career on taking bribes and kicking in teeth. The man was poison.

To find he'd been transferred over to our patch was the worst news I could have got, and I got it in the worst way, when Rodney (proud owner of that year's Doziest Twonk award) invited him back from the Nag's Head. Course, Rodney didn't know who he was, even a dipstick of his calibre wouldn't have invited Slater into our home if he had. Still, he was there and, predictably enough, out to cause as much grief as he possibly could. After asking us about a consignment of microwave ovens that had recently fallen off the back of a lorry, he bundled Rodney, Grandad and I off to the local nick, determined to play one of his stupid little games. And it was stupid. I mean, what did he think he was gonna fit Grandad up with? Being in possession of a forged bus pass? Demanding protection money from the local Darby and Joan Club?

But it was me Slater was really after. Rodney and Grandad were just what they call 'unilateral damage'. He had all three of us interrogated, spinning us in circles, trying to trip us up any which way he could.

Finally he threatened to plant some drugs on Rodney and have him put away. It shouldn't have surprised me. I'd known a lot of coppers and never had a problem with 'em. I mean, I weren't mates with 'em or anything, but they played a fair game. And then there was Slater. The only way out, he said, was if I agreed to become one of his informants. The fact that I'd sooner be six feet under than be one of his lapdogs made it all the more enjoyable for him. He knew full well I'd always been one to keep my nose, and everything else, clean, and he was relishing every second of having me in his trap. Now, I'd been stuck between plenty of rocks and hard places before, but I won't lie, as diachotomies go, this one was forty-two carat! The idea of having

Slater on my case for ever was more than I could bear. He'd have me running all over the place, getting me to stitch up anyone I could. I couldn't have that. No way, Pedro!

He was just about to get the charge sheets typed up when I had the idea. I told him that I did know of something he could use: the name of the bloke who had nicked the microwave ovens. But I told him I'd only give him the name if we could cut a deal. For his part of the deal he'd have to let Rodney and Grandad go, and sign an official document granting me immunity from prosecution. He couldn't believe his luck. His face lit up like a sprog's on Christmas morning at the thought of having me in his grubby little pocket. A while later he put the official document in front of me, so I signed it and gave him the name: Derek Trotter!

He had no choice but to let us all go. As it turned out though, Slater was only the first of two unwelcome visitors from my past that year and, however unpleasant it had been dealing with him, the second bad penny was much, much worse.

CHAPTER 14

LONE RANGER

I've always loved Christmas time. The lights, the carols, the goodwill between all men (and birds). Granted, all I'd ever got from Saint Nick growing up was an orange and a clip round the ear'ole, and I now had to brace my stomach for the annual onslaught that was Grandad's Christmas dinner (he'd been cocking it up ever since Mum died, bless 'em both). But despite all that, Christmas still made me feel warm inside. That particular year the Trotter household was all set to receive wise men bearing gifts. We got a wally with a disease instead.

I was down the Nag's Head, enjoying a seasonal Singapore Sling when Rodney came rushing in to tell me that Reg had turned up at the flat. Now, as far as I was concerned, Reg Trotter wasn't welcome. He'd run off and abandoned us all. That was his choice. Coming back into our lives? That was *my* choice. Rodney did his best to calm me down on the way back but all I wanted to do was grab the old bastard by the scruff of his neck and throw him back to wherever he'd come from.

'He's not the man you remember,' Rodney said. 'He's dishevelled and pathetic, he seems frightened.'

I promised I'd let the old man have his say, though I nearly went back on my word when I clocked him sat in my chair, wearing one of my shirts, drinking a glass of my brandy and smoking one of my cigars. Dishevelled and frightened? He was just where he wanted to be, sitting pretty.

'Your dad had a bath and a shave, Del,' said Grandad, 'then he found he was low on clothes.'

'He'll be low on teeth before he's much older,' I promised.

'He only wants to stay for one night,' said Grandad.

'When he closed that front door all those years ago, he closed it for good,' I told him.

'Don't I get a say in this?' Rodney asked.

Knowing how to manipulate a soft mark, Reg jumped in. 'Let's hear what Rodney has to say.'

'What's to be said, Rodders?' I asked him. 'You know what he's like. I've told you often enough.'

'Yeah,' he said, 'and that's all I know. I wouldn't mind the opportunity of judging him for myself.'

'I may not have been the best father, Rodney,' said Reg, 'but I tried. And remember one thing: I never raised a hand to your mother, except in self-defence.'

I couldn't believe it! He was wheedling his way back in!

'He deserted you when you were just a sprog, Rodney! And not just you. He walked out on his own father! In all that time he didn't even know if Grandad was alive or dead.'

But Grandad had already decided to forgive him. Having a son of my own now – not that you could compare the two, Damien's an angel – I understand, but at the time I couldn't believe Reg was getting exactly what he wanted.

I stared at Reg. 'Give me one good reason why I shouldn't chuck you out by the scruff of your neck?'

'I can't think of one, Del,' he said. 'I'm not proud of what I did. I'm ashamed, and sorry. I've been lying in that hospital bed, night after night, reliving the moment I walked out of here. It hurts, Del. It *hurts*.'

Course, that set Rodney and Grandad right off.

'Hospital bed?' Grandad said. 'What's wrong with you, Reggie?'

'A few months ago, they took me into hospital for some routine checks,' he said, handing over a medical card issued by Newcastle Infirmary.

'I've been living up there for the last year or so.'

That was the point he started to reel *me* in 'n all. Maybe, when it comes down to it, it's as hard for a son to abandon his father as it is for a father to abandon his son. Well, in most decent people's cases, Reg Trotter never struggled with it.

'What's wrong with you then?' I asked him.

'They discovered I've got some hereditary blood disorder,' he said. 'It's called...' He shook his head. 'I don't know, it's a medical word. A long one. They don't think they can cure it so I live on in hope. That's about all I have left.'

'Come on, Dad, these doctors can do miracles these days,' Rodney said, 'you've just gotta be brave... Hang on... did you say hereditary?'

'That's the reason I rushed down here!' he said. 'They told me I had to warn my children immediately. You'll both have to have blood tests as soon as possible.' He looked at me with a soppy look in his eyes. 'I've done right by you this time, ain't I, Del?'

'Yeah,' I said. 'Thanks a bunch.'

He got up out of my chair and made off to my bed. 'I'm feeling a bit weak,' he said, 'I think I'll climb in. Night, boys.'

'Do you think I'll have to have a blood test?' Grandad asked.

'It's hereditary!' Rodney said. 'That means it's passed forwards, not back!'

The next morning, Rodney and I went to see Dr Becker. He took a pair of samples and sent them off to be tested. As for Reg, his 'just one night' showed no sign of coming to an end. Christmas Day had come and gone and he was still making himself comfortable in the flat, helping himself to whatever took his fancy. I tried not to let it get to me, after all, if what he said was true I could hardly begrudge him a few meals and a loan of my wardrobe.

On New Year's Eve our results arrived. I'd been out, trying to bring a few more quid in now we had an extra mouth to feed, but Grandad pointed them out to me when I got back that evening. Both the envelopes were torn open.

'You can't blame him, Del,' said Grandad, 'I suppose he was too worried to wait for you.'

'I suppose so.' I gave Rodney his envelope and let him go first. 'Go on then, Rodders, what does it say?'

'All clear!' he shouted. 'Go on, my son!' I didn't blame him for being happy, but when I saw my result my heart sank.

'It says I'm… "Negative".'

I thought of everything I'd hoped to achieve in life, all my great plans, all my dreams. All ruined because of some poxy disease! Rodney then pointed out that 'negative' meant all clear. Bloody doctors! I'd assumed it was a medical term for 'curtains'. Still, it was good news and Rodney went off to get changed so we could go out and celebrate the New Year, now we knew we had one.

'That's weird,' Grandad said, staring at the test results. 'Your blood group's AB, but Rodney's is A.'

'Can't be,' I told him, 'we've got the same parents so we'd have the same blood group, wouldn't we?'

I checked the papers. He was right.

'We're brothers,' I said, 'so we should have the same blood! I mean, we had the same mother and we had the same fa…'

I'd had an 'orrible thought. Like most 'orrible thoughts, it only took a few seconds for it to grow in my head and become an 'orrible fact. When Rodney came back in, looking all blond and really tall and not even slightly like me, he could immediately tell something was up.

'I suppose you've got a right to know,' I said, 'but I want you to understand that it don't make a blind bit of difference. Rodders... that man you call your dad... ain't.'

'Ain't what?'

'Your dad.'

He shook his head. 'Are you trying to tell me that that man isn't our father?'

'No... he just isn't yours.' I showed him the test papers.

'So I've got a different blood group, what does that prove?'

'It proves you're a "whodunnit", Rodney!'

Just then, Reg came in.

'Been for a drink, Reggie?' Grandad asked.

'Yeah I've been for a drink, Dad. I've got bloody good reason to, ain't I?'

'What are you moaning about now?' I asked him, though I reckoned I could guess.

'I can read, Del Boy! Earlier this morning I happened to notice them medical reports. I thought, *That's funny, different blood groups!* So I checked my group with my donor's card, then I checked your grandad's with his old army records. And what do I discover? We've got a Lone Ranger in the family... If your mum was alive now I'd kill her!'

I was about to escort him to the balcony to find out if the EEC had changed the law on gravity, when Rodney and Grandad stepped in.

'Try and see it from my point of view, Del!' Reg said. 'How would you like to have a son who you loved and cared for, who you fetched up as your own, only to find years later that he's a mystery?'

'Loved and cared for him?' I shouted. 'You walked out and left Rodney when he was five years old! You didn't care if he had shoes on his feet or food in his belly!'

'I dunno what you're talking about Rodney for,' he said. '*You're* the mystery!'

It knocked the wind out of me.

I had to get out of there, I couldn't stand that old devil staring at me, as if I could give him some answers. I didn't have answers. I had nothing.

I wanted to avoid people for a bit, the last thing I needed was for mates to start asking questions. I was thinking of Mum and what people would say about her if they knew. See, she'd gained a little bit of a reputation towards the end of her life, but that was only 'cos people didn't really know what she was going through. Mum and Dad had always had problems, but it weren't surprising, Mother Teresa would have been hitting the bottle if she'd shacked up with Reg Trotter. But had the problems really gone as far back as before I was born? Had Reg had good reason for the way he was with Mum? Nah, he'd not known anything about it, had he? He was just a bastard. Worst thing was, right then, it seemed he weren't the only one.

I gave Trigger a bell and ended up kipping round at his place. I had no worries with Trig. I could have drawn him a diagram and he still wouldn't have had a clue what was going on.

The next day I went down the market but I was well off my game, so I headed over to the Nag's Head. The barmaid knocked me up a Grand Marnier and grapefruit juice, telling me what a giggle Reg had been at the party the night before. 'He got up on stage and sang a few

Adam Faith songs,' she said, 'he was good! He did a brilliant version of "Someone Else's Baby".'

I was gutted I'd missed it.

Then the three of 'em came in, thick as thieves, Rodney and Grandad laughing over one of Reg's stupid stories. Rodney came over to say hello. He could see what I was going through, and a part of him was hating it almost as much as I was. I didn't blame him for spending time with the old man though. They had a lot of time to make up for, although I did think their trip to the zoo was taking it a step too far.

'Look, Del,' he said, 'why don't you just come home, eh?'

'How can I, Rodney?' I said. 'He'll never let me forget that I'm a Lone Ranger.'

'He hasn't mentioned it, honest.'

'Maybe not to you but I know him, the minute I let my guard down he'll be shouting, "Hi Ho Silver!"'

'Listen,' he said, 'I remember during a biology lesson at school, the subject of genetics came up, and the teacher said that children of the same parents can have different blood groups. Why don't you get some advice from Dr Becker?'

'Because then he'd know!' I told him. 'He treated Mum when she was ill, I don't want him thinking badly of her.'

Rodders was just trying to cheer me up. For all his general wallyishness, he really is the jewel in Mum's crown, and I told him so. In the end I felt no better, but Rodney's chat had made me realise one thing: I couldn't let Reg beat me. Derek Trotter may be a lot of things, but he ain't a man to just roll over. I'd done more to keep that flat going, keep the *family* going, than Reg ever had. If he wanted me out he was gonna have a fight on his hands.

Reg called Rodney over to play cards, and, deciding to be the bigger man, I joined them. I managed about half an hour and then had to leave before I did something to get us all barred.

Needing to get my head straight, I took a leisurely toby back to Trig's place. By the time I arrived I knew exactly what I had to do.

That evening I went home feeling much better.

'All right, Grandad, all right, Rodders!' I said, full of the old bounce, 'good evening, Reginald. Stick a pizza under the grill, would you, Grandad?'

'You in for the night then, Del?' Grandad asked, shuffling off to burn me a pizza.

'Yes I am!'

'Good,' said Reg, 'we can have a family sing-song.' He looked at me and grinned. 'You can join in if you like.'

I just smiled as he buggered off into the kitchen after Grandad.

I could tell Rodney was in a bad mood.

'What's up with you?' I asked.

'It's Dad,' he said, 'earlier on I showed him my GCE certificates. He said he was proud of me. Then he went and wrote a bet on the back of one of 'em!'

'I told you Rodney, he's the devil.'

'I'm beginning to think you're right.'

Reg came back in, moaning that there was no booze left in the flat, and asked me if I fancied popping out to get some more.

'No, Reginald,' I said, 'I don't. I went to see Dr Becker this evening.'

Grandad came in. 'Something wrong with you, Del?'

'Yeah, see, for the past week or so I've been suffering from a pain in the arse.' I stared at Reg. 'So I decided I should get a second blood test just to check whether there had been a mistake with the first. But Dr Becker said there was no need because, as you so rightly said, Rodders, a person's blood group don't mean a thing. A mother and father could have three children and they could all have different blood groups.'

'Rubbish!' said Reg. 'What does he know anyway?'

'Oh he knows a lot!' I said. 'For example: he knows my blood group is A.'

'Why'd he write AB on the results then?' asked Grandad.

'He didn't. Someone else added the B.'

'It must have been someone at the clinic having a joke!' Reg could see his advantage slipping, but he weren't going down without a fight. 'The letters arrived by post, the envelopes were sealed!'

'Until you opened 'em!' Grandad said.

'I just wanted to check that my boys didn't have the same illness as me!' He suddenly, very conveniently, grew weak.

'Oh yeah,' I said, 'Dr Becker was very interested in this disease of yours so he phoned Newcastle Infirmary to find out exactly what was wrong with you. What do you reckon they said?'

'They'd never heard of him?' asked Rodney.

'How did you guess, Rodney? They ran his name through their computer and found they didn't have a patient called Trotter, but they did have a *porter* called Trotter! He left a couple of weeks ago, with fifty-seven blankets, one hundred and thirty-three pairs of rubber gloves and the chief gynaecologist's Lambretta.'

'I don't feel all that well,' said Reg.

'Dr Becker mentioned that too. He recommends lots of fresh air, new surroundings and plenty of exercise, like taking a long... brisk... walk.'

'Maybe he's right,' Reg said, looking at his watch. 'Is that the time? I really ought to be on my way.'

'So soon?' I asked.

'Don't want to outstay my welcome, Del. I'll get my things together.'

'You do that.'

I popped a few quid in his pocket – he may have been the devil, but he was still family.

⁂

I won't deny that over the years I wondered what had happened to him, wondered if he would turn up again. He never did. I suppose he must be dead now. Reg Trotter, you were a lousy dad, in fact you were a lousy human being full stop, but still… whatever you did and wherever you went, I hope you didn't have it too bad.

CHAPTER 15

GHOSTS AND BOOMERANGS

Remember June, my old fiancée (well, one of 'em) from back in the sixties? Well, it was around about this time that she and I got briefly reacquainted. Rodney had started dating this young bird, Debbie, who worked in the local newsagents. Well, I say dating, basically he'd been lurking round the shop for about a month like a lost cat in a parker, pining over her from behind the Slush Puppie machine, and she'd finally took pity on him. I had to hand it to him though, she was a pretty girl, and she didn't even seem to mind his ever-growing collection of 'adult art' magazines. She was a real keeper. Anyway, it turned out that Debbie's mum was none other than June Snell. Junie had recently moved back to the estate and had a place over in Zimbabwe House, just across the precinct from us.

I popped over to her flat one night and it was clear right from the off that even after nineteen years apart there was still a spark between us (at one point that evening I even considered popping home and getting my Sheena Easton LP). The years had been kind to June, well, civil at least. She looked smashing, in a loud, slightly scary sort of way, and when I started firing up the old charm generators I could almost see the sweat begin to glisten on her skin. To be fair though, she'd put on a good few pounds since we'd last met so that might have had something to do with it. We had a really nice chat, catching up on what had been happening in our lives, reminiscing about the good old days. Even Rodney turning up to see Debbie couldn't spoil it. Junie and I decided to leave the young lovebirds to it and went for a drink down the Nag's Head for old times' sake.

I'll be honest, it weren't all fun seeing June again. It had stirred up some mixed emotions in me. If you recall, the last time I'd seen June was just after Albie Littlewood's funeral. He'd been my best mate, and it had cut me up pretty badly, especially coming so soon after I'd lost Mum. Junie and I and Albie and his bird, Deidre, had been having a right laugh up to then, going on double dates and what 'ave you. But the thing that had bothered me most about what happened was that Albie had been on his way to the pub to see me when he died. Another thing I couldn't help but still wonder was why June had dropped me so suddenly after it had happened, without a word of explanation. I brought it up over our drinks, but she didn't want to discuss it. I couldn't blame her. Sometimes the past is best left where it is. She'd had her reasons, and that was that. So I decided to change the subject to something more cheerful.

'What did they put your old man in prison for?' I asked.

'He stole some watches,' she said. 'We're getting a divorce when he gets out, the marriage never worked right from the start.'

'Oh I dunno,' I said, 'it must have lasted quite a while.'

'No, we've only been married seven years.'

'Seven years? But Debbie must be... Sorry, I didn't mean to—'

'He's not Debbie's father,' June said.

'I'm sorry.' I tried to explain. 'I wasn't trying to... y'know.'

I'd put my foot in it, so I decided it was time to change the subject again. I went and got us some more drinks, and up at the bar I bumped into Mickey Pearce. He said he'd just come from an evening class where he was learning Aikido (which was a load of rubbish 'cos when I asked him to say something in Aikido he just stared at me gormlessly). He then happened to mention that he'd got an invitation to Debbie's nineteenth birthday party. Well, it took a second or two to register, but when it did I went numb. June and I had broken up *nineteen and an 'alf* years ago. It couldn't be… could it? Then it all suddenly started to make sense, and I knew why June had left me so suddenly.

I needed some space and fresh air, so I made a quick dash to the bog. Pacing back and forth in front of the urinals I ran it over and over through my head, and no matter what way I came at it, the answer was the same: Debbie was *my* daughter! I suppose you never know what you're gonna feel when you discover something as life-changing as that. I imagine some blokes would feel panic and want to run away, but right then, standing there in the Nag's Head lav, Trigger standing next to me washing his hands, all I felt was… well, maternal. This in itself came as a bit of a surprise to me. I'd never really thought of myself as a dad before, maybe 'cos every time I'd tried it reminded me of Reg. But then I suppose I'd been a dad in a way to Rodney, but… bloody hell! Rodney!!!

I piled Junie into the van and sped back to the estate. I had to stop Rodney before he did something we'd all end up regretting, and I managed to drag him off just in the nick of time. Of course, he weren't best pleased when I finally got him home, and even had the nerve to accuse me of being jealous. I had to put him straight, didn't I? He didn't believe it at first. So I filled him in on the dates, and he still wouldn't have it that Debbie was my kid.

'But she's a pretty girl,' he said.

'I know that,' I said, 'I can see Mum in her.'

It finally sunk in.

He took it about as well as any bloke who's just found out that the woman he's fallen head over heels in love with is actually his niece could.

'I had to tell you, Rodney,' I explained. '"Cos that sort of thing just ain't allowed. It's… well, it's incense.'

Poor Rodney. Him and Debbie had even been planning on getting married.

'You can imagine the kind of problems that would have caused,' I told him. 'I'd have been your father-in-law. Your mother-in-law would have been your aunt, your wife would have been your second cousin… God knows what that would've made Grandad, the fairy godmother I s'pose!'

He made me promise to talk to June to make sure it was definite, then headed off to bed. 'I bet I have a nightmare,' he said when he reached the door. 'I bet I have a nightmare where my wife keeps calling me Uncle Rodney.'

The next evening I went to see June to have it all out in the open.

'If you've come 'ere to drag up the past, just forget it!' she said.

'But, Junie, there are things that need to be discussed,' I told her.

'What things?'

'Like are you going to tell Debbie or shall I?'

'Tell her what?'

'Oh come on, Junie,' I said, 'don't play the innocent with me – tell her that I am her father.'

That stopped her in her tracks.

'Oh, Del,' she said, 'Debbie's not your kid.'

'But she must be, she was born six months after we broke up,' I said. 'I mean if I'm not her father then who is?'

'Albie Littlewood,' she said.

I couldn't believe it. I had to sit down. Albie Littlewood! My bestest friend in all the world. We were blood brothers. And all the time he was doinking my bird!

'We were just kids,' June tried to explain. 'We were just playing games. At least you don't have to feel guilty no more. The night Albie died he wasn't coming to meet you, he was coming to meet *me*!'

She had a pretty good point too, and since the confessions had begun, I decided it was as good a time as any to make one of my own. Y'see, I'd always felt guilty over Albie's death, but not just 'cos I thought he'd been on his way to see me at the pub. It was 'cos I hadn't been at the pub. I'd been round his bird Deidre's place.

'You were with Deidre?!' June said.

Well, what did she expect? After all, we were only playing games.

⚜

Family. Sometimes you don't think you'll ever lose them. Sometimes you wish you could lose them. But when you *do* lose them, well, it knocks you for six, don't it? It's like getting hit by a giant wave, you get swept away, and it takes a while after just to get your bearings. And different people deal with it in different ways. Some people throw themselves into work, some into the bottle. Others just shut down for a bit. Sometimes anything you can do to distract yourself can be better than just... well, feeling. For me it was laughter I turned to. That sounds weird, I know, but the thing is I never learned any other way. When the angels came down and took Mum away, I was on my own. I had Grandad, yeah, and he tried his best, bless 'im, but he was about as useful as a pair of sunglasses on a bloke with one ear. Then there was Rodney, poor little sod, he was too young to really understand what was happening. So the best I could do was to put a smile on my face and make him giggle. That's what I did, and it's what I've been doing ever since.

I used to think nothing would ever stop Grandad. Disease? He'd already got most of 'em. They were probably what kept him going. But as much as Rodney and I didn't want to admit it, it was clear that the years were finally catching up on him. His health kept getting worse, then one night he was heading to bed when he toppled over in the doorway. When Rodney and I had got him into bed, he didn't know where he was. He'd had a stroke. When people on the estate asked after him, of course I stayed positive. 'Just a pulled ligament of the wallet!' I said, or a 'severe fraying of the trilby, be right as rain in a week.'

He weren't. He went from the hospital to St Mary's Hospice, just like Mum had before him. He was only there a week before the time had come for him to say bonjour to this mortal curl. It hurt. Of course it did. He was family, and the whole place just weren't the same without him. But the thing is, even though he weren't there any more, part of him still hung on in the flat. You could sense it the minute you walked in, and it was especially strong in his bedroom. Still, it was nothing a can or two of Febreeze couldn't fix. See, I'm doing it again. Joking. I can't help it.

We made sure the old boy had a decent send-off, and the vicar played a blinder. He talked about Grandad and everything he'd achieved in his life, but like I say, other than that it went really well. Course, I bunged the vicar a few quid to see him right, and I'm glad I did, 'cos I heard later that right after the service had ended some git nicked his hat. Some people, eh? Makes you sick.

We had the wake at the flat. The new manager of the Nag's Head, Mike Fisher, smashing bloke, had offered the use of the pub, but I wanted to keep it small. I bunged him a few quid to cover the booze though. Eventually.

Rodney didn't get it, not then anyway, he's older and wiser now. Well, older. But back then he couldn't believe it, all the people at the wake, laughing and joking, sharing a bottle and a few old stories.

'How could you get over it so easily?' he asked me.

Of course I hadn't. I hadn't even started.

Most of the usual crowd were there. Cousin Stan, from the north London branch of the family, turned up, which was nice. He brought his wife Jean 'n all, but I didn't hold it against him. They'd also brought Grandad's brother, Albert, who was living with them in their mobile home. He looked a bit like Captain Birdseye after a breakdown. Bald as a cue ball on top but with a beard you could stuff a king-size quilt with. From a distance he looked like he had his head on upside down. I'm sure Grandad had mentioned him a couple of times, but he never went into detail. We quickly discovered though that, for a man nobody ever talked about, our Great-Uncle Albert had lived a very full and rich life. He'd been everywhere: Russia, Australia, Kenya, the Isle of Wight! Going by what he said it seemed he'd also been present at every single major battle of the last half-century. Listening to him going on about all the ships he'd gone down with made you wonder whose side he'd been on. Apparently he'd had a nickname amongst the crews: 'Boomerang Trotter' 'cos he always came back.

It was nice to meet him.

That said, when we discovered later that, while Uncle Albert was sleeping off his hangover in Rodney's room, Stan and June had hitched the mobile home onto the back of the Volvo and sped off to God knows where, it was a sobering moment for us all. And according to Albert, it weren't the first time it had happened either. Apparently he'd once lived with a cousin, Audrey, until she sent him to the shops one afternoon and then emigrated before he'd even stepped foot on the return bus. Another time some woman he'd moved in with set fire to her house. I'll be honest, I didn't much like the idea of him moving in. The last thing Rodney and I needed at that moment was more bad luck, and this was a bloke kamikaze pilots gave a wide berth.

And it weren't just paranoia on my part, it all came from the old duffer's own lips. Not only had he at some time or another managed to sink everything and anything that had ever floated, he'd also been shot at, torpedoed and dive-bombed (once all in the same morning), he'd leapt from towering infernos, escaped from smoke-filled engine rooms, and had had run-ins with aircraft carriers, cannibals and the kind of sea monsters that would've given Sinbad nightmares – and there he was in my front room unpacking his duffel bag and talking about which bed he'd prefer!

A cold realisation dawned on me in that moment. I can only imagine it must have been how a turkey felt when it caught Bernard Matthews grinning at it. Don't get me wrong, it was perfectly understandable him wanting a bit of stability in his old age (I mean, there's only so many times a person can be blown up before it starts to get a bit annoying), but the previous Christmas when Reg had shown up was still fresh in my mind, and I was bound to be a bit cautious, weren't I? Besides, after everything with Grandad, the last thing I wanted was someone else to be responsible for. Someone else to grow old and die and leave you staring at six foot of freshly dug, Peckham dirt.

It's not like I had much choice. Not really. I tried though. I gave him a few quid and packed him off to the seamen's mission (Rodney, always the angel, looked at me as though I'd just shot Bambi's mum). But true to his nickname, the boomerang came back in no time and, well, I'm just too soft for my own good sometimes, ain't I?

A few weeks later we were discussing the pros and cons of Rodney's latest investment. There was thick frost out and a wind blowing in that would have had Nanook of the North climbing in the fridge to warm up. Not to worry though, 'cos Rodney had blown all the firm's capital on a deal so shrewd it was all I could do not to drown him in it: we were sitting on a monkey's worth of bleedin' suntan lotion!

'I bought it as an investment!' Rodney said, proving yet again what a fur-lined, gold-plated, ocean-going, forty-two-carat plonker he really is. When I explained to him that the best thing about his investment was the cardboard boxes it came in – 'cos the way things were going we'd soon be living in 'em – he tried to blame our bad fortunes on Albert.

'It's him, innit?' he said. 'Ever since he come to live here we've had nothing but bad luck.'

He was right in a way, we had had nothing but bad luck, but it weren't Albert's fault. And in fairness, the old goat even tried to help.

'I was reading in the Sunday papers about them fellas what pick up these rich old widows,' he said, 'toy boys! You wanna see the stuff they get for presents. Solid gold watches, sports cars, money! Might be worth considering?'

Rodney pointed out to him that he might be past his prime for that sort of thing. 'I'm not talking about me,' Albert said, 'I meant you.'

'What? I'm not selling my body to some old tart!' Rodney said.

I set Albert straight.

'Listen, Uncle. You came to stay with us for a few nights, about four weeks ago, so you don't know us very well. So let me explain something to you. You can't expect Rodney to go and do something like that! I mean, even I wouldn't expect Rodney to do something like that!'

'I suppose it was too much to ask,' admitted Albert, 'sorry, Del.'

'That's all right,' I assured him, happy to explain. 'You see, Rodney can't even give it away, let alone flog it!'

CHAPTER 16

IF AT FIRST YOU DON'T SUCCEED...

Say what you like about Rodney (I do) but he was slowly beginning to show that he did have some ambition. He picked his battles, mind you. You'd be on a hiding to nothing trying to get him to do some proper work, but when there was something he wanted, he kept at it all the way to... well, usually to the part where he didn't get it. That's the definition of a tryer though, innit?

As for me, you'll have realised there ain't much I can't turn my hand to. Then again, when you have the skills I have you need to branch out, and not just to increase your portfolio, but also because genius can't be caged. It demands to flourish in all directions.

I like to think that I'm the Simon Cowell of the business world (minus the Botox and the silly trousers). Now there's a man who knows an opportunity when he sees one. And like Simon has revolutionised the music industry a good few times over already, I've very much done the same to the world of business. Obviously a lot of people don't realise that, but how can I compete with a bloke who's got his own

TV show? I mean, he got Sinitta, I got Rodney. It's hardly a level playing field, is it?

Anyway, when Rodney announced he was playing drums (well, packing crates) in a local band, I seized an opportunity to help us both out. I'll admit I was a bit put off though when I found out that the lead singer was Mental Mickey (known to his mum and the local law enforcement as Mickey Maguire). Mental had a bit of a reputation, based mainly on the time he chewed some bloke's ear off. Having listened to him sing though, it could be said the bloke who was one down in the lug'ole stakes got a good deal. I'd have sacrificed both my ears just to make it stop. Still, I weren't the market and I weren't so long in the teeth that I couldn't appreciate a bit of aggressive noise either.

Then I heard a bit of news that set me on the path to music management, and Rodney on the path to fame and fortune. Earwigging down the Nag's Head, I'd found out that the Shamrock Club was lacking a band for St Patrick's night. Their regular band, the Dublin Bay Stormers, had got in a ruck the weekend before and were currently beating their washboards at Her Majesty's Pleasure. St Paddy's was the biggest night of the year for the Shamrock, but without a band they were sunk. So I made a little phone call to the manager, Liam, and happened to mention that I knew of a local band that might get him out of the Guinness. Of course, he was over the moon. It gives me a very special feeling when I know I'm really helping someone out. And if that someone is willing to cough up three hundred notes for that help, well, that's lovely jubbly too, innit? But it weren't all about the money. I've always been passionate about music, and not just The Who (who, let's face it, can't be whacked), but also rare old classics, like 'Old Shep'. I love 'Old Shep'.* As songs

---

* It'll probably be played at my funeral. It's on the shortlist, along with Carly Simon's 'Nobody Does it Better', Chas 'n Dave's 'Gertcha' and 'I Get Knocked Down' by Bumbajumba.

about dead dogs go, it's my absolute favourite. I only have to hear a few bars and I feel happy (in the 'the dog's dead and I'm so sad' sense of the word).

Anyway, deal done, I went down the community hall to break the exciting news to the band. I caught them right in the middle of rehearsing their latest song.

'I'm very impressed,' I told them, 'but you know you're gonna flop like a jelly on a wet mattress, don't you?'

'Why's that then?' Mental asked, sizing up my earlobes.

''Cos you're undisciplined,' I explained. 'You ain't going nowhere until you get your act together.'

'Yeah?' said the guitarist, Charlie, a young mush with hair like a basting brush. 'Well, my mate's cousin works for a record company and he reckons he can get us a contract!'

'My mate's cousin's a doorman at Chelsea,' I told him, 'don't mean he can get me a game though, does it? You're still rough around the edges, take a butcher's at yourselves.'

'Shut it, Trotter!' said Mental. 'We like looking like this! We're Marxist Trotskyite Anarchists!'

I could tell this was news to Rodney, but he had the good sense to keep schtum.

'How come you want to be superstars then?' I asked.

''Cos we want to be *rich* Marxist Trotskyite Anarchists.'

'Not too rich though,' said Charlie.

'Yeah,' the bass player piped up, a confused little herbert called Stew, 'just a *bit* rich. Money ain't everything.'

'No it ain't,' I agreed, 'takes the sting out of being poor though, don't it? Strikes me you need someone to steer you in the right direction and look after your interests. A manager! That's what you need. Don't look at me though, I mean, the bloke who becomes your manager has gotta get you all brand-new equipment. Costs an arm and a leg, that does.'

'I thought you said we were good?' Stew asked.

'You are!' I told him. 'You've got raw talent!'

'Not willing to put your money where your mouth is though, are you, Trotter?' said Mental.

'You think I'm not the kind of bloke to back my instincts? You know me! He who dares wins! Truth is though, things are a bit tight at the moment.'

'Yeah yeah,' Mental said, 'we've heard it all before – you're all talk.'

'All right!' I said. 'I'll be your manager, and I'll get you bookings, you just see if I don't! I'm gonna make an investment in you lads. This time next year we'll be millionaires! Oh, by the way, you don't happen to know any songs by The Bachelors, do you?'

They didn't, but that was all right. As far as Liam was concerned any band was better than none, even if that band did sound like a cat being doctored without anaesthetic.

I stuck to my word, got some gear together and kitted them out with some decent clobber, which I conveniently already had in the lock-up. I also came up with a name for them, something that perfectly encapsulised their sound and attitude in one simple phrase: 'A Bunch of Wallies'. And surprisingly enough, that bunch of wallies didn't mind it. According to Stew, it was 'well punk' which endorsed my choice every which way you looked at it really.

We spent a fair old time rehearsing and I like to think I helped shape their sound. I felt like how Brian Epstein must have felt when he started moulding The Beatles. Mind you, as insects go, this lot were more wormy than anything else (actually 'The Worms' had been on my shortlist of potential names for the group, but Rodney weren't keen). Every now and then I tried to slip something a bit Paddy-Night-friendly in there, you know, a dollop of Gilbert O'Sullivan or what 'ave you, but it turned out they weren't as open to suggestions as I'd hoped. Charlie stormed off in a sulk when I asked him whether he'd ever thought about having a bash on a fiddle, so I decided to drop it. They'd play whatever they wanted to play and that would just have to be good enough.

I can't pretend that the Shamrock gig was a complete success. As anyone who saw the police report from the night in question could see, A Bunch of Wallies went down in the Shamrock Club about as well as a pube on a pizza. Still, the Shamrock Club being the kind of venue where you judge how successful a night has been by how many chair splinters you have in your back, Liam must have been expecting it. Personally speaking, it was the warm crunch of notes in my pocket rather than the notes in my ears that saw me through. It came to a bit of a sticky end when the fighting really broke out. Mental seemed to be in his element though. The last I saw of 'im in my rear-view mirror as the rest of us made for the hills was the look of joy on his face as someone broke a bottle of vodka over his head.

It was to be my one and only gig as manager of A Bunch of Wallies. I was gutted, naturally, but I did get some comfort knowing that I had at least left my mark on them. It was Rodney I felt most sorry for. Shortly after the Shamrock riot (as the press named it), he was forced to leave the band due to what he called 'creative differences' (i.e. Mental tried to chew his face off). What really hurt him (and me too, mind) was when he later discovered A Bunch of Wallies had actually made it into the charts. Yeah, I couldn't believe it either! Their success was limited though, taking a pretty sharp nosedive after their first and only appearance on *Top of the Pops*. But that's the music business for you. It's a hit and miss game that can trip up the best of 'em. At the end of the day I don't regret it. Simon Cowell had Robson and Jerome, I had A Bunch of Wallies.

It's learning from your mistakes that matters.

⁂

Undeterred, Rodney signed up for one of them evening classes, nothing useful, art, but as I said, at least he was trying. Either that or he was just looking to cop off with some bohemian sort. I hadn't been doing too badly at the time. See, my mate Abdul's cousin's girlfriend's brother's mate's mate was a keeper at a private zoo, and Monkey Harris's sister's husband's first wife's stepfather worked at an animal food company. So naturally I'd put the two together and set up a nice little tickle. It weren't ideal having Uncle Albert heaving two ton of hay about while Rodney was at his class, but at least it got him out of the house for a bit, and he didn't moan any more than he usually did, even when a camel tried to eat his beard.

I must admit, when Rodney announced that he'd been assigned to make a student film, me and the boys weren't convinced he could pull it off, especially when he told us Mickey Pearce was directing it 'cos 'he had experience in films' (he once had a Saturday morning job on the photographic counter at Boots). More worrying though was that Rodney was planning on writing the script.

Rodney had previous when it came to writing. A few years back he'd knocked out a novel called *The Indictment* which had never got published, partly – all right, *mainly* – because I'd thrown it down the rubbish chute. I felt bad after, and I made it up to him by getting him a full year's subscription to *Penthouse*, but I'd read *The Indictment* and I just didn't want him being destroyed by all the rejection letters. He was a sensitive lad, he'd already lost his mum and dad, and when it came to birds he'd been blown out more times than a windsock. I was worried any more rejection would have finished him off.

'It was an indictment of a failing system!' he told us. 'All right, it was a first effort so it probably didn't have the same social impact as, say, *Cathy Come Home*.'

'It didn't have the same social impact as *Lassie Come Home*,' I told him, remembering how I'd forced myself through the first couple of chapters, following the adventures of some depressed artist going on political rallies and trying to get his end away. Which would have been fine if he'd ever succeeded. Don't get me wrong, Rodney had his talents, maths, art, winning ugly bird competitions, things like that, but he weren't no Jackie Collins.

Still, I wanted to support him in his latest project, so I picked him up a lovely little typewriter down the auction. Proper vintage it was. It even had a crest on it, showing it had been made by royal appointment. Admittedly the queen in question was Victoria, but they made things to last in those days and as long as you gave the keys a proper hard whack (and you could get by without any 'T's or 'A's and didn't mind your fingers bleeding a bit) you were laughing.

I even gave him an idea for his story. One of my best to date. It was called 'There's A Rhino Loose in the City', and it was all about this rhino that gets loose in the city. See, it escapes from the zoo and heads right for London. After a few days they start finding these bodies lying about and no one knows who's done it, so they get hold of this private detective, a Charlton Heston-type geezer, to try and solve the crime. He pairs up with the zookeeper who's this very attractive woman, so, before you know it, old Charlton's giving the sort what for (and there's your romantic interest). Rodney weren't impressed.

'A rhinoceros?' he asked.

'Yeah!' I told him. 'Only they don't know it's missing.'

'How can they not know it's missing? If you've got a rhinoceros and then one day it ain't there, you *know* it's missing.'

'Don't be a plonker all your life!' I said. 'The zookeeper bird ain't got just one rhinoceros, she's most likely got two or three of 'em.'

'What about the eight million people living in London? Don't none of them spot it?'

'Yes!' I said. 'But the ones who spot it are the ones that get trampled to death.'

'But what about all the people in offices, the people in cafes, the people sitting on tops of buses? It's a rhino, Del!'

'Yeah… but it only comes out at night!'

'Where does he live during the day?' Albert asked.

'In a lock-up garage in a backstreet somewhere.'

'Leasing it, is he?' asked Rodney.

'No,' I said, beginning to wish I hadn't opened my mouth in the first place, 'it's a disused garage in a backstreet where nobody ever goes. The detective finds it though, only… it's at night!'

'And the rhino's popped out?'

'Right!' I actually began to think he was getting it. 'So the old detective is that bit nearer to solving the mystery. You see, not only is it a love story, it's a whodunnit as well!'

'Whodunnit?' Rodney asked. 'We know whodunnit! The rhino done it!'

'All right,' I admitted, 'some of it needs working out a bit, but it's got all the essential qualities of a hit! Suspense, lots of killings and a bit of humpty dumpty. I mean, this is a disaster movie!'

'It's a bloody calamity, Del.'

'I'm only trying to help,' I told him. Clearly he needed it, he'd been working on the script for a couple of days and hadn't written a single word yet.

'I appreciate that, Del,' he said, 'but I've only got a small budget.'

'But that's the beauty of it,' I explained. 'I know where there's a rhinoceros going cheap!'

Truth be told it had seen better days, that's why Abdul's cousin's girlfriend's brother's mate's mate was trying to get shot of it. But still, with a few camera tricks, some clever lighting and a lot of actors screaming, I reckoned we could make a star out of the poor old sod yet. Rodney wouldn't budge though.

I was feeling frustrated, the way one only can when they've promised to do a mate a favour and take a rhinoceros off his hands and then had to break that promise. Still, my problem was nothing compared to the one Boycie was facing. See, him and Marlene had been trying for a sprog for years but had had no joy. Boycie had always blamed Marlene for this, but the doctors had just confirmed the problem was actually Boycie's. Apparently he had what they call a 'low count'.

'It means he's been firing more blanks than the Territorials,' Marlene explained when we bumped into her while picking up a Chinese takeaway.

Course, you couldn't help but feel sorry for anyone who finds out they're a Jaffa (you know, seedless). Well, anyone but Boycie. Still, a mate's a mate, I promised him I wouldn't spread it around and I've always stuck to that promise. After all, it's in bad taste to talk publicly about someone else's personal problems. It's the sort of stuff they put in those celebrity biographies to make 'em sell. Can't be doing with it.

With the rhino deal knackered,* and in desperation, I started doing a bit of business with Mickey Pearce. As director of Rodney's new

---

* Rodney was more interested in Boycie and Marlene's situation and started making notes on childbirth and artificial incrimination and all that game. He finally managed to knock out a script, and I helped him out with the title, but nothing came of it.

film, the council had lent him the use of a load of camera equipment and, as Rodney was still pondering the first blank page, I thought it only right that Mickey should get a bit of practice in. I popped down the town hall and did the rounds of the local churches, taking notes of the banns, then got in touch with a few of the brides-to-be and offered them the chance to have their happiest day recorded for posterity. So at least we had some money coming in. What I didn't count on was that Mickey was also working for Boycie, who, at the time, was doing a sideline in home video entertainment. Thing is, Boycie's sideline had a sideline, which was providing entertainment of a more… intimate biological nature. It's a market I steered well clear of, and especially on this occasion as Boycie was being backed in the venture by none other than Danny and Tony Driscoll, aka the Driscoll brothers. I'd known 'em since way back, and they were dangerous company. Rumour had it that Ronnie Kray once advised them to calm down. I'm not sure which of 'em was worse. Tony was little, but he was vicious, and he really didn't care how big the bloke he was up against was. What he lacked in height he lacked even more of in brains. Example: I once overheard him hit on the brilliant idea of chopping his own fingers off to avoid leaving prints at a smash-and-grab he was planning. Nobody was too keen to do the chopping (or to ask how exactly he was gonna grab anything when he didn't have any fingers), so he said he'd do it himself. Then Danny pointed out that once he'd chopped off one lot of fingers he wouldn't be able to hold the cleaver to do the next. That put him off. As Tony said, he's an all or nothing sort of bloke. So Danny was the brains of the outfit, which says a lot considering the time some guru predicted that the world would end in a month, and Danny bet a grand that it would!

Anyway, despite the moody tadpoles, that week Boycie had hired the Nag's Head for a party to celebrate his and Marlene's twentieth wedding anniversary.

We'd all had a few sherbets when Boycie sent the word around that there would be a private viewing of his latest 'specialist' movie in the room upstairs. All the lads sat down, Boycie put the tape in and we prepared for the premier screening of *Night Nurse*. The film started and immediately the boys were cheering as our medical star returns to her flat after a hard day of taking temperatures and feeling pulses. At some subconscious level I could tell something weren't right, but I was getting a bit carried away in the moment and it didn't register. As the plot usually demands in these movies, it weren't long before the leading lady found a reason to take her bra off. And it was at that moment, as the camera cut to a wide shot of Nurse Naughty baring her Bristols, that some dozy twonk having a panic attack walked into frame. For a split second I thought, *That's weird*, then it dawned on me that the twonk in question was Rodney, and the nurse's flat was *my* bloody flat! I could guess who the cameraman was 'n all!

Of course Rodney swore blind he knew nothing about it and, in all fairness, I believed him. If you knew someone was shooting a porn movie in your front room you wouldn't suddenly pop out of the kitchen and stroll in front of the camera, would you?

Luckily I managed to get hold of the tape and made sure *Night Nurse* never got a second screening by flushing it down the bog.

We never did get to make *There's a Rhino Loose in the City* (though we did a smashing poster). But who knows, if this book does all right I might give it a bash as a novel.

CHAPTER 17

A PRAYER AND A WING

It had been a grotty year all told. Business was down, times were hard, we'd lost Grandad, we'd gained Uncle Albert. Sometimes life just keeps giving you a slap, don't it?

So you can imagine how much it improved my mood to hear about the fall from grace of Roy Slater. Far be it for me to take pleasure from the misfortunes of others, but I was skipping for a week when I heard he'd been done for corruption. Apparently Slater had been running a diamond smuggling racket out of Amsterdam. I couldn't believe it (not the bit about him being corrupt, we all knew that, but that he'd been stupid enough to get caught). It was difficult 'cos there were so many stories flying around, even one where – can you believe it? – I was involved! This particularly stupid bit of tittle-tattle had it that Rodney and I were the middlemen in the deal. As though that weren't daft enough, it also went that we'd pulled the whole thing off by – get this – hiring a boat and sailing over to Holland ourselves… with Uncle Albert as skipper!

Anyone who knows me would know just how ridiculous a story this was. As if I'd put mine and Rodney's lives in the hands of a man who once managed to get into a fender-bender with an aircraft carrier!

More's the point, as if I'd get caught up in anything like diamond smuggling! Me? I've never even been to Amsterdam, and that's a fact that can be easily proven by checking my passport records or talking to any number of people who will swear blind (even in a court of law if it comes to it) that I was right here in Peckham the entire time the caper was going on.

Anyway, uplifted by the news, I decided I should do something to pass that goodwill on. It's easy to get selfish in this game, we're all just trying to put food on our own tables, ain't we? 'Pull the ladder up, Jack, and sod the rest,' as Shakespeare once said. Well, not me, I've always tried to give something back to the manor, and I'd stumbled across the perfect opportunity to do just that.

I'd recently bought some gear and I was beginning to think the deal weren't quite as on the level as I'd been led to believe. Being the honest bloke that I am, it was keeping me up at night. I went out for a mosey to clear my mind when I just so happened to pass St Mary's Church, and bingo! What better way to cleanse the spirit than a spot of confession? Plus it had just started pissing down, so two birds, one stone and all that. What a lot of people don't realise about me is that I'm a deeply spiritual person. I mean, I don't read the Bible or go to church if I can help it (I've never understood those people who take it to extremes), but I'll always watch a repeat of *The Ten Commandments* if I catch one.

So there I was in the box, laying it all out to Father O'Keith, puffing on a Castella to calm the nerves, when he mentioned that the church was having a fund-raising do to try and save the hospice.

'It's got dilapidated over the years,' he said. 'They've estimated it'll cost a quarter of a million to repair it. I'm sad to say we've little or no chance of reaching our target though.'

'Hang about,' I said, 'maybe we could organise a charity darts match for you at the Nag's Head. How much more money do you need?'

'£185,000.'

'Maybe we could throw a raffle in as well.'

'That's very kind of you, Del, but I really do think this is one battle that we've lost.'

'But they can't knock it down!' I said. 'What's gonna happen to all the old and sick people living there?'

'They'll move them out first.'

'I know that! But to where?'

'The four quarters of the metropolis probably,' he said. 'They'll be far away from their friends and relatives, it's all local people at St Mary's.'

He didn't have to tell me that, not after what had happened to Grandad, and Mum before him. I couldn't believe they could just knock the place down.

'It's out of our hands,' he said. 'I'll be honest with you, Del, since hearing about the plans for the hospice, my faith has been severely tested. All my efforts and prayers have failed. I feel I've let the people down.'

'Don't talk like that, Father,' I told him, 'something'll turn up, remember the old saying: "he who dares wins".'

On the way out I stopped to pop a score in the collection box, when I heard him shout.

'Del! Come down here quickly!'

He was staring at one of them statues they have, you know, Mary and Child, looking all fed up. Only this one was especially depressed 'cos, no word of a lie, there was a *tear* flowing down Mary's cheek.

'It's a sign!' he said.

'Yeah,' I told him, 'it's a sign we can make a fortune! An authentic deluxe miracle! They go for a bomb these days.'

'How can you talk about money at a time like this?'

'What do you wanna talk about?' I said. 'Your holidays? Don't you see the opportunity you're being presented with here? The newspapers and magazines would pay through the nose to get this sort of thing on their front pages.'

'I don't know if it's right, Derek.'

'Those old people down at St Mary's Hospice would think it was right, wouldn't they? With the money you could earn out of this you could have that place repaired, redecorated and get Samantha Fox to reopen it for you!'

'Do you really think we could?'

'Of course! I mean, she don't come cheap, but I'll see what I can do.'

'I mean save the hospice!'

'It'll be a doddle,' I told him. 'Where's your phone?'

'I don't think I could exploit something like this.'

'Of course you couldn't, Father,' I said, giving him a reassuring pat on the back, 'but I'm shit hot at it!'

It was an absolute gift from God, my chance to help the local community and save the hospice that had looked after my own when they'd needed it most.

You'll have Rodney pegged well enough by now to guess he didn't exactly greet my news of the Miracle of Peckham with the sort of enthusiasm I was after. He thought I'd flipped. I had more important spiritual concerns to worry about than what that Moby thought, things like praying, opening my heart up to Jesus and getting on the blower to the Peckham Echo to bring them up to speed.

As predicted, we had a right rush on. The media couldn't keep away. To begin with they were a bit septic but once they'd seen the miracle for themselves they left as converts to spread the word and sign the cheques.

The miracle didn't always happen though, it weren't a permanent thing, but I developed a sense in my gut, almost like the Big Man himself was giving me a nudge and a wink when things were likely to kick off in the weeping statue department.

As happy as I was to spread the word, I'd promised Father O'Keith I weren't gonna be soft about it. I was taking no prisoners as far as the reporters were concerned. They signed a contract and paid in full before I'd so much as let 'em twitch a biro in the presence of the Almighty. Some of them kicked up a fuss but once old Mary turned the waterworks on there was no holding 'em back. Within a week or so we'd gone global. We had people coming from all over the world to catch a glimpse of our damp Virgin. I was giving serious consideration to going on the lecture circuit, when the Miracle of Peckham ran dry.

It was a reporter from Belgium that ruined it. Apparently he'd spotted that the Virgin only cried on days when it was raining. It didn't take him long after to find the leak in the roof from where some local villains had helped themselves to the lead.

I won't pretend it weren't disappointing, for a while there we had a real piece of magic but, you know what? We made enough money to save the hospice and, contractually, nobody could touch us. So, while I was sorry to scrap my plans for adding a Derek Trotter wing to St Mary's, I suppose it all worked out for the best.

As an added bonus, it just so happened I'd recently done a deal on a load of lead so I could help out there 'n all. God, eh? He don't 'alf work in mysterious ways.

<hr />

Uncle Albert had been in the dumps. I thought he'd heard sales of fish fingers were down or something, but then one night in the Nag's

Head, he explained to me and Rodney that Aunt Ada had been rushed into hospital.

'Who's Aunt Ada?' I asked him.

'My wife!' he said.

'*That* Aunt Ada!' I said. 'But you haven't seen her for years!'

'She told the rest of the family that if she saw you again she'd kill you,' Rodney said.

'Well, yeah,' he admitted, 'but she was annoyed when she said that. I'd like to go and see her.'

'Well why don't you then?'

''Cos she might not be as ill as they say.'

You couldn't argue with logic like that so I decided to take him out for a Chinese to cheer him up. However miserable Uncle Albert was, he always perked up when you slung a few sweet and sour prawns his way. Stopped him from singing too, so it was a win-win.

We were just about to head off when we bumped into Trigger, who mentioned that his niece, Lisa, was in town. I could half remember her from when she'd been on the estate, but it was her mum I'd really known. I forget her name now, but I'd nicknamed her Miss 999, 'cos I only called her in an emergency. Fair sort though.

Anyway, turns out Lisa had grown into something a bit more special (well, by estate standards. She reminded me a bit of a young Madonna, just uglier). So when she waved over to us from the bar, Rodney's eyes went all goggly and he started dribbling, bless 'im. Not that he stood a chance with her of course, Lisa was clearly out of his league. So I decided to chat her up myself. Course, he immediately decided to try it on too.

'It's lovely seeing you again,' Lisa said. 'I always remember that day, years and years ago now, you drove round to my nan's in a brand-new three-wheeled van. I remember you saying, "This time next year it'll be a Mercedes." I was so impressed.' Well, she was only human. 'Did you ever get a Mercedes?'

'Nah, I went off 'em. Got myself a nice little two-seater these days.'

'Yeah, two seats, three wheels, it's the same van, innit?' Rodney chipped in.

'It is,' I admitted, 'and I sometimes let Rodney borrow it when he's behaved himself, 'cos of course he can't afford a car of his own.'

Looking back now, I can see how childish and stupid it was, the two of us competing over her like that. After all we'd been through, and whatever our differences, falling out over a bird was ridiculous. At the time though, things got a lot worse after we invited Lisa round for tea at the flat. Uncle Albert tried to warn us, reminding us that the main reason him and Grandad had fallen out all those years ago, was because they'd fought over Aunt Ada.

'Back then,' he said, 'me and your grandad weren't just brothers, we was mates. We went everywhere together, got up to some right capers. Then, one night we met your Aunt Ada at the local palais. She was a beautiful woman, a bit like Ginger Rogers... Last time I saw her she looked more like Fred Astaire... We both ended up having a few dances with her, then we both wanted to take her home. We ended up fighting in the street over her. He never spoke to me again from that day to... he never spoke to me ever again.'

It was all very touching, although part of me couldn't help but feel a bit for Ada, I mean, having to dance with both The Old Man of the Sea and The Old Man of the Settee.

Anyway, at the time I was doing a lovely line in home sunbeds. We had one set up as a display in the front room, and Rodney, fed up with looking like a blood donor who couldn't say no, and wanting to impress Lisa, decided a nice healthy bronze was the way to go. Well, he must have pressed the wrong button or something, 'cos he ended up a deep, chorizo-sausage red (his head mainly). I could tell something weren't right when I entered the flat and noticed a singed smell in the air. For a minute I thought Uncle Albert had accidentally set fire to his beard again (stone me, that thing was flammable!). Then I heard a whimpering sound coming from the bathroom. The door was ajar, so I popped my head in and there was Rodney standing over the sink looking like a Swan Vesta with eyes. It was a sight, and even more so when that evening he got dressed up for our date with Lisa in a white suit. Maybe it was the artist in him, you know, going for the contrast, but it did him no favours. Lisa and I tried our best not to laugh, but it weren't easy. He made David Dickinson look ashen. Course, he claimed I had something to do with it, but then he would, wouldn't he? It was a lot easier for him to say I'd waited until he'd fallen asleep and altered the timer than it was to admit that he's a total wally!

Whatever had happened, the damage was done, and that conniving little git bided his time, waiting for the opportunity to get his revenge. And when we offered to drive Lisa back to Hampshire the next day, that opportunity arose.

Admittedly, I hadn't done myself any favours when I'd bigged myself up a bit over tea. I can't remember exactly what I said, but it was something along the lines of me being an ex-paratrooper. Thing is, Lisa had been banging on about some friends of hers that were members of a hang-gliding club and I was just trying to keep the conversation going. I definitely didn't say I wanted to go hang-gliding. That would have been Rodney.

And now I come to yet another brush with death, and this one was *all* mine!

The way I see it, God never intended Man to strap a kite to himself and jump off things. It's stupid. But Lisa had it in her head that I was desperate to go soaring through the clouds, and once we were there up on that hill with all her hang-gliding mates watching, well, I couldn't show 'em I was scared, could I? So I had to find a way of getting myself out of it without looking like a right dipstick. The main bloke, Andy, was giving me all this spiel about airflows and how I was supposed to steer and land and generally not die, but he could have been talking Botswanan for all it mattered. All I was worried about was keeping my feet firmly on the old terra cotta. Eventually I got a moment alone with Rodney, and after mulling it over for a bit, he came up with what, on the face of it, was a full-proof plan to keep my pride and, more importantly, body intact. The only snag, and I should've spotted it at the time, was that the plan's success depended entirely on Rodney and some crucial timing. See, I was gonna get myself done up in all the gear and let them strap me into the glider thing, pretending I was all ready and eager for the off, but then, just as I was ready to hurl myself into the sky, Rodney was gonna come rushing up and say we'd had an emergency call on our car phone and that we had to return to Peckham immediately. Brilliant! Well, it would have been, only the second, and most important, part of the plan never materialised.

I remember glancing over at Rodney as the glider gathered pace, my Hush Puppies dragging through the mud, but he never said a word. He just watched with this self-satisfied little smirk on his face. Then the glider must have caught an updraft 'cos seconds later I was off. I can't recall too much of the first half hour of my flight, on account that I spent most of it praying really loudly, but by the time I'd composed my senses a bit I was closing in on the Atlantic. I knew I'd set off in a southerly direction, and sure enough there was the Isle of Wight looming large off to my left. It dawned on me then that, if I continued on the path I was on, the next bit of land I'd come to would be the Falklands, which at the time was still a military exclusion zone. My head was suddenly filled with images of anti-aircraft fire and heat-seeking missiles... and Rodney grinning like a Cheshire cat. I then started to wish I'd paid a bit more attention to Andy's tips on steering. You'd have thought they'd fit these gliders with steering wheels, but no, they have to go 'n make things bloody awkward.

Still, I tried everything I could to change direction. I wriggled and kicked my legs and nodded my head and swayed my hips, and the glider went up, down, sideways, backwards and every which sodding way but the way I wanted to go! Then, by the grace of God, a gust of wind banked me round so that I was facing the mainland. For the next few miles or so I was joined by a herd of seagulls who adopted me as their leader. I'm pretty sure one of 'em fancied me.

Overall I was in the air for the best part of three hours. I circled over fields and towns, I did barrel-rolls over motorways and fly-bys past office buildings. Kids in parks and people sitting in traffic were waving at me. My voyage finally came to an end when I nosedived into some big aerial transmitter thing in Redhill. Luckily enough I didn't break anything (well, not on me, but I heard the good people of Reigate had to make do without BBC2 for a few hours).

I was very lucky also in that my fall from the transmitter was broken by a Ford Sierra. Not so fortunate was the unsuspecting courting couple who were inside it at the time. I had a bit of a chat with them as we waited for the ambulance, you know, to help keep the shock (mine and theirs) from setting in. Nice couple. Anyway, I was taken to hospital and given the once-over, X-rays and all that, but apart from a few cuts and bruises I was fine. Mike and Trigger came down to pick me up. I could have made my own way back, but the doctor was worried I might suffer a bit of delayed percussion, and said it was best I was with someone.

Back in the flat Rodney had lost his smirk, but if I hadn't just had a strict warning from the doctor not to do anything too strenuous, it wouldn't have been all he'd lost. To top it all off, Trigger then mentioned that Lisa was engaged to be married 'to some bloke called Andy', and had been for a few months now. Apparently she'd only come up to London to look for a wedding dress. Well, I don't know who felt the bigger tit, me or Rodney.

On the upside we did get an invite to the wedding, which would mean another trip down to Hampshire. It's a lovely county from what I'd seen, and believe me, I'd seen all of it.

CHAPTER 18

G'DAY MATE

A few weeks later I popped into the Nag's Head for an emergency amaretto and dandelion and burdock, when who should I bump into but Jumbo Mills! Turns out he'd gotten into the motor game down under and was back to do a deal with Boycie on some new stock. If he'd asked me I'd have pointed him in a better direction. Still, Jumbo was a shrewd boy so I had no doubt he knew what he was doing.

The years had been kind to Jumbo in places, brutal in others. He had a gut on him and was wearing enough gold to show he weren't short of a shilling, but his hair had gone AWOL and had been replaced by a syrup that looked like a metrosexual hamster. It was good to see him, even if he had managed to wind everyone up in the pub from the minute he'd walked in. That was always the problem with Jumbo, heart of gold, but loud and obnoxious, which is probably why he'd got on so well in Australia.

He'd had a pop at Albert's singing (which was fair enough, nobody liked Albert's singing, but he loved nothing more than getting on the old joanna and having a good howl. The council sent someone round once 'cos Mike didn't have a music licence. They came in, listened for a couple of minutes, realised what they were hearing didn't count as music and told Mike to forget about it). Jumbo had also got up Mike's nose by insulting his beer and food (which, again, was a hard one to argue), but like I said, it was good to see him.

'You remember that 'orrible little kid brother of mine, Jumbo?' I said. 'The one with the funny haircut, all snot and Marmite?'

'Yeah,' said Jumbo, looking at Rodney, 'he ain't changed a bit, has he?'

That was Rodney in a mood with him as well.

Of course, once Jumbo and Boycie had finished their meeting, one drink had led to another and we were still sat there come closing time, catching up, swapping stories, hatching plans, just like in the old days.

'I take it you never did become that millionaire you were always talking about?' he asked.

'Well, no,' I admitted, 'not yet.'

'"This time next year I'll be a millionaire,"' he smiled, 'they were the last words you said to me before I emigrated. You should have come with me. You're wasted here. This country's old, decrepit. The stench of defeat is everywhere.'

'Maybe,' I said, 'but it's a British stench and I happen to be proud of it. All right?' He was always having a pop at the homeland, and as far as I'm concerned the only people who have the right to call this great country of ours a dump are those who have to live in it.

'When our business broke up and I decided to emigrate,' he said, 'I'd have gone to Australia potless if it weren't for you. You gave me your last two hundred quid.'

'Yeah well, I told you at the time to forget it, didn't I?'

'Well, I didn't. Even when times were hard I used to lie in bed at night and think to myself, *One day I'm going to pay Del back, with interest!* And now I am. I want us to re-form our old partnership.'

'You want to set up another fish stall?' I asked.

'No!' he said. 'I'm setting up a business importing prestige European motors. Rollers, Mercs, that kind of thing. I want you to come to Australia as my partner. I want you to front the business, Del Boy, deal with the public, give 'em that old razzamatazz just like you used to.'

'Australia?' I couldn't get my head around it.

'I've got the money, I've got the site and thanks to my deal with Boycie I've got the motors. All I need is you.'

'I don't know,' I said, 'Australia? It ain't half a long way away. It'd cost a fortune to move there.'

'I'm paying,' he said.

'But I've got family ties, ain't I?'

'So bring 'em with you. Put young Rodney on the payroll.'

'Well,' I said, 'he has got two GCEs.'

'That don't matter, we'll find something for him to do.'

I still weren't sure, as much as I loved Jumbo we'd spent a lot of time rowing.

'So we'll still row,' he said. 'Our biggest argument will be who's got the most millions.'

He spat in his hand and held it out. I stared at it for a second and then made up my mind.

'All right, you old bastard,' I said, shaking his hand, 'let's do it!'

We polished off a bottle of champagne (Dillinger's 75, Prince Charles's favourite, and mine) and I went straight back to the flat to tell Rodney and Albert the good news. They were sat in front of the telly when I burst in.

'We're going to Australia!' I shouted.

'Triffic,' said Rodney, 'I'll just finish watching this first.'

It took a little while to convince him I meant it, but finally he got it.

'So he wants us to help run his business?' he asked.

'Not help run it, no! I'm gonna be a partner. Jumbo's gonna be behind the scenes, handling the money, and I'm going to be the sales director. I'll have my own executive office, swivel chair 'n all that game.'

'So what's my job?'

'Rodney, you're going to play a very vital role in the organisation and I know, I just *know*, that you can handle it.'

'What is it?' he said, hardly able to contain his excitement.

'Well,' I said, 'you know when all them Rolls-Royces and Mercedes come trundling off the ship? What's the first thing they're gonna need?'

'Import licences, customs clearances, all of that?' he said.

'No, what's even more important than that?'

'Re-registering!' He was almost jumping up and down with excitement now. 'New number plates, logbooks, all of that!'

'What are they going to need *even more* than that?' I asked, but he was all out of answers so I put him out of his misery: 'Cleaning!'

'I'm going thousands of miles to be a car cleaner?'

Sensing the wind had gone out of his sails a bit, I tried to beef it up.

'No! Not *just* a car cleaner! A *prestige* car cleaner! You'll be in charge of it!'

'What, with staff under me?'

'Eventually, yeah. I mean, this is a growing business, Rodney, and in a year from now I won't be able to afford to have you down there with your cloth and bucket. I'll need you up in the boardroom. And you'll have your own in-car celluloid phone and everything!'

'And a secretary?'

He was getting excited again, the randy little git.

'Yeah, all of that.'

'What about Albert?' he asked. 'We'll have to find something for him to do.'

'I shouldn't worry, boys,' Albert finally piped up, 'I'm not going.'

'What do you mean you're not going?' I asked him.

'Listen to me, son,' he said, 'I've spent three-quarters of my life sailing around this world. Now all I want is a place to settle down. When I came to live with you two I hoped I would end my days here. It's a young man's opportunity. I'll be all right here on my own.'

And with that he shuffled off to bed. Rodney and I just stared at each other for a bit, not knowing what to say. So I got out the pictures of Jumbo's place that he'd given me and that soon put the spring back in our step. After all, if Albert didn't want to go, then that was up to him, weren't it? It would be unfair for Rodney and me to miss out on the opportunity just because he'd decided to stay behind. That sounds harsh, I know, but I've always done my best by family, and this could have been the making of both me and Rodney.

As it turned out, Uncle Albert weren't the only problem. Rodney and I applied for our visas and I sailed through (well, they knew a citizen worth having when they saw one). Unfortunately, Rodney didn't, on account of his drugs record.

'I'm sorry, mate,' he said, 'I've messed it all up for you, ain't I?'

'No you haven't,' I told him, 'there'll be a way round it, Rodney, there's always a way round these things.'

'Really?'

'Yeah,' I tried to reassure him, 'don't worry… I'll find another car cleaner.'

Well, this weren't the reassurance he wanted and he went into a right sulk.

'Look, Rodney,' I said. 'This is my golden opportunity to fulfil my potential. I've got to go, ain't I?'

I tried to sweeten him up by reminding him that once I'd gone he would become the sole proprietor of Trotters Independent Traders, but that didn't seem to lift his spirits.

'Look at all the great stuff we've got!' I said. And it was true, we were sitting on some blinding stock. We had twenty-four computers! All right, they didn't actually work, but they looked lovely. We also had a smashing Persian rug that'd come up a real treat after a going-over with some bleach.

'I'll tell you what else I'll do,' I said, 'I'll give you my little black book. It contains the names and addresses of all my birds!'

I couldn't say fairer than that, could I?

'So that's my lot, is it?' he said, 'Twenty-four computers that don't compute, the only rug in the world with a sell-by date, and the script to *101 Dalmatians*. Thanks a lot!'

I couldn't believe it, after everything I'd done for him.

'Don't you think I've sacrificed enough for you?' I asked him. 'When dear Mum died, who was it that stood by you?'

'Oh yeah, I remember it well,' he said. 'I remember standing in a damp graveyard wondering what the hole in the ground was for. I remember all the other people saying, "What's going to happen to poor little Rodney?" But I had no need to fear, did I? 'Cos suddenly a vision appeared from beyond the silhouette of the gasworks. Is it a bird? Is it a plane? No! It's Del Boy!'

I let him have his moment. He just needed to get it out of his system.

Later on Albert pitched in with his penny's worth. 'You've gotta go, son,' he said. 'If you don't you'll spend the rest of your life wondering what might have been.' And he was right. It was my dream. My chance to become a millionaire! How could I just say bonjour to it all? Rodney would be all right on his own, wouldn't he?

I spent the rest of the day thinking it over. Then I remembered something. It was a kind of hazy flashback, like the ones I get the morning after a heavy night at the One-Eleven Club. It was a couple of days after Mum died, and I'd never felt so bloody useless in all my life. I had to get out of the flat, I couldn't stand to watch the old man as it slowly dawned on him that the 'little' woman he hated so much had actually been the backbone of the family. So I decided to go for a walk.

Anywhere would do, I just wanted to be on my own for a bit. I was down to my last sixpence anyway, so I couldn't have done much even if I'd wanted to. I was crossing the precinct when I noticed Rodney following me. He was just a little nipper then, you know, all odd socks and eczema. I told him to go home but he wouldn't. He just kept following me. Eventually I decided to stop and sit on a wall and wait it out till he got bored. But he didn't. We must have sat on that wall for at least an hour, in silence, me wishing I could go into the nearest pub and get smashed to pieces, Rodney just kicking his heels, watching the world go by. It was Rodney who finally broke the silence.

'Look, Del,' he said, holding a finger up at me.

'What is it?' I asked.

'A bogey.'

'Bloody hell, Rodney, that's 'orrible!' I said. 'Get rid of it!'

'Where?'

'I dunno, flick it somewhere, just not at me!'

The silence returned for a few more minutes.

'Del, where's Mum?' he asked.

'I told you, she's gone to Cornwall for a few weeks.' It was the best I could do.

'What's a cornedwall?'

'It's a place where people go to rest when they're tired.'

'Can we go there?' he asked.

It was killing me inside, but I couldn't let him see that, could I? So I took out my James Dean shades and slid them on. Just then an ice-cream van pulled up across the road, and of course, Rodney's eyes lit up.

'Del, can I have an ice cream?'

'Not now, Rodney,' I told him.

'But I want one.'

'I know that but I can't afford one.'

'I like ice cream,' he said, watching as a few kids from the estate came running up to the van to place their orders. 'Can we get one?'

'Not now, maybe another day.'

'Can I have a Flake in mine?' he asked.

'You can't have an ice cream, Rodney, 'cos I can't afford an ice cream, stop going on about it!' I said. And he did stop. Eventually.

That afternoon as we headed back home together, we were both feeling a little bit better. Rodney 'cos he had his ice cream, Flake 'n all, and me 'cos I'd realised I weren't completely useless after all, even if I was completely skint. My mood did dip a bit though when we got in and Grandad pointed out that I had a bogey stuck to my jeans.

<hr>

I phoned Jumbo and told him the deal was off. Rodney came back in later that evening, half-cut and full of apologies, telling me I ought to go, but it was done now, weren't it? And maybe it was the chance of a lifetime, but the way I look at it there are chances of a lifetime every single day, you just have to spot 'em. And if I had gone to Australia, all the good things that came afterwards, well... none of it would have happened, would it? I think sometimes you just have to appreciate what you've got and stop worrying about what you ain't.

CHAPTER 19

GOLDEN OPPORTUNITY

With the dream of an adventure down under knocked on the head, I settled back into the old routine. It took a while, but I finally managed to offload one of the computers to Mr Jahan who ran the local funeral parlour. I also managed to get Rodney a bit of work out of it too. Rodders, always one for an evening class, had quit the art course and moved on to a diploma in computer science. He'd failed the exam, but he'd shown a bit of initiative and when I told Mr Jahan about it he looked very impressed. You know Rodney though, as soon as I told him I'd got him a job he got argumentative.

'I don't want it!'

'After all my time and effort, that's the thanks I get,' I said. 'This ain't just a job anyway, it's a career move.'

'I haven't got a career!'

'You would have if you took this job, and it'd be moving!'

'What sort of job was it, Del?' Albert asked.

'He would have been a trainee computer programmer... eventually. Mr Jahan even mentioned your CV, can't be bad, eh? Nice little Citroën as part of the package? You'd have had to start at the bottom, of course, work your way up.'

'Doing what?' Rodney asked, his interest growing.

'Delivering basically, with some computer work on the side.'

'Where will I be working?'

'You know that new office block in Wilmot Road, the one with all the smoked glass and the lairy cars?'

'Where all them young birds come out at lunchtime?' Albert asked, and Rodney's enthusiasm shot up a couple of notches.

'That's the one,' I told 'em.

'I know it!' said Rodney, chomping at the bit.

'Well,' I said, 'right opposite it is an alley. At the bottom of the alley is a yard, pop your head in there Monday morning, ask for Mr Jahan, and he'll give you your duties and uniform.'

I dashed off then, 'cos I'd found the best way to negotiate with Rodney is to give him the details then make yourself scarce before they have time to sink in. It helps to avoid pointless arguments.

<hr />

That weekend Trigger's niece, Lisa, was getting married down in Hampshire and we were all invited. It was a lovely service, not a hang-glider in sight. We ended up giving the vicar a lift from the church to the reception. It was a bit of a squeeze getting him into the back of the van, as there was already a couple of computers and Uncle Albert in there, but with a bit of strategic manoeuvring we finally managed to wedge him in. I tried to get him interested in one of the computers but had no joy, which was a shame 'cos I'd already shoved one in his vestry during one of the hymns. Never mind, I told him, he could have it on a fortnight's approval.

The reception went down a treat, proper classy do, and as the night rolled on I had a right laugh on the dance floor wrestling with Marlene to a bit of Wham.

Then I bumped into a blast from the past, Mum's best mate, Reenie. Course, we had a right old catch-up, talking about the past, what was and what might have been.

'He seems a nice kid,' she said, looking over at Rodney.

'He's a diamond,' I told her. 'Clever 'n all, GCEs, the lot.'

'Well,' she said, taking a swig of port and lemon, 'he's had you there to guide him. He wouldn't be in the position he is today if it hadn't been for you.'

'I've done my best by him,' I said. 'Kept my promise to Mum.'

'She would have been so proud of you two.' A sad look came over her. 'Just think, if things had worked out differently you and Rodney could have been millionaires by now. I remember visiting your mum in hospital and her saying to me, "If only I knew where he'd hidden it, Reen. My boys would be set for life!"'

'Hidden what?' I asked.

'The gold!'

'What gold?'

'His gold!'

'Who's "*he*"?'

'Freddie the Frog! You know, Freddie Robdal.'

Now, you've heard a bit about him already and probably wondered if he'd turn up again. Well, here he is! Dramatic, innit, this writing lark? Don't get confused in a minute though, just remember that back then I didn't know anything about it, which is why I said to Reen:

'Who's Freddie Robdal?'

'You mean your mum never told you? Oh my God, me and my big mouth, forget I said anything.'

'How can I forget it now? You may as well tell me, I'll only get it out of someone else.'

So she told me most of what you already know, about Freddie, how he was a bit of a villain that Mum had befriended, about how he used to have a holiday place down here on the coast, and how he'd died tragically.

But here's the bit you don't know: just before he died, Freddie and his gang had broken into the vaults of a bank in the city and got away with a quarter of a million in gold bullion! Given how long ago that had been, I quickly conduced that it had to be worth at least a million by now, probably more. Now, after Freddie had died, they'd opened up his will and found that he'd left everything to Mum. Most of his stuff, the stolen paintings and jewels and what 'ave you, were found and handed back to the rightful owners, but *nobody ever found the gold!* So, by rights, it was still mine!

'Well, yours and Rodney's,' Reen said.

'Same thing,' I told her. 'I can't believe it... I'm a millionaire!'

'Yeah,' she said, 'bloody shame nobody knows where it is, innit?'

Which was putting it mildly. But I decided there and then that I wasn't going to give up easily, that gold was our birthright and, one way or another, we were gonna find it.

❦

Back home the next day I couldn't think of nothing else. I bumped into Trigger and Boycie in the market and asked them about Freddie the Frog but the name didn't mean nothing to them.

I was about to call it a day when I spotted a funeral procession begin to pass by. On closer inspection I noticed Rodney leading the solemn march, dressed up like something you'd stick on top of a wedding cake. Considering all he had to do was stare ahead and walk, you'd have thought it would've been a doddle, but no. He suddenly became all irked and started hurling a load of verbal at me! Before you knew it, he'd taken the procession the wrong way up a one-way street and caused a traffic jam that ended up bringing pretty much the whole of Peckham to a standstill. Honestly, dipstick ain't the word.

That night, back at the flat, he was still moaning.

'You said I'd be a trainee computer programmer!'

'And are you not programming his computer?' I pointed out.

'Oh yeah, I'm programming his computer, I'm also an apprentice pall-bearer, a fully fledged chief mourner and the bloke what makes the sandwiches!'

'I don't want to talk about it,' I said, 'I've got more important things on my mind.'

'We're not going back to Freddie the bleedin' Frog again, are we?'

'Yes we are!' I said. 'There's a million quid's worth of gold bullion out there and it's ours!'

'But how do you know it hasn't been found? At some time or another, every policeman and underworld figure in the country must have been looking for it.'

'And what would they have done with it, eh?' I asked him. 'They'd either have put it through a fence, meaning it would have been public knowledge within a month, or they'd have smelted it down themselves and sold it on. That amount of bullion coming on the market causes the kind of ripples that would be remembered!'

'What about the police?' Albert asked.

'I'm talking about the police!' I said.

Then Albert decided to mention that he'd known Freddie Robdal.

'Over the years I'd bump into him every so often, usually in one of the pubs near the docks. He was a likeable fella. Generous too.'

'But what about the gold?'

'Well,' he said, 'he robbed a bank in the City.'

Stone me!

A couple of days later, Rodney stumbled on the next piece of the puzzle. He'd been asked by Mr Jahan to transfer all his old paper files onto his computer and he'd found something so interesting he'd taken an early lunch and come running into the pub to find me.

'It's one of Mr Jahan's old order forms,' he said, handing me a piece of paper. 'Look who ordered a specially made coffin five weeks before the bullion robbery: Freddie Robdal.'

I checked the form. 'Hang on, Robdal only paid for it. The coffin was for some bloke called Alfred Broderick.'

'Yeah! But look at the two names closely – it's an anagram!'

An anagram, as it turned out, is a posh word for when you mix up the letters of one word to make another, like what they do on *Countdown*. And Rodney was right!

It was all beginning to make sense. Freddie, the crafty old so-and-so, had obviously put the bullion in the specially made coffin, buried it and then accidentally blown himself to kingdom come.

'If what you're suggesting is right,' Albert said, 'he'd have needed permission from the authorities and official documentation. Where did he get all that?' Trust Albert to piss on the chips just when things were getting good.

Then it dawned on me. Mum had done the filing at the town hall. She could have got hold of the documents Freddie needed *and* given them the rubber stamp.

Just then, Mr Jahan came in looking for Rodney so I took the chance to quiz him.

'I remember Mr Robdal well,' he said. 'He was a very charming man. Also, the casket he ordered was very unusual because it was extra-large.'

'His friend Mr Broderick must have been a big chap!' I said.

'I wouldn't know,' Mr Jahan said, 'we didn't handle the funeral, just the coffin.'

'So you don't know where it was buried?' I asked him.

'No idea.'

And we'd been doing so well.

⚜

A few days later we had to pop back down to Hampshire to see the vicar. Apparently he'd been having a few problems with the computer I'd loaned him and wanted to wash his hands of it. I took a look at it, gave it a whack, but he still weren't interested.

'But there are thousands of people pouring out of London to live in the new housing estates in your parish,' I told him. 'Your flock is increasing daily and you'll need something to keep a track of 'em all!'

'I only wish that were true,' he said. 'Unfortunately few of them seem to need the spiritual services of the church. If only they could be more like our mutual friend Mr Robdal.'

You what?

'I apologise,' he said, 'but I couldn't help overhearing you and Mrs Turpin mentioning him at the wedding. When I first came to the parish, he had a holiday home just a few miles from here. He'd always call in when he was in the area. A charming and very generous man. He donated the stained-glass windows. In fact, he loved this church so much he had his parents buried here.'

Something told me this was the break I needed. 'Did you ever meet his friend Broderick?'

'Alfred Broderick? Yes – well, not in the conventional sense. It was my sad duty to lay the poor man to rest.'

BINGO!

'He must have been a rather large man, it took eight of us to carry him from the hearse.'

This was it! The final piece of the puzzle! I could almost smell the bullion!

'Could you tell me where he was buried? I'd like to pay my last respects.'

'Of course, I'll check my records.' He went looking for one of his ledgers. 'Mr Robdal must have been very close to Mr Broderick,' he said. 'I'll never forget the way he constantly patted the coffin, containing his grief behind a smile.'

'Yeah,' I told him, 'I bet he was well choked.'

Then he found the entry and told me what I needed to know.

I rushed back out to the van, calling for Rodney and Albert.

'I know where it's buried!' I shouted, leading them round the church and into the graveyard. I took 'em right through the graveyard, over the fence at the end and on through the field behind. I stopped when we hit the sand.

'This is where he buried it!' I said – pointing out to sea.

'A burial at sea?' Rodney asked. 'How did he ever hope to get the gold back?'

'Well, there are a few minor details our dear uncle forgot to tell us about,' I explained. 'Like he told us he met Freddie the Frog but he didn't tell us *where* and *how*.'

'It was when he was doing his national service in the navy,' Albert said.

'Yes, Uncle!' I said. 'I know that now. And you also omitted to tell us why he was nicknamed Freddie the Frog.'

''Cos he was a frogman.'

'Why didn't you tell us?' Rodney asked.

'Well, you know me,' said Albert, 'I don't like talking about my days at sea.'

At that moment I had to fight the urge to give the old duffer a swift kick back into it.

'We knew Freddie had a chalet down here,' said Rodney, 'if we'd also known he was an ex-sailor and deep-sea diver we could've probably put two and two together!'

'It's beautiful, innit?' I admitted. 'He had all the kosher paperwork, a pukka ceremony with an authentic vicar, he even had two off-duty policemen to help carry the coffin to the boat! The sea shall not have it! I will bring it back to the surface!'

'But where are you going to start searching, Del?' Albert asked. 'You're looking at five hundred square miles of ocean! It took 'em seventy years to find the *Titanic*, what chance have we got with an outsize coffin?'

Albert was right. I was gutted! To have your birthright lost in Davey Smith's locker and with no way to get to it. To have been within a hair's breadth away of riches and success and to have been forced to say bonjour to it.

Story of my bloody life, innit?

CHAPTER 20

LITTLE JOE

Despite knowing our fortune would remain at the bottom of the big blue, things were going well. Sometimes Rodney and I were like a pair of King Minuses, everything we touched turning to gold. I liked to savour those moments. I had to 'cos they never lasted long. Right then though, even Albert getting his box of old photos out and dragging Rodney and me on a long stagger down memory lane couldn't dampen our spirits.

Usually when he got that box out it meant some epic tale of stupidity on the high seas (with a gang of killer sea bass thrown in for good measure) was on the cards, but this time there was one photo in particular that was on the old sea dog's mind. It showed a young Albert and his shipmates celebrating his birthday on board HMS *Pilchard*, I think (I forget now, but it was one of the HMSs) somewhere in the South Pacific. According to Albert, just a few hours after the photo was taken, a Japanese submarine appeared on the scene (enough to ruin anyone's birthday that, innit?). Albert's ship was there to protect an American aircraft carrier anchored offshore, but when the alarm was raised they panicked and crashed straight into it instead.

'You went and whacked into the boat that you were there to protect?' I asked him.

'Yeah,' he said, 'it was a good job she was there really 'cos she picked up most of the survivors.' Course, the authorities blamed Albert for the incident and tried to get him on the trivial technicality that he was on watch at the time, and that it was in broad bleedin' daylight! 'I wasn't close enough,' Albert explained.

'You must've been reasonably close, Unc, you hit it,' Rodney pointed out.

'Yeah, but I weren't on deck, I was down in the radar room watching the screen. I couldn't make head nor tail of it... it was all blibs and blobs. Anyway, the Japanese sub had it away a bit lively.'

'I s'pose it didn't feel needed with you around,' Rodney said. 'Did you get in trouble for it?'

'Court martial,' Albert said. 'The papers were sent to naval headquarters in Singapore.'

'You were court-martialled?'

'No, as luck would have it, before my trial the Japanese invaded and I never heard another thing about it – and the blokes on my lifeboat used to say I was unlucky!' He walked off to his bedroom, laughing that old laugh of his – it sounded like someone trying to push-start a Lada.

Rodney then noticed the date on the back of the photo. The sly old sod was trying to slip us a little reminder that his birthday was coming up, hoping we'd arrange a treat for him. Rodney suggested we get him an electric razor, but I reckoned I could come up with something better.

We were in the Nag's Head the following afternoon listening to Boycie going on about having recently joined the Freemasons. Naturally, I was well pleased for him.

'What did you wanna go and join that bunch of dipsticks for?' I asked him.

'It is a great honour to be chosen,' he said. 'It's changed my life. I'm involved in a lot of charity work, helping the needy and underprivileged – but it's got its good side as well. Us Masons vow to help each other in business whenever humanly possible.'

'It sounds like a load of old snobs trying to clone another load of old snobs,' said Rodney.

'We're not snobs,' Boycie went on, 'we've got all walks of life at our lodge; we've got an estate agent, a judge, a television director—'

'What's he do, film the secret handshakes in case you wallies forget?' Rodney said, doing his best to wind the snobby git up.

But before Boycie could answer, Trigger walked in wearing a suit and holding a bunch of flowers. I weren't sure if it was Comic Relief again or if someone had died.

'I've got a date,' he announced.

'You wanna watch those stones,' Rodney warned him, ''cos Del got one stuck in his throat once.'

'No, Dave,' Trig said, 'I've got a date with a woman.'

You can imagine it came as a bit of a shock to us all. But it turned out Trig had recently joined a computer dating firm called the Techno-Match Friendship and Matrimonial Agency. Apparently they'd fed all his information into their computer and it had come up with a bird who matched. Frightening, innit?

Anyway, a bit later I was on my way to the betting shop when I spotted Trigger and his date entering a restaurant on the high street, and stone me – she was a *woman!* What I mean to say is she was a normal-looking woman – own hair, teeth, two eyes, no humps that I could see. Well, it got me thinking about my own situation. Truth be told, my love life had been going through a bit of a drought, and though I obviously didn't need an agency for that kind of thing, I thought I'd throw my hat into the ring anyway and see what occurred. After all, if they'd found a decent-looking bird for Trigger – a man who gives pet names to his teeth – they'd be laughing with me.

I sailed through the signing-up process, although I did tell a couple of little white lies about myself. Well, I wanted to make sure it was worth my time: it weren't cheap, and I didn't want to end up being lumbered with some bow-wow who couldn't tell the difference between a Liebfraumilch and a can of Tizer. So they took all my info, fed it into the computer and within seconds it came up with a name: Raquel Turner. Raquel just so happens to be my most favouritest name ever, so we were off to a triffic start. She was an actress, which, what with me being a man of the arts, was right up my street too.

The agency geezer suggested Raquel and I go for lunch and recommended we meet under the main clock at Waterloo station. Apparently this was traditional and romantic 'cos it was where some bloke called Trevor once met a bird called Celia (no, I didn't know what the soppy sod was going on about either). I was having my doubts though, 'cos the last bird I met at Waterloo got mugged on the escalator.

The day of the date arrived and, determined to make an impression, I put on my very finest clobber. 'You going out, Del?' Albert asked, as I stood in front of the mirror making some last-minute adjustments to the old barnet. 'No, I'm going to bleed the brakes on the van,' I said.

'I thought it might be a special occasion, like a birthday or something,' he said. 'I used to have some smashing birthday parties when I was a lad.' Subtlety never was Albert's strong suit.

As it turned out, romance was also in the air for Rodney. He'd got himself a date with a new barmaid at the Nag's Head, 'Nervous' Nerys, lovely girl, blonde, had a look of permanent terror etched on her face. I'd bought Raquel a big bouquet of flowers and booked a table for two at the Hilton Hotel, Park Lane. Yeah, it was a bit extravagant, but she was an actress so I thought I'd better spruce up a bit. Rodney had always had his own unique ways of impressing women – doing silly walks, talking to them about dead painters, things like that – but on this occasion he took it to a whole new level by reinventing himself as a sort of down 'n out Arthur Fonzarelli.

'It's the fashion,' he said. 'It's what they call "the James Dean look".'

'Yeah but when they said the James Dean look they meant *before* the crash,' I said.

I must admit I felt a bit of a wally myself standing around under that clock at Waterloo. Raquel was running well late and there I was all suited up with a gigantic bunch of flowers in my hand. I was just about to call it a day when a voice behind me said, 'Hello.' I turned round and there was this lovely brunette smiling back at me. 'Raquel?' I asked, wanting to be doubly sure as I'd noticed there was a good few prostitutes on the prowl. But it was Raquel. She was full of apologies for being late, but all I could notice was her big brown eyes. I remember thinking to myself, *blimey! She's really, really... nice.* It was a bit awkward though as we walked off together to find a cab.*

'This is a bit like *Brief Encounter*, isn't it?' Raquel said, eyeing up our surroundings.

I'll be honest, I couldn't see it myself, but she was an actress and must've known what she was talking about, so I agreed.

---

* I'd let Rodney use the van. Well, I could hardly pull up outside the Hilton in it, could I?

'That's my favourite film,' she said.

'Oh yeah, mine too,' I said. 'My favourite bit is when the big space-ship comes down and all the little Martians come out.' I forget what she said next but it was obvious my knowledge of films had impressed.

Lunch was lovely (no chips on the menu, and they were fresh out of Malibu, but still lovely), and Raquel and I soon relaxed and got to know each other better. I was surprised that someone with her looks, career and talent needed to use a computer dating agency, and I told her as much. 'I could say the same about you,' she said, 'a successful man, managing director of his own import–export business.* I suppose I was grabbing at straws really. I've been married before, and that was a disaster.'

'I just thought that being an actress you'd be meeting lots of people on the film sets and all that,' I said.

She was upfront with me then, admitting that, while she tech-nically was an actress, she'd never made it big time. 'I had one line in a *Doctor Who* about ten years ago,' she said. 'I was a lizard person.' I remembered the episode, and she was bloody good!

'I had to give it up for nine years when I was married,' she con-tinued. 'My husband was one of those old-fashioned types who thought there should only be one breadwinner.'

'My dad was like that,' I said, 'he used to get up at six every morning to make sure my mum got off to work.' It weren't a joke, but she laughed anyway.

'Recently I've been trying to pick up from where I left off,' she said, 'but I can't see anything coming of it.'

'Au contraire, Raquel,' I told her. 'This time next year you'll be a star. She who dares wins! If you want something enough, you'll get it, as long as you don't stop believing.'

---

* Little white lie no.1.

By the time we'd finished eating we were starting to relax properly, and I could tell there was something special in the air. Raquel felt it too.

'This is nice,' she said. 'There's a lovely feeling of... honesty.'

It was nice, so much so in fact that when the head waiter came over to inform me that I had an important call from my New York office,* I told him it'd have to wait. Raquel went on, mentioning she was a big fan of the works of Shaw (who ain't?) and some other foreign-sounding things.

Before we left I asked her if she'd like to see me again Saturday night. 'I can't do Friday or Saturday evenings, I teach drama class,' she explained.

'What about Monday night then?' I suggested.

'I'd love to,' she said, 'why don't you come round to my flat?'

The rest of that day I couldn't stop thinking about her. As you know, I'd been prone to falling hard and fast for birds in the past, but this was different. It weren't just physical, it was a meeting of minds, and that was a rare thing for me. Up till then I'd never had such interesting and intellectually simulating conversation with... well, anyone. Fair enough, a lot of what Raquel had said might as well have been in Vietnamese for all the sense it made to me, but that weren't the point. My brain had been massaged on a deep and meaningful level, and it wanted more.

Rodney clearly had something on his mind too. I asked him how his date with Nerys had gone, but he didn't want to talk about it (she was off work for a couple of days so I'm guessing it went about as well as most of his other dates).

That night I lay awake in bed thinking about Raquel and her situation, and I came to a decision: I was gonna join the Masons.

---

* Little white lie no.2.

Well, she was clearly a talented actress, but talent ain't nothing unless someone gives you a chance to show it off. If I joined Boycie's lodge I could get that television director he mentioned to give her that chance.

The second date with Raquel was smashing too. She cooked a lovely meal, duck à l'orange (which has always been my favourite flavour of duck), and told me all about the latest book she was reading. I forget what it was called and what it was about, but it was a classic. After dinner I told her about my plans to help her out by joining the Masons. She weren't too sure, but decided to leave it to me to do what I thought best.

So I got on the blower to Boycie.

'No, Del,' he said, after he'd stopped laughing. 'Only the most respected members of our society can join my lodge.'

'But I'd make a very good Mason,' I explained. 'Masons are supposed to do each other favours, so you do me this favour and I'll do one for you.'

'And what might that be?' he asked.

'I won't tell Marlene about that bird in Sheffield,' I said. The line went quiet for a few moments, as I knew it would.

'No, Del,' he came back on, 'you might be many things, but you are not a grass. I don't think we have anything else to say to each other, goodbye.'

He was just about to hang up when I heard Marlene in the background telling him not to. 'Del?' her voice came on the line. 'About Albert's birthday, what d'you think he'd like as a present?'

'Well…' I said, knowing Boycie would be earwigging, 'he does like a bit of fishing, and he was talking about getting himself a proper angler's knife, but it must be made of *Sheffield* steel.'

'Sheffield?' she said. Then there was a scream and a commotion as Boycie wrestled the phone off her. He came on the line and was only too happy to help me out. Funny how quickly people's minds can change, innit?

The next evening I had to go down the lodge and meet the committee members. I broke the ice with a joke (the one about the 'twelve-inch pianist', always goes down a treat) and dazzled 'em with a bit of the old *Bouillabaisse, Mon Amie*, to let them know they weren't dealing with just any old herbert. They were all wearing masks, even Boycie, and referring to each other by numbers, which was a bit off-putting, but apparently these Masons take their secrecy very seriously. Personally I didn't see what the big deal was, I mean, we were in a house on Kings Avenue,* not some secret underground bunker. The whole thing didn't take more than ten minutes, and after getting into a row with Boycie (number 69) over whether or not it was actually him, I was off. I was confident I'd done enough, but I had to bear in mind the possibility that I could end up being blackballed. Y'see, each member had one black ball and one white ball,† and they each had to put one of their balls in a bag. At the end of it all when they emptied the bag, if all the balls were white it meant you was in. If there was just one black ball, you were out. Thankfully, I had other things to help take my mind off it. I'd booked the Nag's Head for Albert's birthday do and needed to take care of some last-minute arrangements.

◆━◆

The do began really well. Albert was on the piano singing… something, it was hard to tell, but apart from that everyone seemed to be enjoying themselves. Except Mike, who had laid down some conditions prior to me booking the pub (that Albert didn't play the piano, sing, drink,

---

* The one at the end with the electric gates and the big marble fountain on the front lawn.
† Snooker balls.

laugh, talk or move). I spotted Boyice and called him over to find out if the committee had come to a decision about me joining.

'I'm sorry, Del, but you were blackballed,' he said.

'Someone put a black ball in the bag?!' I couldn't believe it.

'Well,' he explained, 'when the bag was emptied there was more than one black ball.'

'Yeah? How many?' I asked.

'Let's put it this way,' he said, 'have you ever seen the bottom of a rabbit's hutch?'

So that was that then. How was I gonna tell Raquel?

'Listen,' Rodney said, 'if Raquel's as talented as you say she is, she don't need you bribing some TV director, her talent will win through.' He was right. Masons or no Masons, Raquel was gonna make it.

I was starting to feel a bit better when a couple of naval officers, a big, serious-looking geezer and a blonde sort entered the pub and headed straight for Albert.

'Able seaman Albert Trotter?' the geezer said. Albert went pale, as though he'd just spotted a U-boat off the starboard bow. 'I'm placing you under arrest,' the male officer continued. 'You'll be taken to the naval stockade, Portsmouth, where you'll await court martial.'

'But why?' Albert asked.

'Dereliction of duty. 19 November 1941, while serving in the Royal Pacific fleet, you did wantonly abandon your watch duties, thus causing the sinking of a ship of Her Majesty's fleet and considerable damage to the American vessel U.S.S. *Pittsburgh*.'

'But I couldn't understand the radar screen,' Albert pleaded. 'It was all blibs and blobs.'

The officer wasn't having any of it and he turned to his fellow officer. 'Read the charges, Petty Officer.'

'Aye, sir,' she said. 'Able seaman Albert Trotter, you are hereby charged by the Queen, by the High Lords of the Admiralty and by all your friends and relatives to have a very happy birthday!' And with that she whipped off her hat, burst into song and started to get her kit off! You should have seen the old git's face, he didn't know whether to laugh or cry. I'd seen one of those strippergram adverts in the local paper and I'd done 'im up like a right kipper! 'I'll get you for this!' he called over to me, but he was loving it, the randy old goat! I was too until I caught sight of the stripper's face and realised it was Raquel. Shock ain't the word.

'Raquel?' I said.

'Del?' she replied.

'Oh,' Boycie chipped in. 'So this is the *actress* you've been telling us all about, is it, Del?'

Everyone in the pub started laughing then. It was a nightmare so I made a quick exit into the car park where I took my anger out on the van. Rodney came out and tried to calm me down. 'Come on, Del, don't get out of your pram about it,' he said.

'Get out of my pram?! She's just humiliated me in front of all my friends!' I said.

'But you booked her,' he said.

'I booked a *stripper*! She said she was an actress!'

Raquel came out then, carrying her wig.

'You lied to me!' I told her.

'No I didn't, I never told you I *wasn't* a stripper. Besides, that's the pot calling the kettle black, I just found out your surname is Trotter. You told me it was Duval!* And I suppose this is your Ferrari,† she said, pointing at the van.

---

* Little white lie no.3.
† Little white lie no. 4.

'All right,' I said to her, 'I might occasionally tell the odd porky or two, but I tell you what I don't do, I don't go around pubs dressed in stockings and suspenders flashing my boobs at geezers, do I, Rodney?'

'No, he's never done anything like that.' Rodney backed me up.

'I only do this a couple of evenings a week to help pay for my drama lessons,' she said. 'I'm sorry you don't like what I do for a living, this may come as a surprise to you, but I don't bloody like it either!'

'I got blackballed for you.'

She didn't know what to say to that.

'Look,' she said eventually, 'this may be a stupid question, but do you want to see me again?'

'Of course I do,' I said, 'but next time I'll pay at the door like all the other punters.'

She left then, and I immediately wished I hadn't said it.

What a wally!

***

A couple of days later I was in Sid's café, aka 'The Fatty Thumb', having a fry-up. Can't say I was enjoying it. But then nobody really ever enjoyed one of Sid's fry-ups, you just did your best to get through it and prayed there wouldn't be any comebacks. Then Raquel walked in. Deep down I was glad, but I didn't let her know that, 'cos I was still angry. She took a seat opposite me.

'If I'd known your real name, I'd never have taken the job,' she said.

'You still didn't tell me what you did for a living,' I said.

'I was hoping I wouldn't have to. After I met you and I realised we were becoming… close, I'd planned to pack the stripping in and you'd have been none the wiser.'

Fair enough, I thought, but still, it was the principle.

'Listen, Del,' she said, 'I'm going on a tour, and you won't have to worry about bumping into me, it's a tour of the Middle East.'

'Oh, use your noddle, Raquel,' I said. 'You read about that sort of thing in the Sunday papers. You'll probably get kidnapped and end up in a harlem.'

'It's an official tour, all above board.' She went quiet again for a moment. 'I just want to say thanks,' she said.

'What for?'

'For being the only man I've met who wanted me to keep my clothes on, for getting blackballed for me, for giving me back some self-esteem,' she said. I was gonna mention the *Very Best of Sandie Shaw* LP I'd got her, but I thought it best not to interrupt. 'I used to wake up in the morning,' she continued, 'I'd look in the mirror and I'd think, *Oh, you again*. After I met you I used to think, *Great! Another day, you're going to be someone. This time next year you're going to be famous*. Thanks for that.'

I didn't know what to say, so I offered her a bit of my fried bread.

'I leave tomorrow afternoon,' she said, after managing to swallow the bread. 'It doesn't have to be the end. If you want me to stay, I will. If you like the idea, be at my flat tomorrow. If not, I'll understand.' And off she went.

I was taken by surprise. I could feel this ball of turmoil churning away inside of me, and for once it had nothing to do with Sid's mushrooms. I went home that afternoon and spent the rest of the day thinking it over. And I came to a realisation.

The next day in the Nag's Head I was talking to Rodney about it. 'Raquel's had a tough old life,' I told him, 'her old man was a right roughhouse, none of the other blokes she's met have been any better, she's had nothing but bad luck, and then she met me.'

'Bloody hell, life's a bitch, innit?' he said.

'That's where her luck changed,' I explained. But maybe he had a point. I'd been thinking back over the birds I'd known, and I'd brought 'em all bad luck.

'I'm a bit like that Little Joe,' I said.

'What?' Rodney asked.

'Little Joe, you know, in *Bonanza*.'

'You ain't, Del, you're nothing like him.'

'Not in looks,' I explained, 'he's an ugly-looking git, but when you're watching an episode of *Bonanza* and that Little Joe falls in love with a woman, you *know* that she's either gonna catch the fever, get trampled in a stampede or the Indians are gonna get her.'

'That's not gonna happen to Raquel,' he said.

And that was the realisation I'd come to: that, whatever happened, Raquel weren't gonna end up full of arrows. So I decided to have a couple of quick liveners and shoot round to her flat. I was just about to leave when a couple of young police officers, a bloke and a bird, came in. Rodney shot out the front door so fast he created a breeze, but considering the state of Mike's pipes, I just thought he'd come down with a case of the two-bob bits.

'Is your name Trotter?' a voice behind me asked.

I turned to face the officers. 'Yes, that's me,' I said.

'Is that your van parked outside?' the female officer asked.

'What, the one with "Trotter" written on the side of it? Yeah, that's mine.'

Apparently a van very similar to mine had recently shot some traffic lights and caused an accident, and they wanted to question me about it. Course, I didn't take it seriously. 'You'll have to do better than that, Uncle, you crafty old git,' I called over to Albert, who was sitting there doing his best to act shocked.

'Mr Trotter,' the female officer said, acting all stern, 'you don't seem to be taking this very seriously.'

'Come on, darlin',' I said, 'I'm a bit pushed for time, so can we get on with it?'

'What do you mean?' she said.

'You know what I mean,' I said. 'Get 'em out!' And I pulled open her blouse. 'You disappoint me, Uncle, I thought you'd have come up with something a bit more original than that.'

'It's got nothing to do with me, son,' he said.

Then I noticed the police car out the window.

<hr />

They let me have one phone call at the station, but by then, and like most things in my life, it was too bloody late!

CHAPTER 21

GROOVY!

Having naused things up with Raquel, the drought in my love-life continued and I went into a slump. But then I had an apothecary… Sometimes a great man realises it's time to reinvent himself. Like Bono when he became the Fly, or Lily Savage when he packed in the skirts. Usually it's triggered by a major event, something so deep and mind-bending that you have no choice but to listen to your gut and make the change. For many it's a near death experience, for others it's finding God. For me it was Michael Douglas. I'd watched him play that giant of business, Gordon Gekko, in *Wall Street* and it really blew me away. It was that 'can do' attitude that suited me right down to the ground. Nothing got the old adrenalin pumping like shifting a few million quid's worth of stocks and shares… I imagine. So I got myself a Filofax, slapped on a pair of red braces and went out to get a copy of the *Financial Times*. It was very much a case of 'I was blind, but now … I'm not.'

***

I'd just done a deal on a lovely line of Turkish raincoats, but they weren't shifting. Rodney reckoned it had something to do with the

'Dry Clean Only' on the labels. He might have had a point. Not that he was putting the effort in. He'd just enrolled in a computer science course (again!) at evening school and was too busy poncing about on his computer to worry about little things like putting food on the table.

Still, when I received a letter from the council saying they'd accepted my offer to buy the flat it cheered me right up. The way I saw it we'd been living in the flat for so long it had become a part of us. It weren't just the Trotter home, it was the Trotter *heart*, so it was only natural I'd want to own it outright. And if I could then flog it on to some chinless wonder for an exorbitant amount, well, lovely jubblies all round!

See, Peckham was becoming a very trendy area. There were wine bars and posh restaurants opening up everywhere, and it would've been stupid not to take advantage. After all the flat was in a perfect location, fifteen minutes from the West End, fifteen minutes from the motorway, fifteen minutes from the... ground. Course, Rodney got his nose out of joint and started banging on about it being immoral 'cos council flats had been built for the poorer classes and where would they go if they were all sold off? Wherever they liked, I told him, once they'd got a fortune for flogging their flats.

One day I was driving Rodders to his evening class when I decided to take a quick detour up Kings Avenue, just to give him a lesson in how the other half lived. As avenues go, the Kings Avenue had always been the Capo Del Monte, lined with massive gaffs filled with guest suites, swimming pools and Jacuzzis. All we had at the time was a put-you-up, a damp patch and a Jakhazi!

'We'll be in one of these one day, bruv,' I told him.

'What you got lined up, a decorating job?' he said.

I ignored the sarcasm. I was riding a wave of new-found optimism, channelling the PMA (positive mental attitude) like what I'd read the yuppies were doing at the time, and I knew that with an 'alf-decent break, we'd be millionaires!

After dropping Rodney off I decided to try out one of the new watering holes that had just opened up across the street. Blinding place, full of cufflinks, aluminium briefcases, glamorous businesswomen… very me. I ordered a Beaujolais Nouveau in a loud voice, just to make sure people noticed a new player was on the scene. And I made sure the barman made it a '79, didn't want them thinking I was just any old philistine.

I was still there when Rodney dropped by after his class had finished, all flushed 'cos he'd bumped into some sort called Cassandra. I wasn't paying a lot of attention at the time 'cos, well, you know what Rodney's like, he fell in love with women on advertising billboards.

He headed off but I decided to hang around, chance my luck and stake my claim on the place. A few minutes later, who should pop in but Trigger! Apparently Mike had kicked him out of the Nag's Head for stealing a pork pie. Which just goes to show how stupid Trigger was. Not for getting caught, but for wanting one in the first place. Mike's pork pies were like knuckles wrapped in plywood, eating one was the sort of thing you did for a bet when you were pissed.

I pointed out a pair of trendy sorts who had been giving us the eye and considered moving in for the kill, but weighing up the situation I decided against it. Trigger was wearing one of his 'special' suits, bright blue it was, and what with the neon in the bar, I didn't really fancy going in for the kill with a six-foot warning signal standing next to me.

Rodney had fared better, bumping into Cassandra again in a nightclub he'd gone on to. He'd even danced with her!

She gave him a lift home and, after all the cobblers he'd been giving me about the flat, the dipstick went and pretended he lived on the Kings Avenue! Had a right long walk home too. In the rain! He was the gift that kept on giving, he really was. No matter how bad an evening you thought you'd had, all you had to do was ask what Rodney had been up to and you'd feel better. Rumour was that Terry Waite had given Rodney a bell first thing after his release just to put things into perspective.

For all of that, Rodney and Cassandra hooked up. They even went out for meals together (the last time Rodney had taken a girl out for a meal, she got a free toy with it). Every day I'd wait for the news that one or the other had jacked it in, but it didn't arrive. So, when the chance arose to help 'cement' things a bit more firmly between 'em, I jumped at it.

I'd been going through a bit of a competition phase. They seemed to be everywhere back then. On every food packet, in every magazine, someone was giving something away.

It was all about the odds, ninety-nine times out of a hundred you wouldn't get a look-in but, if you sent off everything you could find, you'd end up winning something eventually.

As you know, Rodney had always fancied himself as an artist, and every now and then he'd drag out some of his old schoolwork and try and impress the girls. Some of 'em weren't too bad, like the painting he'd titled *Marble Arch at Dawn*. What was really impressive about that one was that he'd originally called it *Arc de Triomphe at Sunset*, then realised he couldn't spell 'Arc de Triomphe'. So he scrubbed out the Eiffel Tower, threw a double-decker bus in, and Bob's your uncle, a few thousand miles and a dab of red paint later and he's got himself a GCE! Goes to show that when he really tries he can pull a fast one.

Anyway, when I spotted an art competition on the back of a Mega Flakes box, I thought I'd see what the judges would make of Rodney's *Arch*, so I sent it off and forgot all about it.

I'd been seeing a bird called Petula who I'd bumped into at a car boot sale (four boxes of roof tiles, a lightly chipped dinner service and a promise of a bit of how's your father, not a bad morning's business) and even Albert had a regular thing going with some old girl called Elsie Partridge who he'd met at bingo. She was a local psychic-medium who he'd apparently known before the war, but then he'd gone off to fight and she'd gone off to get married. Now, years later, they had a chance to make another go of things. And that was it, he was popping the Sanatogens like they were Smarties.

So when the letter turned up announcing that Rodney had won the competition it was a proper bolt from the blue. I couldn't wait to tell him and Cassandra that they were going on a free, all-expenses paid holiday to Majorca! And that I was going with 'em! Well, the holiday was for three people, and I had been the one to send it off so fair dos. It was a good time to be out of Peckham anyway as there was a lot of bad luck going about. I'd heard on the grapevine that some spiv had been going round stitching people up with a non-existent deal involving gold chains. Actually there were a lot of weird stories doing the rounds at the time, like the one about exploding inflatable sex dolls. Apparently a batch that had been accidentally filled with propane gas had gone missing from a factory in Deptford. There'd also been reports of a loud explosion coming from the rec just down the road from us, but I never heard nothing. Some poor bastards had to deal with those dolls though. Sod their luck!

Anyway, where was I? Oh yeah, Rodney and Cassandra couldn't believe it. Rodney was particularly shocked he'd won the competition 'cos he hadn't known he'd entered it. I told him not to worry and got a bottle of champagne in.

It weren't long before Rodney started panicking. He was suspicious about the fact that the holiday was for three people. He just couldn't get his head around it (mainly 'cos I hadn't shown him the second page of the letter announcing that he'd won, but we were celebrating and I didn't want to bore him with a load of small print).

Cassandra got a week off work, we packed our cases, trotted off to Gatwick, and before you could say *Muchos Grassyarse* we were touching down in La Palma.

As we got through passport control and approached the Mega Flakes greeting party, Rodney noticed something about the group of winners.

'That's strange,' he said, 'they're all mums and dads, they've all brought kids with them.'

I decided it was probably a good time to mention the small detail I'd held back for fear of ruining the holiday.

'It's not the parents that are the winners,' I explained, 'it's the kids.'

'What do you mean?' Cassandra asked.

'Well, the thing is, Rodney's painting won first prize in the under-fifteen category.'

'They think I'm fifteen?'

'No, Rodney, they think you're fourteen and a half, 'cos that's what you wrote on the bottom of the painting. I sent it off in good faith, didn't I? It's your fault for writing it.'

'How was I supposed to know that years later you'd enter it into a bloody cornflakes competition?'

'How was I supposed to know it was gonna win?' I told him. 'Come on, Rodders, kids today look much older than they used to, and with your boyish good looks we'll waltz it.'

'That's why there's three tickets, ain't it?' he asked. 'One each for Mummy and Daddy and one for the sprog!'

'Well, you can't expect thirteen- or fourteen-year-olds to go on holiday on their own, can you? So when the cornflakes people rang up and said you had to be accompanied by your parents, well, I got a bit flustered and… you'll laugh at this,* I said I was your dad.'

'Who the hell does that make me?' Cassandra asked. 'His mum?!'

'No! Of course not.' I explained. 'I told 'em Rodney's real mother had passed away, which is true, innit? I just told 'em I'd met a much younger woman who had become a very important part of our lives.'

After a bit more huffing and puffing, I finally convinced them to play it cool. After all, it was done now, weren't it? And if we told them the truth we'd have been stuck in Majorca airport for a week waiting for the flight home. Anyway, once we got past the official greeting stage we'd be straight on to the hotel and then we could just crack on and have a good time.

The two reps in charge, a bloke called Alan and a bird called Carmen, were obviously a bit taken aback by Rodney's size, but I told 'em his old mum had been a big girl, clocking in at 6'3", and they were too polite to go on about it.

Alan then handed Rodney a badge that gave him lifetime membership to the 'Groovy Gang' (he just couldn't stop winning), a stipulation of which was that every time either Alan or Carmen asked him if he was having fun, he had to shout 'Groovy!' Rodney didn't really go a bundle on this, so I shouted it for him a couple of times, you know, trying to encourage him into the spirit of things. Then it was announced that the kids were going to travel together on a 'Fun Bus' so they could eat hamburgers, compare acne and sing songs and stuff (I don't know what they thought kids were getting up to at that age, when I was fourteen I was sat at the back having a Capstan, but bless 'em for trying). Rodney didn't fancy this too much either, but with some further encouragement, a bit of nudging, and a lot of effing

---

* He didn't.

and blinding, I managed to get him onto the bus just in time to enjoy a groovy rendition of 'Viva España'.

At the hotel reception I bought us all a few lottery tickets (well, we were on a winning streak, weren't we?) while Cassandra went upstairs to unpack. I thought it best to give her a bit of space as she weren't in the best of moods. By the time I joined her she was having a right moan about the sleeping arrangements. Being a family room there was one main bedroom and a small single room. I tried to calm her down, telling her I'd take the single room (though I'd take the picture of Prince down first, I couldn't relax with his ugly mug staring at me), then her and Rodney could get comfortable in the king-size. Finally we agreed that she'd sleep in the kid's room while Rodney and I shared the king-size. I did point out that it would look a bit funny if the maid came in and saw me and Rodney bunking up together, but as the alternative was the maid catching him shacked up with his stepmother, I admitted she was probably right.

We still hadn't seen Rodney at that point. Actually, that's not quite true, we caught a brief glimpse of him from the hotel window, disappearing over a hill on a skateboard.

Carmen stopped by to let us know about the junior disco she'd arranged, and then a few minutes later, Rodney burst in with his skateboard, looking like a deranged Eddie the Eagle.

'What's up with you?' I asked him.

'I'll tell you what's up with me, Del,' he said, 'thanks to you I'm a twenty-six-year-old man who just came second in a skateboard derby!!!'

'Second? You were in front when we saw you.'

'I fell off.'

Served him right for showing off.

'I also have a thirteen-year-old Bros fan called Trudie who's got the hots for me and tomorrow I start the first of three cycling proficiency lessons, and I'm gonna kill you!'

I ducked into the bathroom at that point, locking the door just to be safe. I'd never been bludgeoned with a skateboard before, but I reckoned it'd hurt.

It went a bit quiet so I popped my head out to make sure everything was all right.

'Git!' he shouted at me. At least he'd calmed down. I tried to reassure him that things would eventually ease off on the Groovy Gang front, but he then reeled off the full week's itinerary, which included a trip to the splash 'n slide, go-karting, a ping-pong championship and a break-dancing competition. Bloody reps sticking their oar in. Couldn't they understand that sometimes a fourteen-year-old just wants to kick back with a nice fag and a Scotch or two?

And then the devils themselves turned up, wanting to double-check Rodney's passport. 'Just Spanish regulations,' said Carmen, a load of old pony but that was OK, I was prepared.

'My date of birth's on my passport!' Rodney whispered.

I tipped him the wink. 'S'all right, bruv, I went over it with a biro.'

And, right enough, they couldn't find anything wrong so they left us to it. A Trotter plans for all eventualities!

It weren't a bad week, in between all the moaning. It was on the fifth night that I was demoted to the single room, so that Rodney and Cassandra could get some alone time. I didn't mind, it was nice to have a bed to myself. I hadn't been getting much kip sharing the double with Rodney – it was a comfortable enough bed, it's just I was worried he'd strangle me to death in my sleep. Anyway, that night in the single room I thought I'd hear something, you know, a little bit of noise to indicate that things had got fully under way in the old 'cementing' department. But I didn't hear a thing. Not that I was trying to listen, I'd never pry into something as personal as that, whatever they were doing out there it was none of my business whatsoever. I just found it strange how silent it was. Even when I put my ear to the wall I couldn't hear anything. I tried a glass next and still nothing. It was so quiet you could've heard an ant fart. *Rodney was probably just knackered from all the activities*, I thought. Still, like I said, it was none of my business whatsoever.

The next morning I was expecting to find Cassandra all smiley and relaxed, but she was more miserable than ever, and I almost started to wish I'd let 'em come on their own.

Sometimes you just couldn't please Rodney. There he was, being chauffeured around on his own bus, having days in the sun packed full of exciting activities, being crowned champion of ping-pong tournaments, all for gratis, and all he could do was moan! How about me? It weren't half cramping my style having to pretend I had the missus in tow. I'd caught the eye of a few of the local señoritas, but it weren't as if I could give 'em the full charm offensive, was it? If Alan or Carmen caught wind of it I'd have dropped us all in it. On the third day I'd even got chatting to a blinding beautician from Hull (I was definitely in there, she fluttered her eyelashes at me so much one fell off into her rum and Coke) but I played the game and kept my nose clean.

Come the night of the junior disco, Cassandra had such an ache on her face I was considering filing for divorce.

'Cheer up,' I told her, 'he's obviously enjoying himself.'

'He's not,' she said, 'he cried last night.'

'Why do you think he's carrying on with this pretence?' I asked her. 'He's only doing this for you, sweetheart!'

'For me?'

'Course. He only wants to see you having a good time. The least you can do is smile and let him know his sacrifices haven't been in vain.'

He came out then, needing a drink, and I told him the same thing. 'She's only pretending to have a bad time for your sake, Rodney,' I said, letting him have a crafty sip of my Cointreau and Dr Pepper. 'The least you could do is act like you're enjoying yourself a bit so she can relax and make the most of it.'

Soon enough they were both smiling at one another and heading off for the finals of the break-dancing competition.*

Job done, I thought, happy that I'd been able to help.

Later on that evening a couple of sorts at the hotel bar asked if I knew any good clubs in the area, so I decided to do my civic duty and forget about the marriage for a few hours.

I got back the next afternoon, feeling a bit rough. I was planning on having a quiet day in bed with a cold flannel and a packet of Nurofen, when Rodney and Cassandra turned up, shouting and jumping around.

'What's up with you two?' I asked.

'We've won!' Rodney said.

'The break-dancing competition?'

'The lottery! You remember? You bought some tickets when we arrived.'

'Yeah…' My brain was struggling to keep up.

'They won!' Cassandra shouted.

I've tried a few hangover cures in my time, most of which involve bacon and Alka-Seltzer, but the only one I've ever known that had an instant effect was being told I'd won a million pesetas. So there's me and Rodders dancing around the hotel bar singing 'If I Were a Rich Man', when Alan came in.

'I'm sorry,' he said, 'but you can't claim a penny of the money.'

'But we've double-checked it!' said Cassandra. 'It's definitely the winning numbers.'

---

* Rodney came third. He would've won if he hadn't tried to do a head-spin and spun off into an old dear on a mobility scooter.

'The numbers are fine,' he said, 'but the ticket's in Rodney's name and under Spanish law you have to be over eighteen to gamble.'

Oh well, it's only money, innit?

CHAPTER 22

IS ANYBODY THERE?

Dark days were upon Nelson Mandela House. It began, as so many dark days do, with a letter from the council. All my recent investments had gone sideways and I was still a long way off buying the flat so I'd slipped behind on the rent. The council, being nice and understanding, threatened to evict us. I was doing my best not to let the strain show – once your competitors know you're teetering on the edge, they can't wait to give you a good hard shove. I'd always thrived under pressure anyway, I told myself, all I needed was one decent break and the Trotter star would soon rise again. But then my belly started giving me jip. To begin with I brushed it off. *Just a touch of yuppie flu*, I told myself, nothing a good burp wouldn't cure. But it didn't go away. I tried everything, Tums, Andrews Liver Salts, special fried rice, but it just kept getting worse.

Things were still looking up for Rodney though. Cassandra hadn't dumped him yet, and he was acting all soppy, blowing kisses down the telephone and what 'ave you.

Albert's romance with Elsie Partridge was blossoming too. She was a lovely old girl, Elsie, a bit like Mystic Meg with a Zimmer frame. But when Albert one night told Rodney and me that he suspected the bathroom in the flat was possessed, it was obvious her psychic powers were starting to rub off on him. He'd even got Elsie in there to investigate, and she'd picked up a chill in the air. I tried to explain to him that it was probably something to do with the fact that the council had put the extractor fan in the wrong way round, but he wouldn't have it. Even Rodney started to fall for it.

'I reckon there's more to this occult lark than meets the eye,' he said.

'Oh leave it out,' I told him, 'no self-respecting ghost is gonna haunt our bathroom, especially after Albert's been in there.'

'Elsie has powers, Del,' Albert said, 'back in the sixties she used to hold regular meetings. People would come from miles around and pay thousands of pounds to use her power of communication.'

And there it was. The sign I'd been waiting for. It often happened like that, a blinding white bolt out of the blue. I felt like St Paul on the road to Tabasco. Course, Rodney and Albert tried to talk me out of it, but I made them see sense.

'Me and Elsie Partridge, what a team! The pensioner with a priceless gift, and the yuppie who's brassic flint. We could make each other a fortune!'

I got on the blower to Elsie and filled her in on my vision. She might have been getting on a bit, but she was game. Well, she'd donated most of the money she'd earned back in the day to Battersea Dogs Home and only had her pension to live on, so you can't blame her really. That night I worked it all out. We'd begin small with a tour of south London and the Home Counties, and then go from there. I worked out a price list: neighbours and family friends, three quid, relatives a fiver, spouses and pets a tenner each, and a score for Elvis Presley. I even got Rodney to design a poster, 'The Séance', it read, above a drawing of a spooky face, 'Make Contact or your Money Back. Admission: £2.50'. Lovely jubbly!

A few days later we had a trial run in the room above the Nag's Head. There was me, Rodney and Albert, Mike, Boycie and Trigger. Up till then I'd never put much stock in psychics and séances and all that. I still don't really. I was a fan of that TV programme *Most Haunted*, you know, the one where that Scouse hairdresser went around having fits in the dark, but apart from that I've always filed it under Cobblers (Load Of). But even though I'd written Elsie off as some scatty old dear who made it all up as she went along, I quickly discovered that she was good. Very good!

There we were, all sitting round the table, lights dimmed, hands on deck, fingers touching, all that lark, when Elsie suddenly started to make a weird groaning noise. Mike panicked a bit 'cos she'd had one of his pork pies for lunch, but Albert explained she was just going into a trance. She kicked things off with a vision of an old black and white photograph that showed a tall, elderly man wearing a black coat and hat.

'He wishes to speak to someone called Aubrey,' she said.

We were all looking at each other, mystified, when suddenly Boycie spoke.

'I am here,' he said.

'Aubrey?' Rodney said.

'It's my middle name,' explained Boycie.

'Bloody hell, you kept that quiet,' I said to him. Up till then I hadn't known he had a middle name. In fact, I weren't even sure he had a first name. I remember seeing his passport once and I'm sure all it said was 'Boycie'.

'You'd keep your middle name quiet too if it was Aubrey,' he said, and he had a very good point.

'There's an odd-looking boy in the photograph with him,' Elsie continued, 'five or six years old, evil face.'

'Boycie, it's you and your dad,' I said.

'Yeah, he was the only one who ever called me Aubrey.'

'There's a sadness about the photograph,' Elsie went on, 'as though something's missing… of course, your mother isn't with you. Had she passed to the other side?'

'No, she was taking the photo,' Boycie said.

'Your father says he is worried,' Elsie said. 'He says you must look after your child.'

'Is he having a pop at me or what?' Boycie said, getting irate.

'Boycie and his wife can't have kids,' Albert explained to Elsie.

'They've been trying for years, but nitto!' I added.

'They've had tests, things frozen, everything,' Rodney expanded.

'The hospital's just about given up on him,' Mike chipped in.

'He's "low" on something,' Trigger chipped in further.

'Do you lot mind not discussing my personal life in front of… strangers?' Boycie snapped, shooting up off his chair. 'You can tell my old man to keep his nose out of my business. He was always having a go at me for not giving him a grandchild!'

'All right,' I said, 'calm down, Aubrey.'

'I'm going to get a drink. It's all a load of old cobblers anyway!' he moaned, leaving the room.

On Elsie's order, we closed the circle, and she closed her eyes to see if there were any other spirits who fancied a chat.

'A woman has stepped forward,' she said. 'Tall and slender, long, golden brown hair, fingers covered in ruby and gold, bracelets adorn the wrist.'

I couldn't believe it. Mum was slender, and she had golden brown hair… sometimes. I'd also bought her a gold ring with a ruby in it a couple of weeks before she died.

'It's Mum,' I said to Rodney, who looked just as gobsmacked as me.

'She says she is proud of her children,' Elsie continued. 'She says you have both worked hard to succeed, but never mind.'

I was getting a bit choked up by this point.

'She is concerned for you, Derek,' Elsie said.

'Me? I'm all right, Mum.'

'She says you are not well. She feels your pain.'

'No, that's just a bit of jip,' I tried to explain. 'Most probably an onion bhaji lodged somewhere, that's all.'

'She wants you to go and see a doctor,' Elsie said.

'I don't want to, you know I don't like doctors,' I said.

And with that, Mum faded away. Elsie couldn't get her back, and we wrapped the whole thing up. Course, Rodney was straight on to me about the message from Mum, telling me I should go and see a doctor.

'Oh, do me a favour,' I told him. 'You don't believe all that, do you?'

'Well, you seemed pretty convinced,' he said. 'At one point I thought you were gonna suck your thumb and throw a paddy.'

I'd only gone along with it for Elsie's sake. I mean, yeah, I had got taken in a bit, but that's what these séances are all about, ain't they? And Elsie probably genuinely believed she was receiving all these messages, but at the end of the day it was still a load of old rubbish. After all, she'd told Boycie he had to look after his kid, and we all knew that Nelson's Column had more chance of knocking out a nipper than Boycie. Thing is though, when we got down to the bar, there was Marlene beaming proudly with the news that she was pregnant!

Now, I should make it clear that I'm not scared of doctors, I just don't like 'em. Well, it's not that I don't like 'em, it's just I don't like what they do to you, you know, sticking things in you, taking things out of you, telling you you're gonna die, that sort of thing. But just to shut Rodney and Albert up I booked an appointment to see

Dr Meadows. I didn't mind him. He was a doctor, yeah, but he was more, I dunno, human, than most of the others I'd known. So, I get there and, just my luck, I discovered that Dr Meadows had left the practice two years earlier, and I now had to deal with a Dr Shaheed. A woman!

Well, I told her in a roundabout way about the pains I'd been getting in the old New Delhi, which confused her a bit 'cos it turned out that's where she was from. She asked the usual questions, like what sort of pain it was.

'Well, it hurts,' I explained.

'Do you smoke, Mr Trotter?' she asked.

'Not just now, Doctor, I'm trying to cut down,' I said.

She then told me to strip off so she could examine me. I don't know what it is with doctors, they always want to get you naked. I went to one with an earache once and he immediately tried to give my plums the once-over.

'Do you have any trouble passing water?' she asked.

'I had a dizzy spell going over Tower Bridge once,' I said. It went straight over her head.

After the examination she told me I had a very high pulse rate. I was flattered and thanked her, but she said she was concerned about it.

'It's almost as if you're frightened of something,' she said.

'Me? What have I got to be frightened about?' I asked her. 'It's probably just 'cos I jogged down here from the gym, that's all.'

I was fibbing, but I didn't want her to panic and send me to hospital. Problem was she then panicked and sent me to hospital. The doctors there took samples of my... well, samples of everything, then they stuck me on a ward and made me fast while they did 'further investigations'. There ain't much to do when you're laid up in a hospital ward but think and worry about things. The pains were coming thick and fast, and the quacks were keeping schtum, so I was bound to think the worst, weren't I? *Maybe*, I thought, *I'd picked up one of those computer viruses I'd been reading about. I mean, Rodney had one in the flat. Maybe he was the carrier!* The next morning the doctors started asking me questions about my love life, and, well, that was it. I knew. I decided the time had come to put my affairs in order, so I asked the nurse for a pen and some paper and then mapped out what exactly I'd leave behind, and who I'd leave it to.

That evening I woke to find Rodney quietly and carefully slipping the bacon sandwich I'd asked him to smuggle in under my pillow. As he sat down next to my bed I noticed his eyes were looking a bit red. I told him he didn't have to hold the tears back for my sake. He said he wasn't and that he'd just got a bit of bacon fat in his eye. I told him that I was proud of him but he didn't have to make excuses. He said he wasn't making excuses and that he really did get some of the fat in his eyes and that it was stinging. I told him to shut up going on about it.

While Rodney nipped off to the toilet to rinse his eyes out, I made sure the matron weren't patrolling and snuck a bite of the sandwich. It was all cold and greasy. Just the way I like it.

When he returned, I told him what was wrong with me.

'Don't be stupid,' he said. 'What makes you think that?'

''Cos the doctors found out I was a bachelor and started asking questions about my "social activities",' I explained. 'I didn't tell 'em nothing, I made out I was an amateur monk. But I've been laying here thinking about my past.'

'What's the point in depressing yourself?' he said.

'I've been thinking back to some of the birds I've knocked about with. Blimey, Rodney, some of 'em had been round the track more times than a lurcher. Then there's that unisex hairdressers, the one in the high street.'

'What about it?' he said.

'Well, I went in there last month for a trim, thinking I was gonna get one of the dolly birds in the miniskirts, but I ended up with some mush called Jason.'

'I don't believe you, Del,' he said, 'you can't go around making accusations against innocent people. Anyway, you can't catch it off a comb.'

'No,' I said, 'but say he nicked the back of my neck with his razor or something.'

'Well, as long as he didn't kiss it better, you're laughing,' he said.

He did his best to calm me down, and it did help, a bit. Course, he was right, I was being stupid (what did I know about these things back then?), but until I knew for definite it was hard to rule anything out.

The next morning, as I lay there imagining what heaven was like, Dr Meadows turned up to see me. Apparently he'd come to work at the hospital after leaving general practice, and, despite everything, it was good to see him. He said he'd come across my file and was a bit surprised by some of the info it contained, like that it said I was a non-smoking, teetotal, celibate vegan, that sort of thing.

'Why did you lie to your GP, Del?'

''Cos she's a doctor,' I said, 'you don't tell doctors the truth, otherwise you'll end up in hospital.' Course, he pointed out that I *was* in hospital, but I didn't mean for that to happen, did I?

'Del, if you had told the truth in the first place, my colleagues could have diagnosed your problem in a quarter of the time,' he said.

'So you know what's wrong with me then?' I told him not to pull any punches and give it to me straight from the shoulder. And he did, telling me that I had an irritated bowel syndrome.

'Well, I'm not surprised with you lot pulling it about,' I said.

He went on to explain that it had been caused by my lifestyle, the late nights, the booze and the fried food. He also said that stress was a major contributor and that a lot of yuppies suffer from irritated bowels. I knew then that he'd nailed it right on the head. He'd even talked to Albert who told him about the rent situation and then to the council who had agreed to give me a bit of breathing space. What a smashing bloke!

And that was it, I was sent home with some pills and told to get lots of rest. And after stopping off at the Star of Bengal to celebrate (that fasting lark don't 'alf make you hungry), that's what I did. I'd always known deep down that it was nothing serious. Still, I couldn't help thinking that, however much it was a load of old cobblers, Mum was looking down on us all and making sure we were all right. And that alone made me feel a hundred times better.

While I was laid up in dock, my dreams of making Elsie Partridge a star went straight down the Kermit. People had seen the posters we'd put up and thought The Séance was a band. Apparently a load of heavy-metallers had crammed into the Nag's Head for the opening night expecting to see an Iron Maiden-type mob, then Elsie Partridge walked out in her hat. She remained in a trance throughout the riot. Albert popped round to see her the following morning and she was still in it. She was all right in the end though.

Tony Angelino (middle), the singing dustman
– style aided by props from Lilley & Skinner,
Crown Toppers and Mattesons.

The holy version of
sliced bread. Trotters
Pre-Blessed Wine.

Tap water my arse!

Rodney and Cassandra on their wedding day, 1989.

A star is born. Damien Derek Trotter, ten minutes of age. 1991.

Even Rodney's getting the renouncements arse-about-face couldn't ruin a blinding ceremony. Damien's christening, parish church of Peckham, St Mary's, 1991.

Lights of my life, fruits of my loom. Me, Raquel and Damien.

John Harrison's Lesser Watch.
I don't know why he thought so
little of it, I thought it was a corker.

A step up from Benidorm.
The Trotters hit Monte Carlo.

A la Brochette!!!

You little beauty!
Joan Trotter, 2003.

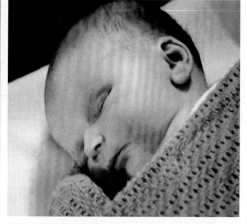

Denzil, Mickey Pearce, Marlene, Sid, Boycie and Trigger.

A recent pic of me
and my Raquel.

By yours truly, a portrait of Rodney, which I titled 'Rodney'. I gave it to him as a
Christmas present and he was well chuffed. Less than twelve hours later it was
destroyed in a freak accident involving a council gritter.

Jonathan Ross explains the rules. My appearance on the television quiz show *Goldrush*. Rodney let me down massively.

Beckham in Peckham, 2014. Me and my mate Dave off for a spot of pie 'n' mash. I'd obviously just said something extremely witty here, but then again it ain't difficult to get the soppy sod giggling, bless him.

JOAN · MAVIS · TROTTER

FELL ASLEEP
MARCH 12 ~ 1964

WIFE OF REG

MOTHER OF DELBOY AND RODNEY

GRANDMOTHER OF DAMIEN

AND JOAN

A final update for Mum's obelisk.

CHAPTER 23

BEST MAN

I'd never thought Rodney would get married before me. In fact, I'd never thought Rodney would get married. But when him and Cassandra decided to tie the knot, I was over the moon for 'em. Everything was falling into place for Rodney, he'd even passed his computer diplomacy exam, after convincing himself he hadn't. Apparently the exam had called for him to mock up a flight plan for an unmanned space probe to Venus. So, Buzz Trotter tapped in all the measurements, only he got confused between litres and gallons, and NASA ended up getting detailed readings of Dartford just before the probe crashed. Just to be sure though, I went to see his headmaster at the evening school and he explained that (just as my gut was telling me) he'd made a mistake and that Rodney had in fact passed with flying colours.

With the diploma in the bag he then got offered a job at Cassandra's dad's, Alan's, printing firm. Alan was expanding the computer section and wanted Rodney to help run it. And if that weren't cushty enough, the bride- and groom-to-be had just seen a flat they'd fallen in love with. They needed to put down a six-grand deposit: Cassandra's mum and dad were giving 'em two grand as a wedding present, Cassandra was taking two grand out of her savings, which left Rodney to come up with the remaining two. Course, I could have left it to Rodney to sort out, but then I decided to spare us all the time and agony, and told him I'd give it to him instead. Well, it's not every day your kid brother gets married, is it? And it was no big deal, I'd just call in my debts, namely the dosh Boycie still owed me for the video recorders I'd recently sold to him. Once he gave the money to me, I'd give it to Rodney, and it would all be *rez de chasse* as they say in the Dordogne.

Things were also looking up for Trotters Independent Traders. I'd just done what I was certain, at the time, was a brilliant bit of business with Mickey Pearce and his mate Jevon. They'd recently got into trading and, being a bloke who likes to help the less fortunate, I thought I'd do 'em a favour by taking a load of executive mobile phones off their hands. And if you put aside the fact that they didn't always work (something to do with the statelite technology back then), that they made your TV go funny and that the aerials shot out faster than a bullet, they were pukka phones. The really brilliant thing though was that they retailed at £199.99, and Mickey and Jevon were letting 'em go for twenty-five nicker each. Well, you'd have to have been a total dipstick not to get in on that, so I bought a hundred of 'em on sale or return.

The only cloud in the sky was the video recorders. Don't get me wrong, they were at the very forefront of electronic technology (it was Bulgarian electronic technology, but still, they had all the buttons and the flashing lights and what 'ave you). The problem was they only worked on a continental electric supply. Not one to be held back by small things like electrical fires and the odd exploding VCR, I'd been chatting to a Chinese kid who lived across the way in Desmond Tutu House. He reckoned he could knock up an adaptor that would solve the problem and leave me with a lock-up full of top-quality kit. I say full, that weren't quite true, as I mentioned Boycie had bought a load off me and still owed me the money. Course, he was kicking up a fuss (something about his curtains catching on fire, I don't remember exactly). But now I'd solved the problem with the voltage it would be happy days.

I was in the Nag's Head trying to drum up a bit of business when Rodney's future father-in-law, Alan, walked in, sporting a nasty-looking black eye (something to do with the aerial on his new phone, again, I can't remember exactly). He wanted to discuss the plans for Rodney and Cassandra's wedding reception. Pam, his missus, wanted something flash, cricket club pavilions, champagne and caviar and all that. He wanted a down-to-earth bash in the Nag's Head, jellied eels and a few quid behind the bar. So did I really, I can't stand those people who do things just for effect. Besides, if you stuck Rodney in a cricket club people would confuse him for a wicket.

Alan's a good bloke, but he'd be the first to admit he can't handle his drink. He'd been off the sauce for years but being back in the old manor and hanging out with the sort of crowd he'd known when he was a lad brought the thirst out in him. And it was the same this time, within an hour he was singing Chas and Dave and reminiscing about whelks. He booked Mike's place and we bundled him into a cab.

Which is when I spotted Mickey and Jevon. You couldn't miss 'em. Mickey had his arm in a sling and Jevon had one of them neck braces on.

'You two still haven't got the hang of revolving doors, have you?' I said. They weren't in the mood for laughing, and neither was I after I'd finished talking with 'em.

Turns out they'd got the mobile phones (the ones I'd taken off them) from the Driscoll brothers, and now they wanted their money. And just to prove how *much* they wanted their money they'd twisted

Mickey and Jevon into positions humans just ain't built to be in. That was sort of a Driscoll brothers trademark, leaving the face alone and knocking seven shades out of the body. But, of course, Mickey and Jevon didn't have the money, 'cos I hadn't made it yet. And, of course, they let this slip to the Driscolls.

Now, I've mentioned the Driscoll brothers before and you know I've been very careful to have as little to do with 'em as possible. Yeah, I'd helped their mum out with a few bags of coal during the winters when they went away to a young offenders' home, that was just civic duty. I certainly had no interest in doing business with 'em, no interest even in being under the same roof as 'em. So the idea that they were looking for me didn't exactly put a spring in my step. Still, I thought, if I could keep my head down for long enough they might just forget all about it. The thought lasted about ten seconds, as no sooner had Mickey and Jevon broken the news, Trigger gave the warning that Danny and Tony's Merc had just pulled up in the car park.

In a panic, me, Mickey, Jevon and (God knows why) Trigger darted upstairs and hid in one of Mike's function rooms. A couple of minutes later we heard the door open and Danny and Tony started poking about. I reckon we'd have got away with it if Trigger hadn't knocked me and sent the aerial on the phone in my jacket pocket on a one-way, high-speed trip up my left nostril. I tried, but the pain (and shock) was too much and I gave the game away.

'He's got one of our phones up his nose,' Danny said.

'That's a good idea, innit?' Tony said, reaching up to pull it out. He'd have preferred to do it via the other nostril, but I told him not to worry and managed to dislodge it myself.

They told Mickey, Jevon and Trigger to clear out, leaving me on my own with them.

I explained I hadn't known the phones were theirs, that I didn't have the money but I'd pass it right on when I did, but it didn't wash.

'Let me explain something to you, Del,' Danny said. 'When Tony and I were kids we were very poor. Our old man used to work in one of them big mansion houses, from six in the morning till eight at night, and for what?'

'A shilling a day and an 'orseshit sandwich,' Tony clarified.

'One day there was a robbery at the mansion,' Danny continued. 'The old bill arrested our old man, but there weren't any evidence.'

'Just fingerprints,' Tony added.

'Just fingerprints,' Danny confirmed.

'And eyewitnesses,' Tony added.

'Couple of eyewitnesses,' Danny confirmed, 'they found the jewels on him.'

'It was a plant,' Tony added.

'A right fit-up,' Danny confirmed. 'He died in a police cell with a fractured skull. They said it was a suicide attempt that went wrong – or right, whatever way you look at it. They claimed he tried to hang himself with his braces and smashed himself to death on the ceiling. And the day he died Tony and me swore that no one would ever dump on us and we'd never be poor.'

I reminded 'em how I'd seen right by their mum all those years ago, and that they at least owed me a bit of time.

'He's right,' Danny admitted.

'No he ain't,' Tony begged to differ.

'Tony,' said Danny, 'we had an agreement. I do the thinking – you *don't*.'

They agreed to give me a bit of time and off they went, leaving me to count all my limbs and come up with a surprisingly happy number.

They hadn't been gone a minute when Boycie ran in.

'Mickey Pearce just told me you got some electrical equipment off the Driscolls,' he said.

'That's right,' I admitted.

'It's not those video recorders, is it?'

I was about to set him straight when I was hit with a sudden, all-consuming urge to get my bloody money off him.

'Yeah.'

He got this look on his face then, as though he'd just invited Marlene out to dinner only to find he'd double-booked the table with his bit on the side.

'Do they know you sold them on to me?'

'I haven't told 'em yet, Boycie, you're a mate, but they want to give someone a good hiding—'

'Here!' he said, shoving a wodge of notes into my hand. 'I thought I was skint but I suddenly realised I had three grand in my pocket. Square it with 'em, Del.'

'Leave it to me, Boycie,' I said, the cheating git, 'what are friends for?'

With the odds of me losing really precious bits of myself shortened, I was feeling a little bit better. And by the time Rodney's stag night rolled around I was actually starting to feel cocky. I was still lumbered with the phones and the video recorders, but I'd got the money to keep the Driscolls happy, and an extra grand to keep the cold off.

I also had a soppy, beered-up Rodney leaning on my shoulder fretting about whether they were gonna announce his middle name at the ceremony.

Denzil spotted the Driscolls walk in and, diamond that he is, offered me backup.

'I've got their money,' I told him, 'let 'em wait a while.' I weren't having Rodney's night spoilt for their sake. If anyone was gonna ruin Rodney's night it would be Rodney. He was lying with his face on the table by now, trying to catch a stray peanut with his tongue.

'Del's done everything for me,' he was telling Denzil, 'he looked after me.'

'I know, Rodney,' Denzil said, in that bored way you talk to drunks.

'I'll tell you something else,' Rodney slurred on, 'he's even giving me two grand as a deposit on my flat.'

Which brought me up a bit sharpish. In my panic over the Driscoll brothers, it had completely slipped my mind.

Tony Driscoll pulled himself up over the height of one of the bar stools and gave me a wave. They wanted to see me outside.

What was I gonna do? I couldn't afford to pay 'em both. I was sure Rodney would understand, he wouldn't want me taking a pounding just for the sake of his future happiness, would he? I mean, obviously, that flat meant a lot to him. It was a fresh start, something he could be proud of, something to make his own. Still, if it was a choice between that and me needing stitches?

I stepped out into the car park.

'You got our money, Del?' Danny asked.

I told them.

Well, the way I saw it was you have to take a good hiding every now and then. I'd taken 'em before and I was bound to take 'em again. That's life. It weren't too bad anyway, once I passed out.

I didn't tell Rodney what had happened. The last thing we needed was him getting worried and breaking out in hives on the eve of his wedding. I didn't want him knowing at all, but Mickey Pearce put that to bed a few weeks later, the mouthy git!

The wedding was smashing, just a little ceremony at the registry office. Cassandra's side were more well behaved and reserved, but our lot were a bit subdued too. I think it was just the shock of seeing Rodney actually married.

We went back to the pub once it was all done. It was a good do, even if I did have to stand very still for fear of coughing up a lung. I had to knock Marlene back a couple of times too, she was five months gone by then but she still wanted to get on the dance floor and give Katarina and the Waves a run for their money.

'So how come you never got married?' she said to me during a lull in the dancing.

'Me? I'm too shrewd for that game.'

'You got engaged though, loads of times. So why didn't you marry any of them?'

'I dunno,' I said. 'It was Rodney, I s'pose.'

'Rodney stopped you getting married?'

'Well, back in them days Rodney was just a kid, I had to bring him up.'

'Yeah,' she said, 'you were like a mother and father to him.'

'I breastfed him for the first six months,*' I said, 'it's just all the birds I got engaged to wanted to get married, but they didn't want to bring Rodney up, especially with the way he went through shoes. What was I supposed to do? Marry them and stick Rodney into care? So I elbowed 'em. Well, it's family, innit?'

'You should be proud of yourself,' she said. 'He turned out a real good'un.'

She was right. He was a forty-two-carat diamond! And as I watched and waved as Mr and Mrs Rodney Trotter departed for their honeymoon, I did feel proud. A bit choked too (but that might have had something to do with the large dose of painkillers I'd stirred into my pina colada).

---

* I didn't. It was just a joke.

CHAPTER 24

SOMETIMES THINGS BLOW UP

Just when you think the status quo will never change you find yourself minus a younger brother and with an uncle spending more and more time round at Elsie Partridge's. It was like a mini holiday where I didn't go anywhere but everyone else did.

Rodney seemed to be getting on all right running Alan's computer department (he hadn't been fired, which is always a good sign). His new flat was nice too, modern, pastel colours everywhere you looked. I offered to redecorate it for him but he said not to worry.

Marlene and Boycie dropped the chavvy and, much to everyone's shock, you could tell it was his – always crying and full of wind. Then again, if I'd been named Tyler I reckon I'd be crying and full of wind too.

As for me, I'd finally shifted the mobile phones and the video recorders and started doing a nice new line in in-car stereos. Top-quality gear from Albania, a rising star in the electronics market at the time. They had all the proper dials, you know, MW, FM, ICI, B&Q, the lot! They also came with a pair of state of the art quadrophonic speakers. Chuck in a free Kylie Minogue LP on top of that and I had no doubt I'd flog 'em easy. I decided to wrap one up as a first anniversary present for Rodney and Cassandra. I just hoped it would fit her motor, 'cos it would have looked silly on Rodney's pushbike.

Albert started helping me out a bit. Well, he was hanging around near me while I worked, topping up his pipe and whistling old sea shanties (the theme tune to *Hawaii Five-O*, 'Popeye', that sort of thing). Still it kept him busy when the inevitable happened and his little thing with Elsie Partridge went for a burton. He said she'd been getting too serious, that he'd felt trapped and wanted to keep his options open, which, considering the last time he'd had his leg over Nelson Mandela was in borstal, was probably just another way of saying she'd had enough and had given him the elbow.

Cassandra found herself in line for a promotion at her bank so her nerves started setting in a bit. Rodney found it hard. As a man who had only just found out what a career was, he hadn't quite grasped how important it was to advance one.

For their anniversary dinner, she invited her boss and his wife around and I found we shared a lot of common traits. Stephen was young, driven and finely attuned to the world's financial movements. He was a yuppie and I happily told him so (being full of modesty, he kept denying it, bless him). Alan and Pam were there too of course. Pam was as warm and friendly as always, but I didn't take it personally.

Cassandra knocked up a blinding bit of grub, and Stephen and I had a good chat about business. He was convinced that Africa was where the smart money was and that banana crops were experiencing major growth. This, I told him, could only be good news as you'll always find it easier to sell big bananas than little ones. I think he took it on board.

After dinner we all settled down to play Trivial Pursuit. Being a man of instinct and action, it weren't really my cup of tea, but they didn't have Buckaroo so I just had to make do. Alan and Rodney were obviously a bit worried, trying to convince me we shouldn't play 'cos 'it might be a bit embarrassing'. I told them not to panic, I'd have their backs.

Stephen won, well, him and his missus (lovely girl, I forget her name but she spoke posher than the Queen), then they started rabbiting on about Africa again, wilder beasts and zebras and sunsets over the Serendipity and all that. That's when I mentioned that we were all off on a beano to Margate the following weekend. As you know, the boys had been going on 'em every few years or so since way back in the sixties, so it was a sort of tradition. Stephen's missus mentioned she was going to see her 'mummy and daddy' that weekend, so I asked him if he fancied coming with us. By the look on his face you'd have thought I'd asked him to pull my finger. He made some excuse, but it was probably for the best he didn't go. I could sense that Rodney weren't too keen on the bloke. You could tell he was feeling out of his depth in his company, and a bit jealous of the way Cassandra was keeping him sweet. Course, he was her boss, so she had to keep on his good side.

The bank holiday arrived and so did a rail strike, so we had to leave at the crack of dawn to try and beat the traffic. There were a few grumbles on the coach, mostly non-verbal ones coming from Uncle Albert's vicinity. Then Sid started kicking up a fuss.

'I own a cafe, right?' he said. 'So how come you didn't ask me to make the sandwiches?'

'The explanation is simple,' I told him, 'we plan on eating 'em.'

He couldn't argue with that. I'd got Trigger on the job so God knows what we'd end up with, but it slightly shortened the odds of an E. coli outbreak on the coach, and that was good enough for me.

Harry was driving. He was a good old lad, spent his whole life on the buses. Unfortunately, he took a funny turn when we stopped off at the Halfway House pub to stretch our legs a bit. He claimed he was overcome by fumes coming from the car stereo, but I knew it couldn't be that, after all I'd sold it to him.

Luckily, Denzil's driving licence covered him for the coach so, after a bit of persuasion, he agreed to take over for the rest of the trip. And after getting Rodney out of the nick for kicking a football at a copper's head (what a twonk), we were on our way to Margate.

We had a right laugh. Even Boycie cracked a grin. Trigger bought himself an inflatable dolphin (and then lost it), Alan found a jellied eel stall and ended up eating half the ocean bed (he paid for it later though when he threw it all back up again). We did the rides, the beach, the arcades, and I even managed to squeeze in a bit of light lunch, a lobster vindaloo and a few pina coladas. It had been a smashing day, just what I'd needed, and by the time we got back to the coach depot, I was cream crackered. Everything was going fine, we were all set for the off, and then our coach exploded. Yeah, you didn't imagine you just read that, it really did explode. Thankfully we'd all got off and were standing at a safe distance when it went up, but still, it did put a bit of a downer on things.

Nobody knows for sure what caused it, but it definitely had nothing to do with the stereo (as some suggested). I don't know, time takes its toll on all things, tyres wear thin, shock absorbers stop absorbing, and sometimes, though not often I'll grant you, coaches blow up.

Anyway, what with the rail strike, it left us all in a right dilemma, and we had no choice but to find ourselves some digs and make a night of it. But this was easier said than done. It was a bank holiday weekend and Margate was packed to the rafters.

Me, Albert and Rodney walked the streets until our Hush Puppies were crying but everywhere we looked it was 'No Vacancies'.

Finally, we found a room in a place called Villa Bella. If you're ever in town looking for somewhere nice and clean with friendly staff, good food and reasonable rates, then I can't recommend it. If you happen to be a member of the undead and you're looking for somewhere to stash your coffin, you'll be laughing.

It was run by a woman called Mrs Cresswell. At least I think she was a woman, she was wearing a dress, a lovely little number made out of Crimpolene and cobwebs. She sorted us out a room, with hot and cold running damp, and we booked ourselves in for some dinner.

Inga, Mrs Cresswell's one member of staff, seemed upset about something (probably just life in general) as she led us to our table, brushed off the dust and dead beetles and then brought us each a plate of boiled fish and misery. After playing a little game of 'guess the fish', we decided to get an early night.

'The front door is locked at 11 pm,' Mrs Cresswell explained, 'and not opened again until 9 am.' That was the way HMP Villa Bella did business.

I earmarked the single bed, leaving Rodney and Albert to share the double. They didn't 'alf moan though. Rodney moaned 'cos Albert kept nicking the covers, Albert moaned 'cos Rodney kept getting in the way of his beard, then Rodney started moaning about Cassandra and what she might be getting up to while he was away (to be more precise, he got it in his head that she'd shacked up with her boss, Stephen, the minute he closed the front door). I told him to stop being a tart and that he had nothing to worry about, so then he started moaning about how cold it was in the room. Well, this started Albert off on one of his tales from the Russian convoys, so Rodney and I decided to knock the early night on the head and go out on the town for a bit.

We ended up in a place called the Mardi Gras club, where we washed away the taste of Cresswell's food with some scampi and a few cocktails. Mike, Boycie and Trigger turned up and we were soon having a decent night of it.

The place had a cabaret on and we'd just managed to survive a rendition of 'Windmills of Your Mind' in Really Bloody Flat, when a magician strolled on. Magicians back then were a lot different to what they are now. These days magic is all about scruffy little herberts hanging off the sides of buses, but back then magicians were all sequins, hair oil and funny walks, due to the amount of wildlife they had shoved down their trousers. They actually used to smile. And that's what this bloke, the Great Raymondo, was like. Anyway, there I was watching him pulling pigeons out of places pigeons shouldn't have been, when I happened to clock his female assistant. It almost didn't hit me at first, and I had to stand up and get a better look just to make sure. It was Raquel! I subtly shouted out to her, which caused a bit of a fright, especially for the pigeons who took the opportunity to scatter and look for the nearest exit, but she was well pleased to see me. As soon as the act was finished (which was pretty much immediately), I met up with her at the bar.

I was finally able to explain what had happened, that a little misunderstanding with the police had prevented me getting to her place before she left. She was very understanding and told me all about her 'No Sex Please We're Saudis' tour, how she'd got fed up and come home and started working with Ray. And then the man himself appeared next to us.* He had the right hump about something and, whatever it was, he was blaming Raquel. He was being right sarky about it too. I managed to restrain myself but he was sailing dangerously close to getting a smack in the mooey. Still, Raquel and I weren't gonna let it spoil our reunion, and we ended up exchanging

---

* He didn't just appear out of thin air. He might have been good when it came to pigeons and balloons, but he weren't that good.

phone numbers and addresses. *What a wonderful end to a mostly wonderful day,* I thought.

On the way back to the temple of doom I was feeling so happy I wanted to sing it aloud, and I did. All the old feelings I'd had to compress came bubbling to the surface again. I was so caught up in it all I forgot all about Frau Gruppenführer Cresswell's door policy. So there Rodney and I were standing outside the Villa Bella trying to figure out the best course of action. Neither of us fancied knocking on the door and getting Cresswell out of her tomb, so Rodney came up with the bright idea of throwing a stone up at our window to wake Albert up. The thing is, apart from the odd wobbly, Rodney had never been good at throwing things. So, having found a stone, he took aim.

I have to give him credit here, 'cos he hit his target first time, the problem was that the stone he'd chosen was actually a brick. Well, it was quite late by then and the world was asleep, so you can imagine the commotion it caused when the stone struck the window – and then went straight through it. *Still,* I thought, *it was an honest mistake, people would understand.* Then all the lights started coming on and we heard Mrs Cresswell screaming about calling the old bill, so we legged it!

There was only one thing for it. It was freezing cold and threatening rain, and we hadn't eaten anything for at least an hour, so we headed over to Raquel's flat. She seemed a bit nervous at first, but she put us up in her front room, gave us a duvet and a pillow to share and then went to stick the kettle on. What a woman! I mean, all she had to do was walk in and she lit up a room. Rodney pointed out that when most of my other birds walked into a room they lit up a fag. And he had a point. But this was something else. This was fate at work. This was destiny, this was the Great Raymondo standing in front of me in his jim-jams moaning about the noise… Yeah, I was taken aback a bit. What was this dipstick doing in Raquel's flat?! He went off into the kitchen and I could hear him giving Raquel a rollicking. I had to do something, didn't I? I couldn't just sit there while my dear heart was being bullied. Plus I was finding the thought of him and Raquel being, well, you know, together quite upsetting. So, on Rodney's advice to play it nice and cool, I went into the kitchen and gave him a smack in the eye. Just to be sure he got the message I then threw his suitcase out the window. Well, I must have taken things a bit too far 'cos Raquel weren't exactly chuffed with how the situation was progressing. Ray got up and tried to explain that there was nothing going on between him and Raquel, even having the cheek to say that she weren't his type.

'Not your type!' I said. 'Listen, pal, you could do a lot worse than *that!*'

Raquel then stepped in, explaining that her and Ray slept in different rooms and that even if she'd been the last woman on earth she *still* wouldn't have been his type. A minute or so later it dawned on me. I felt terrible, of course. But I weren't to know, was I? I apologised to Ray and told Raquel that I'd only done it for her, but she just stormed off to bed.

'What did you do that for?' Rodney asked me.

'You know how it is, bruv,' I said, 'he who dares wins.'

'Yeah, well, I reckon this time he who dared cocked it right up!' he said.

And I was thinking the same thing, till Raquel popped back out, said thank you and gave me a kiss on the cheek.

Lovely jubbly!

The replacement coach arrived early the next morning and off we went back to Peckham. I gave Rodney a bit of advice before seeing him off, telling him he had to put his foot down with a firm hand

and assert his manhood a bit more. He obviously took it to heart 'cos when he got in and found Stephen was there he punched him on the nose. Course, Stephen's wife was there too and all they were doing was looking at some holiday brochures, but Rodney hadn't bothered to check. Some people just never learn, do they? So Cassandra sent him packing back to me.

Turns out the Jolly Boys Outing had been quite eventful for more than just me and Rodney. Albert had a nasty-looking bruise on his head after he'd been rudely awoken by a flying brick. Even Mike and Boycie had been in the wars when they'd been walking back from the club the previous night and a suitcase fell out of the sky and landed right on top of them. I don't know what this world's coming to sometimes, I really don't.

CHAPTER 25

I'M THE DADDY

As time went by, Raquel and I grew closer and closer. I popped over to Margate and took her out to dinner, she popped over to Peckham and took me to see a play: *Richard III*. I was a bit lost to be honest, but then I hadn't seen Richard 1 or 2. Then she went and got herself a job touring *My Fair Lady* in America. I missed her, course I did, but I weren't gonna stand in the way of a job like that. Granted, she was only playing the flower seller, but according to the reviews I saw she sold them flowers beautifully. She sold 'em all down the east coast, Miami, New Orleans, Atlanta City! I couldn't have been more proud.

But if things were going well for Raquel, things for Rodney and Cassandra were just going from bad to worse. She'd forgiven him for clumping her boss (Stephen hadn't pressed charges, even though his nose was broken in two places), and she'd taken him back. Actually 'forgiven' might be stretching it a bit. But they were talking, you know, in that really loud way that some couples do. The sort of talking that some people mistake for shouting. *Arguing*, that's the word I'm looking for.

What it boiled down to was Cassandra's job. She was spending a lot of time socialising with her bank colleagues at bank seminars, bank training courses, bank cocktail parties, bank go-kart rallies, bank BASE jumping weekends, you know, the usual stuff. I could understand why Rodney resented it, but Cassandra was a career woman and he knew that when he married her. But he admitted to me one night that he wanted her to look after him a bit more. Course, he'd never really known what it was like to have a mum and have someone spoil him and cook for him. There was Grandad, yeah, but that weren't cooking. I s'pose I could sympathise with both of 'em. I mean, Rodney had got married and was realising it weren't all he'd thought it would be, and Cassandra had got married... well, to Rodney.

It weren't long before she booted him out again and he came back to me, which would have been fine, only by that time Raquel and I were just about ready to take our relationship to the next level. She'd got fed up selling flowers in America and returned to me. She wanted to take things slowly, which just added to the ever-growing respect I had for her. Anyway, waiting to get your card stamped just makes it all the more special when it happens, don't it? So I'd cleared Rodney's room out, got a firm in to fumigate it to within an inch of its life (even the bedside table had a fungal infection), scrubbed out all the stains, gave the carpet a bit of the old shake 'n vac, stuck a pot of pouri on the window sill, and Bob's your uncle, Raquel moved in. But with Rodney back and moping and moaning about Cassandra and banks and rainforests, it was looking like my card would be waiting for that stamp a bit longer than I'd hoped.

<hr />

Rodney had never been much of a drinker, until now. He was hitting the bottle so much he was calling in sick at work. I didn't know what to do with him. One minute he'd be getting lairy and saying it was no skin off his nose, the next he'd be blubbing into his Scotch and saying he'd lost the love of his life. And to top it all off, some bastard went and nicked his bike. I tried my best to talk sense into him but all my advice got drowned out in the alcohol.

He did, as I soon discovered, take the advice of Mickey Pearce though, when, in an attempt to make Cassandra jealous, he got himself a date. I couldn't believe it! And not just that Mickey Pearce was dishing out relationship advice (the last time he dated a bird he'd taken her to a Bay City Rollers concert), but that Rodney had gone through with it. He had it all planned. He was taking his date, some bird called Tania who worked at the local exhaust centre, to the Odeon in the high street to see *Honey I Shrunk the Kids*. It just so happened that Cassandra's bank's squash club was right opposite, and he was timing it just right in the hope that she'd come out and see him and Miss Kwik-Fit smooching in the queue. Even Albert, with all the harrowing experiences he'd had, was appalled (well, he was when I told him to be). I had to do something, anything I could, to get Rodney to change his mind, so I made out Tania had a reputation for being a bit of a dog and that she'd once slept with a darts team, but all that did was send Raquel off on one about women's rights. I tried to explain to her that I was only doing it to put Rodney off, but I couldn't get a word in edgeways. So now not only was that little plonker about to ruin his own life, he'd ruined my evening 'n all. And off he went.

What could I do? There was no way I could let Cassandra catch Rodney with the Michelin woman on his arm, so I went round to their flat to warn her, and, judging by the squash rackets sticking out of her rucksack, I got there just in the nick of time. I broke the news gently, explaining why Rodney was doing it, and she took it well for a few seconds then started screaming and punching things. To this day I'm not sure what bothered her more, that Rodney was taking another bird to the pictures or that she was missing out on seeing

Honey I Shrunk the bleedin' *Kids*! Anyway, I'd done what I could, and, as horrible as it was seeing Cassandra upset, I reckon I'd done the right thing by telling her.

So I was back at the flat and Raquel had calmed down and was wanting to, you know, make it up to me (my card had been well and truly stamped several times over by that point), when I got a phone call from Rodney, telling me he'd changed his mind and cancelled the date with Tania. He'd seen sense and was determined to make another go of it with Cassandra. I told him it was probably best he didn't go back to his flat just yet, but the wally was already there! I could tell he'd been drinking, he was getting all soppy and telling me he loved me. Dipstick!

So I was out the door again and speeding back to his flat, praying I could get there before war was declared, but I was too late. I could hear the screaming before I even got into the car park. And Rodney went right off on one on me, of all people! There I'd been darting about like a tit in a trance, trying to save his marriage, and he was saying it was all my fault! The ungrateful little git! So then me and Rodney were going at it, and, just when I thought things couldn't get any worse, one of their neighbours came out in his dressing gown and started sticking his oar in. I told him where else he could stick it, and the mood I was in by then I'd have happily given him a demonstration.

Stone me! I thought. *I know they say the path to true love never runs smooth, but this is taking the piss!*

It didn't take too long for some of Rodney and Cassandra's luck to start rubbing off on me and Raquel. She'd got herself an audition for a part in a Shakespeare play. Having always been a fan of his work myself, I decided to help her learn her lines by playing all the other characters in the play. She told me off for it, but then I s'pose it ain't easy to learn lines when you have to keep stopping to admire someone else's performance. Anyway, the play she was auditioning for was called *As You Like It* and Raquel was playing some sort called Rosalind. I couldn't quite get my head around it, but it didn't matter what I thought, it was a good part and Raquel knew what she was doing.

While she got on with rehearsing I nipped over to fit a new front door at Cassandra and Rodney's flat, on account of Rodney having come home one day and, finding she'd changed the locks on the old door, kicking it in. Cassandra was very gracious about my offer, practically begging me not to do it, but I couldn't leave her without a front door, could I? I got her a good one too, genuine French Angolan pine, and it was a perfect fit, so long as you didn't try to open it.

While I was there I took the opportunity to put my latest plan into action. The situation with Rodney and Cassandra was tearing me apart. I mean, here were these two lovely people who I cared so deeply for and they were at each other's throats. It was too much to bear. Plus Rodney had been kipping at mine for months now and I wanted my sofa back. So I told Cassandra that Rodney had confided in me that he'd fallen in love with her all over again and wanted to woo her. Naturally she was a bit surprised by the news, but I gave her the address of a little romantic restaurant over Wapping way and said that was where Rodney wanted to meet her that night, just to talk things through and see if they couldn't come to a compromise. She accepted. Later that day I told Rodney that Cassandra had confided in me that she'd fallen in love with him all over again and that she wanted to meet him that night at the restaurant. He acted like he weren't sure, but you could see he was chomping at the bit. Poor sod. The only bit of action he'd seen in the last three months had been when he kicked that door in.

The more submerged Raquel became in her play, the more I noticed her mood changing. It was subtle little things, the odd look here and there, the way she kept telling me to piss off and leave her alone. At first I put it down to nerves. It would mean big things for her career if she got the part. But the warning signs kept coming, and I should have known. It might not sound like a big deal, but there's no telling what a cravat and a codpiece can do to a woman. So when she had to go and meet the play's director, some geezer called Adrian, in one of them trendy bistros, I decided to pop along and introduce myself. Again, I was picking up that it made her uncomfortable, especially when Adrian asked me what I thought of *Hamlet* and I told him I preferred Castellas. She took him off so they could discuss things privately and left me chatting with the set designer (I forget his name, nice lad though, very soft hands).

The rest of that day she had the face ache, and she weren't the only one. Thanks to my little stint at playing Cupid, Rodney and Cassandra had made up. Everything had been going nice and rosy, then she caught him fumbling about with some old tart outside the Nag's Head (God knows who she was, he says he was just helping her get in a taxi, all I know is that she had absolutely nothing to do with me). So, before Rodney could even get his foot back in the door Cassandra had wedged it shut!

But the worst of it came when Rodney, worried about what Alan would do when he found out, and on the advice of Uncle Albert, went and handed in a letter of resignation. His thinking was that Alan would read the letter, realise just how important Rodney was to his firm and reject the resignation. In reality, Alan took one look at the letter and accepted the resignation right off the bat. As you know, there have been many, many times when I have despaired of that little plonker, but not many that compared to this time. He'd had a wife, a new home, a new job, *a new life*, and he'd flushed the lot down the Kermit!

Deciding it was as good a time as any to have it out with Raquel, I let her know how I felt. I knew I was a bit out of my depth with all that showbiz mob and that it embarrassed her. But as much as I tried, I struggled to do all that intelligent, sensitive actor malarkey.

'Derek,' she said, 'will you get it into your thick skull, I'm not trying to meet intelligent and sensitive people, I'm happy with you!' Which made me feel a bit better. Then she told me the play was actually a two-month tour of the country, and I understood then. It was the lure of the theatre, the applause and all that 'the show must go on' cobblers. I say that, but to be honest I didn't want her leaving me 'cos I was worried that if she did she wouldn't come back. But she told me I had nothing to worry about 'cos she'd turned the part down. I felt bad and told her to ignore me, I was just being selfish, but she insisted.

'But why?' I asked.

'Because I've read that play over and over again and at no point does Shakespeare mention that Rosalind is pregnant.'

Well, there's always poetic licence, I thought. And then it hit me. Bloody hell!

'I've done all the tests and everything,' she said. 'It's certain.'

Well, what could I say to that? There weren't enough lovely jubblies in the world to show what I felt at that moment. All I could do was shout and hop about the bedroom like that Scrooge geezer when he wakes up on Christmas morning.

It was the best feeling I'd ever had.

I was finally gonna be a daddy!

CHAPTER 26

STARS IN MY EYES

With Rodney once more dumped in my lap, and the prospect of another tiny little Trotter mouth to feed on the horizon, the time had come to pull out all the stops and earn some proper readies. As you know, I'd had a brief flirtation with music management a few years back handling that bunch of wallies A Bunch of Wallies, and, while that project had floundered somewhat before it could really get going, I was about to take the valuable lessons I'd learned and apply them to a fresh, exciting new venture: The Trotter International Star Agency!

It all came about when I popped in to see my old pal Eric down at the Starlight Rooms, Peckham's answer to the O2 Arena. He's a lovely bloke, Eric, untrustworthy, prone to violence, but a lovely bloke all the same. He'd been stitched up over a singing duo and was desperate to find a new act that'd be ready to roll in twenty-four hours. Well, you know me, if I can ever help a mate in need, I'll do it – especially when that mate in need is laying 600 quid for one night's work on the table.

Raquel weren't too keen on the idea at first but, as I explained to her, I'd already given Eric her word that she'd do it. Besides, she had (and still does have) a lovely singing voice, and gifts like that should be shared with the world. And it weren't like she hadn't done anything like it before. I remembered her once showing me a poster of when she appeared on the same bill as Otis Reading at the Talk of the Town, London. She pointed out to me that it was actually Laurie London at the Talk of the Town, Reading, but that was just splitting hairs. Finally she agreed to do it but only if she didn't have to do it alone. So I got Rodney to draw up a contract (something with plenty of 'hereinafters' and 'forthwiths') and we went straight out on the hunt to find Raquel's new singing partner.

After a few setbacks, we found ourselves in the Down by the Riverside Club, which, if you've been there you'll know, is very much at the end of most lines. And it was there that we saw him. *Tony Angelino, the singing dustman!* I remembered Trigger had mentioned him before, I couldn't remember what he'd said exactly 'cos I'd been doing my best not to listen, but seeing Tony there in the flesh, working the stage in a pink frilly shirt and a pair of trousers that went some way to explaining how he was hitting the high notes, I was blown away! He reminded me a bit of a young David Hasselhoff, just shorter, browner and wetter, and he was belting out his own unique take on that old classic 'Delilah'. Tom Jones wouldn't have lost any sleep over it, but you should've seen the old dears in the audience (come to think of it, the old dears *were* the audience). They were lapping it up. I knew then that if I could get Tony and Raquel up on stage together we'd be on to a winner. Rodney voiced his doubts, even though I'd already explained to him that his duties as road manager went no further than driving the van, fetching the sandwiches and sweeping up after we'd finished.

Anyway, as soon as Tony had wrapped up and left the stage (under a barrage of big knickers), we went to his dressing room to introduce ourselves and talk business.

Tony was well pleased. The Starlight Rooms was obviously a big step up for him, which surprised me a bit at first, but once he'd taken his wig off and removed the jumbo saveloy from his pants, it started to make sense. I could tell he weren't quite as confident as he made out though, when he mentioned how picky he was when it came to the songs he sang, but when I told him he'd be getting a hundred notes for the gig his confidence soon returned. He could sense that he was in safe hands.

With Tony on board, Rodney and I headed over to the Nag's Head to have a little celebration, and it was there, while chatting with Boycie and Mike, that we discovered some disturbing news. Apparently Eric and the Starlight Rooms had been bought out a few months earlier by Eugene McCarthy, a local villain from the Driscoll brothers school of business. Built like a brick shithouse, rumour had it the S.A.S. paid him protection money.

'There were no boardroom negotiations,' Boycie explained. 'Eugene gave Eric a simple choice: take it or I'll nail you to the nearest door.'

'Tomorrow night's Eugene's mum's eighty-second birthday,' Mike said, 'so he's throwing a party for her at the Starlight Rooms.'

'No, Eric's at the Starlight Rooms,' I said.

'He's just the manager now,' Mike explained. 'But with Eugene's reputation for showing his displeasure by doing a bit of extreme DIY on whoever's wound him up, all the agents had a meeting in the local convalescent home and decided to boycott the Starlight Rooms altogether.'

'So,' Boycie added, 'unless Eric can find a mug to supply the cabaret for tomorrow night, B&Q'll be selling another door.'

There weren't much we could do about it. We'd already signed the contract guaranteeing we'd provide the entertainment.

Well, when you've hit your stride you just have to put your head down and keep moving forward. I'd never let a violent maniac stop me before, I weren't about to start then. Rodney, always the thinker, took a more philosophical view on the situation and immediately handed in his resignation and began to seek a deep and meaningful relationship with God.

First thing the next morning, I booked Raquel and Tony in for a whole afternoon's rehearsals at the Jesse Jackson Memorial Hall. I even managed to persuade Rodney to go, just in case they fancied a sandwich or wanted anything swept up. I would have gone myself, of course, but I happened to have an urgent date with a magistrate that I just couldn't get out of (I can't recall what it was about exactly, but I was innocent). Course, my case ended up being the last in the queue. I got fined £65 but then realised I'd left my wallet at home, so I got on the blower to Sinbad and got him to bring it down, and he only went and took a bus! So there I was banged up in a cell and that silly old duffer was fighting his way through the Friday night rush hour on a sodding bus!

Anyway, I got home, whacked on a suit and shot over to the Starlight Rooms just in time for Tony and Raquel's introduction. They were all there, Eugene, his mum and all their mates. Rodney was hyperventilating, trying to say there was some sort of problem, but it was too late. The moment had arrived.

Any feelings of apprehension I had (and there were quite a few) melted away once Raquel walked on stage and started singing the opening verse to that Roy Orbison classic, 'Crying'. Then, as the chorus crept ever closer, Tony stepped into the spotlight, wig and sausage perfectly placed, and lifted the whole thing to another level entirely. Honestly, I could feel the hairs on the back of my neck stand to attention. Then Tony led into the chorus and the hairs shrivelled up and died.

See, what neither Tony, Raquel, Rodney or any other git had told me was that Tony couldn't pronounce his 'R's. There's nothing wrong with that, of course, loads of people can't pronounce their 'R's, it's hardly noticeable, but when you're belting out the song 'Crying' at two hundred decibels to a hall full of gangsters and their mums, it tends to stand out. Now I understood why he was picky about choosing his own songs. But there was no stopping Tony then, he was in the zone and 'cwying' all over the place! I did the only thing I could do: I sped home and hid the hammer and nails.

Raquel had the right hump when she got in. She'd seen it through to the end though. And not just 'Cwying', no, she and Tony's repertoire also included 'Please Welease Me', 'Congwatulations' and 'The Gween Gween Gwass of Home'. Then Tony showed up. I paid him, of course. It weren't his fault. He explained that he usually only sang songs that didn't have 'R's in them, and that sometimes if a song did have an 'R' in it he'd change the lyrics.

'Why didn't you change the lyrics tonight?' I asked him.

'How can I change the lywics to "Cwying"?' he said. 'The bloody song's called "Cwying"!'

I couldn't argue with that, could I? Anyway, just as we'd begun making plans to emigrate to Toga, I got a phone call from Eugene. It turned out his mum had loved it. I don't know, maybe she'd got a bit of wax lodged in her hearing aid or something. Well, that's Tony for you. He's like Marmite. Brown and sticky.

Raquel and Tony went their separate ways after that, and what with her being pregnant it was probably for the best. It was a bloody shame though. They could have been the next Sonny and Cher, and me, well, I could have been the next Phil Spectrum. Tony continued singing in the Down by the Riverside Club, right up till a serious case of fake suntan poisoning forced him to retire (the way he used to slather it on I weren't surprised). He's living in a maisonette in Gandhi Avenue now, between the Nigerian greengrocers and the

Kosovan kebab house. As for Eugene, he met a very sad and tragic end a few years later when he took his own life. At least that was what the police said happened. He shot himself twice in the head and three times in the back.

Ɛ

You'd have thought the news that he was gonna be an uncle would have cheered Rodney up, but if anything it seemed to depress him even more.

I'd thought my latest investment in a job lot of fax machines would have excited him, knowing his love for all things that had buttons, but nitto! Still, determined as ever to be on the cutting edge of technology, I kept one for myself, hooked it up and settled down for the long wait until someone else I knew had one. I finally managed to flog one to Mike at the Nag's Head so at least he could drop me a line. And he did. '*Machine...no... work... prop*' it said. He'd obviously been pressing the wrong buttons so I gave him a bell and told him I'd fax him later on about it.

As Rodney got more miserable, Raquel got more pregnant and Albert kept scaring the neighbours by doing his 'physical jerks' in front of the window. With the state Raquel was in, I decided it was time we became a two-car family (well, one car and a three-wheeled van). The newspapers were full of stories about muggings on the estate and it put my mind at ease knowing she'd be able to get to and fro without having to risk her life. So I bought a smashing little Capri Ghia off Boycie. Granted, it had a few holes in the bodywork, but it purred like a kitten and went like shit off a shovel.

Rodney met up with Cassandra a few times, but they still hadn't reached an agreement on who was getting custody of Barbie and Ken, so the fights continued. Then he took her out for a day at Hampton Court.

Well, if Henry the Eighth's gaff don't inspire matrimonial harmony, nothing will. Course, they got in a row over which was the quickest way out of the maze and that was that. Finally, deciding he weren't quite miserable enough, Rodney decided to become a vegetarian.

I couldn't worry about it too much, I had to get myself geared up for parenthood, so I started attending Raquel's antenatal classes with her. If I'm honest I weren't looking forward to it, but I wanted to show I was willing to get up to speed on all the ins and outs of it all (mainly the outs). They showed us videos of babies being born, and it made a few of the blokes there feel ill. It didn't bother me though. I think it was 'cos of my experience working on a jellied eel stall. And what with all those Christmas turkeys, giblets 'n all, Grandad used to knock up, watching a baby being born was a walk in the park. Raquel didn't seem to appreciate my support though, but then I s'pose she just weren't used to having a sensitive and attentive partner like me. If nothing else, it took my mind off the batch of wigs I'd been stitched up with by Mustapha, an old mate who worked down the Bangladeshi butcher's. I'd had a queue of old dears lining up for 'em, but when I opened the box it turned out they was all blokes' wigs. I did my best, going through my contacts and calling up a few likely buyers to see if they were still bald and wanted to do something about it. I managed to sell one to Trigger (he weren't bald but said he wanted one in case of an emergency). To be honest, they weren't one of my most successful product lines.

Raquel and I couldn't settle on a name for the baby. We originally thought about calling it Rodney if it was a boy, then, realising we wanted it to have the best possible start in life, we changed our minds. I quite liked Sigourney (after the actress) if it was a girl, and I really pushed for Troy. Brilliant bloke's name, that. Troy Trotter. If you were in trouble, your life on the line, and you knew the bloke coming to rescue you was called Troy Trotter, well, it would fill you with confidence, wouldn't it? Raquel stuck the kibosh on it, but then her hormones were all over the place by that point. You know how women get weird cravings when they're pregnant? Raquel couldn't get enough tuna. She'd eat bowls of the stuff. Giving her a kiss goodnight was like snogging Japan.

It was Rodney that came up with the name Damien. I don't know where he got the idea from but both me and Raquel loved it from the off. Damien Derek Trotter. It was Albert who pointed out that it'd make his initials DDT. *At least there'll be no flies on him*, I thought.

One night, Raquel said we needed to go. Albert had just started filling us in on yet another chapter from the Battle of the Baltic, so I thought she meant she needed to get out of the room, but then she said her contractions were getting regular. Remembering the classes, I calmly went and got all the gear and calmly told her to focus on breathing calmly. Then we calmly made our way out to the lifts. They were calmly broken. So we calmly started to make our way down the stairs. Well, Raquel did, I sprinted on ahead to make sure the Capri Ghia would start and get the heating going.

That night Rodney had gone round to see how Cassandra was. Given that she was in bed when I rang I guessed he'd found out. A night for miracles all round. I told her to give him a nudge and get his arse down the hospital sharpish!

It was important that Raquel knew I was there supporting her so I stayed in the delivery room and held her legs in the air, until she told me to stop. I also wanted to keep an eye on the midwife who it turned out was a geezer! Outside, Rodney and Albert settled down with something hot from the vending machine and waited.

You know I said how easy it was watching that video of a baby being born? Well, I soon discovered that the real thing ain't that easy.

I mean, the way they made it look in the video, the bird just laid back, pushed a bit, let out a groan and the baby popped out. I'd passed farts that were more traumatic. But this was sweating, panting, huffing, puffing, spitting, growling, nerve-shredding agony. And that was just me! Raquel was really in the wars. Luckily the nurses were prepared and dosed us up with a load of gas and air. It's amazing really that something as simple as mixing a bit of gas and air together can make you feel all nice and floaty like that. It weren't helping me focus, which is what I should've been doing, but by then I didn't care. Then I saw it. The baby's head was engaged (that's medical speak for 'poking out'). At first I weren't sure if it was just the gas 'n air playing tricks on me. But a couple of pushes later and I saw eyes and a nose and a mouth and ears. An entire head! I got a bit overwhelmed then and rushed out into the corridor to tell Rodney and Albert. Bloody waste of time really 'cos all Rodney could ask was if it had any numbers on it. Typical Rodney that is. Anyway, I got back in for the final push, and there it was. A perfectly formed little human baby. Overwhelmed again, I rushed out into the corridor to update Rodney and Albert.

'We've done it!' I cried. 'We've only bloody done it!'

'What is it, Del?' Rodney asked.

'It's a little baby, Rodney,' I explained.

'No, I mean, is it a boy or a girl?' he said. I shot back in to check… It was a boy! As moments of my life go, it was, and still is, the crème de la menthe. Damien Derek Trotter had finally arrived. It's silly, I know, but I wanted Mum to see him so I took him over to the window. Holding him in my arms, I looked deep into his beautiful little eyes and made him a promise: I promised him the world. I'd never seen so many stars in the sky as I did right then.

CHAPTER 27

TRANSATLANTIC

As it turned out, fatherhood really suited me. I know a lot of people moan about how difficult it is, the sleepless nights, the nappies, all that game, and yeah, Raquel did make a bit of a racket getting out of bed to go and deal with it, but you've gotta take the rough with the smooth, ain't you?

The biggest change was mental. You don't realise until you've got a baby just how many dangers lurk in the home. Little things that would otherwise seem completely innoculous, like a Stanley knife and an open bottle of toilet-duck sitting on a side table, suddenly start ringing alarm bells. I couldn't wait to take Damien out and introduce him to the world, but before I did that I got him a pukka car seat for the van (you just can't be too careful when it comes to that sort of thing). It didn't fit so I had to shove him in the back with Albert.

'Drop 'im and I'll drop you,' I told him.

And it worked. There weren't a speed bump in Peckham that could loosen that iron grip. The old boy was useful in other ways too. Five minutes of one of his wartime sagas and Damien was out like a light (usually along with anyone else standing within a ten yard radius). Course, the change upset Rodney a bit, and he started acting weird,

240

getting paranoid that Damien was giving him funny looks, holding him up in front of the mirror to check that he had a reflection, that kind of thing.

The day of the christening was a very, *very* proud moment for me and Raquel. Everyone was there, Mike, Trigger, Denzil, Boycie and Marlene, Alan and Pam, Mickey Pearce (he was the photographer so he had to be there). And of course, as godparents, Rodney and Cassandra. As is his way, Rodney seemed a bit frightened by the whole thing and got confused with all the renouncing, but apart from that it was a blinding ceremony. After the reverend wrapped it all up, I took the opportunity to discuss a bit of business with him in the vestry. Some people might think that's in bad taste, discussing money in a biblical place like that, but those people obviously haven't read their Bibles, 'cos I instinctly remember from my school days that the Bible actually contains a chapter called 'Profits'. So don't let anyone tell you that God don't know a bit of bunce when he sees it.

It was my latest idea and, like most of the others, it was ground-breaking.

'Trotters Pre-Blessed Wine?' the rev asked, looking a bit stunned. Well, you couldn't blame him.

'Now you know how the people felt when they gazed upon the burning bush or the first Pot Noodle,' I told him.

The way I saw it, Trotters Pre-Blessed Wine was gonna be like the holy version of sliced bread. I'd recently made a new connection with a vintner in Walsall (which, as anyone who knows their wine will tell you, is very much the Noir Valley of England) and he had a contact in Bucharest who was about to ship a new range of Romanian wine into the country. So we did a deal. I had it all planned: the reverend would bless the wine by the lorryload then we'd ship it out to every church and cathedral across the land. The beautiful thing though was that we'd get the wine at £1.39 a bottle and we'd knock it out at £2.50, so before you'd know it the church would be rejoicing, the Reverend would be redeemed, and we'd both be a nicker and a bit in front. Everyone's a winner!

It weren't all about the money. I'd worked it out that what with all the time being spent on blessing individual bottles, the church was losing what amounted to weeks of vicar hours. With my idea, not only would that time be saved, so would thousands of pounds that could be much better spent on the things that really mattered, like roofs and organs and what 'ave you. Anyway, I left him to think about it while I got on with sorting out the arrangements for the first lorryload (well, he'd have to get a bit of practice in).

Things were looking up for Rodney too when he had a little windfall of his own. See, when he started working for Alan, he'd been set up on the firm's pension scheme, and now the insurance company had come up with his repayment: £935. I was well chuffed for him. Things between him and Cassandra were still raw, he was still living at the flat with us, and he deserved a bit of good news.

After the christening we held a bit of a gathering at the Nag's Head, just a few close and dear friends (and Boycie). I'd got Mickey Pearce to go back to the flat and babysit Damien, so no worries there. Boycie wouldn't stop going on about his and Marlene's up and coming three-week tour of America. I must admit I envied 'em. I'd always wanted to go to America. Most of the Americans I'd met had been brash, mouthy gits, but still, I reckoned I'd fit in nicely on the other side of the pond; teach those Wall Street wallies a thing or two 'n all. I wasn't fully aware of it at the time, but already the seed of another brilliant idea was forming in my mind (I know, sometimes I just can't stop). It didn't hit me proper till later that evening when Albert was telling me all about one of his underwater adventures (I found his stories often helped 'cos it gave me the chance to really switch off and step outside myself). I'd already heard Cassandra mention that she'd always dreamed of one day going to America, and I thought, *What better way for her and Rodney to patch things up than a dream holiday?* So, the next morning I got out early to put my plan into action. I found Rodney in Sid's café, harping on about Ozones and fossil fuels. Luckily I'd already popped into the bank to pay his pension money in (well, I didn't want him giving it all to Sting, did I?)

'Listen,' I said to him, 'I've had a brilliant idea on your behalf, 'cos I know how much you like to travel.'

'I ain't going to Romania!' he said. 'Raquel mentioned you had a call from Bucharest last night and when you got off the phone you were all pale and sweaty.'

'It was just a hiccup in the old translation,' I explained. 'Nothing I can't handle. Anyway, listen. I was talking with Cassandra about Boycie and Marlene's holiday and she mentioned how much she'd love to go to America. So on the way down here I called into Alex's and he's got a once in a lifetime offer: return tickets to Miami, 250 smackeroonies! And the cherry on the cake is that two go for the price of one!' I watched him turning it over in his brain, desperately looking for obstacles. 'She'll love it, Rodders,' I continued. 'Just imagine how she'll feel when you announce you're taking her on a holiday of a lifetime. She'll be all over you like a rash!' I was sensing the dam was close to breaking. 'And don't worry about her getting time off work, she told me the bank owe her a couple of weeks.' He said he wanted to phone her just to make sure, but I had a much better idea. 'You take her out for dinner,' I said, 'and when you get to the old Grand Marnier stakes, you whack the tickets down on the table and say "Darlin', I am taking you to Miami." You'll knock her bandy!' And the dam broke.

'I better get down Alex's and get those tickets,' he said.

'Save the shoe leather,' I said, 'I've already got 'em for you.'

'But how did you know I wanted them?' he said.

'Well, I thought to myself that even a plonker like you wouldn't turn your nose up at a deal like this.'

'I don't know what I'd do without you,' he said. 'I wouldn't have thought of that in a million yea... hold on, how did you afford it? I thought you was skint.'

'I am,' I said, 'but I signed one of your cheques down the bank and cashed it.' Well, at this point he was so overcome with gratitude I had to physically restrain him. 'Don't you *dare* thank me,' I told him. 'It's no big deal anyway, forging your signature's a piece of piss!'

That night Rodders took Cassandra out to break the wonderful news. Well, it would have been wonderful if the trip to Miami hadn't clashed with some seminar at Cassandra's bank. Rodney was gutted, and I can't say I blamed him, even though, as Raquel pointed out, it was an extremely important seminar that Cassandra had been working towards for years now.

'It's just my luck, innit?' Rodney said. 'Any other week of the year would have been fine, but it had to be *that* bloody week!' And with that he went off to bed.

'It's a shame he didn't phone Cassandra first and make sure it was all right,' Raquel said.

I didn't want to get into the minor details of it all, my main concern was Rodney, and when he told me a bit later that he weren't going to Miami either, well, there was no way I could stand for that.

'You've gotta go, Rodney,' I told him. 'Otherwise Cassandra'll think you're just a puppet who can't do anything unless she pulls your strings. You've gotta show her you're a man and you can stand on your own two feet.'

'You're right,' he said, and then went off to think about it a bit more.

I'll be honest, as much I couldn't stand to see Rodney miss out like that, I was a bit worried about him going on his own. Albert very helpfully suggested that Mickey Pearce go with him, a smashing idea, the problem was the tickets were made out in the name of Trotter. Then Raquel suggested that I go with Rodney. Well, it hadn't even crossed my mind, but I s'pose she had a point. After all my name is Trotter.

I wrestled with the idea, struggling to find a way out, but there weren't one. Whether I liked it or not I'd have to go with Rodney and make sure he was all right. So I went and told him the news and he was chuffed to bits, naturally, but he did have a few conditions (rules on where we went, what we said, what we did, what we wore, that sort of thing). You know what he's like. I put his mind at rest, explaining to him that things had changed since our Benidorm days. For one, I was a married man and a dad (well, I was a dad) and you can't get a much bigger responsibility than that, can you?

❦

We flew out on a jumbo jet. Not that that was a big deal to me or nothing, it's just when you're going *transatlantic* you need a bigger plane. You could feel the difference though. Not a spot of turbulence the whole way. The only problem I had (apart from Rodney, who was continuing to dole out more laws than Tony Blair at happy hour) was with my seat. It reclined so fast at one point it nearly chinned the old dear behind me.

Anyway, turns out Miami is right up my street. Hot? I'd never known anything like it. We were there no more than ten minutes and even Rodney got a bit of colour in his cheeks. It was a beautiful place, palm trees, golden beaches, tanned sorts in dental-floss G-strings everywhere you looked, harbours chock-a-block with million-dollar yachts. Oh yes, it was very me. First things first though, we had to sort out the living arrangements, so we went to the vehicle hire company that Alex had found for us and picked up our camper van. Rodney didn't go a bundle on it, but, as I explained to him, it did have its advantages, like being very, *very* cheap. And once he'd laid down the further condition that I abstained from curry for the entire holiday, he got on board and we were away!

I must say that I found the roads over there a bit of a nightmare, and every twenty seconds or so I was forced to make an urgent swerve in order to avoid a head-on collision. You should have seen some of the hand signals I was getting. Before that I thought there was only three, but it turns out there's at least ten! It weren't my fault they had it all arse about face, was it? I did my best not to let it get to me, but when some fat mush in a shitty little Honda cut right in front of me, and then had the diabolical nerve to give *me* the finger, well, I'd had enough and I gave chase. Realising he'd crossed the wrong man, he put his foot down, so I put mine down too. Admittedly, it weren't the fastest car chase (we probably didn't break 30mph throughout), but it was still tense.

It was a bit like something out of the *Dukes of Hazzard*, you know, if Bo and Luke had driven a clapped-out old camper van. Rodney was begging me to give up, but I was caught up in the moment, and to tell the truth, part of me was enjoying it. I could tell Rodney was getting a bit of a kick out of it too. I remember looking over at him at one point as I swung us down an alley, and seeing the adrenalin pumping through his eyeballs as he gripped the dashboard with one hand and crossed himself with the other.

Anyway, after about half an hour or so the van started to belch smoke, so we had to stop to let the radiator cool down. Rodney reminding me that the American old bill carry guns also played a part in my decision. It weren't the best start to the holiday, and I regret it now, but these things happen, don't they?

On Rodney's suggestion that we leave the van for a bit and go for a toby, we came across a boat that was offering something called 'Star Tours', which basically gave you a chance to have a butcher's at the back gardens of the rich and famous from a great distance. It was all right, I s'pose. The highlight was when I spotted Barry Gibb doing a bit of weeding. I shouted out to him, but he didn't say anything, just walked off to get something from his shed. I dunno, maybe it was just some bloke with a beard.

That night we came across a really classy-looking nightclub, all pink neon and pukka pot plants. The way Rodney looked at it you'd have thought it was the gateway to hell, but, as I explained to him, we had to go in so I could use the phone to call Raquel and let her know we'd arrived safely.

'And what's wrong with the public phone box across the road?' he said.

'Well, we can't get a drink in there, can we?' I told him.

So there we were sipping our drinks, when this bunch of what they call 'Italian-American' lads came over and introduced themselves. I had my guard up at first, thinking they were mates of the fat geezer in the Honda, but my fears were soon proved to be dumbfounded. They were a smashing bunch of lads, real salt of the earth types, and generous? Rodney and I didn't have to put our hands in our pockets all night. The main bloke – I forget his name now but it ended with an 'o' – reminded me a lot of a younger, Italian-American version of myself: handsome, well turned out, successful, etc. Apparently he was big in stocks and shares also, so that was another thing we had in common. I was considering mentioning the Romanian wine deal to him, but Rodney begged me not to.

We had a really great night, before being brought down to earth with a smack when on leaving the club we discovered some git had broken into the van. All our money and luggage was gone. Thank God, Rodney had kept our passports and tickets on him or we would have been dead lumbered. But just as we thought the holiday was well and truly knackered, our new mates turned up and saved the day. They were obviously embarrassed about the whole thing, and so invited us to come and stay at their place for a few days. I could sense Rodney was getting a bit edgy, and I'll admit, part of me found it a bit odd, but once we saw the place we'd be staying in all that went out the window. It was a proper mansion of a gaff, electric gates, a pool, tennis courts, the works! Up till then I'd often wondered how it would feel to sit on a marble khazi, and let me tell you now, it feels nice. The only downside was that a tropical storm had blown in and downed all the telephone lines in the area, so we couldn't call home. Rodney was a bit suspicious of all the security that was about but I explained to him that, once you reach a certain level of success, you can't be too careful about these things. Besides, it was either this or kipping in the van during the nights and begging on the streets during the days.

We had nothing to worry about though, we had a really brilliant time! They even took us out to a lovely little restaurant overlooking the ocean, ordering Italian dumplings and wine with a bouquet that would have made Interflora wet itself. After we'd eaten, they set me up with a ride on one of those jet-ski things. I weren't completely sold on the idea but it seemed rude to knock 'em back. The one they hired had a few minor problems with it (steering and speed control mainly) but that weren't their fault, you get cowboys the world over. I just hope they got their money back once the coastguard had picked me up.

Then, on about the fourth day, Rodney confessed to a new worry. I'll admit it had crossed my mind once or twice too. I mean, a group of well-dressed blokes living together, not a bird in sight. But as I said to Rodney, they were Italian, and it's a well-known medical fact that there's no such thing as an Italian noofter.* 'They're just men's men,' I told him, 'as long as they don't start dressing up as the Village People and trying to rope us into the YMCA, we're laughing!'

Our holiday was nearly at an end, and Rodney and I decided to get out and take in a bit of the local wildlife. So we scaled a wall and went over to have a stroll through the Everglades. Rodney had been going on about them for the last couple of days, you know what he's like with his nature, but I've gotta say, as glades go, they weren't all that. It was, I thought at first, basically just a massive load of water and reeds, with mosquitos so big they showed up on radar. Then it came to my attention that the Everglades is also what Rodney called 'the natural habitat' of alligators. Now, you'd have thought he would have mentioned this *before* we went in, but no, he mentioned it after we'd bumped into one of the gits! You'd also have thought things couldn't get a lot worse than that, but they did, and then some! First of all, after the brisk jog we made to get away from the alligator, we realised we were lost. Secondly, Rodney said that once night fell a load more alligators would come out looking for something to eat. And then some bastard started shooting at us! It was at that point I started to wonder if I'd have been better off staying at home.

So there we were, doing our best to leg it through the swamps, bullets whizzing past our heads, when we bump into Boycie and Marlene! No, it weren't a mirage, it was actually Boycie and Marlene sitting on some rickety old raft thing with a giant fan on the back.

---

* Not that it would have mattered to me if they were noofters. Straight, gay, bi, tri or transcendental, we're all just human beings as far as I'm concerned.

For a moment I thought about heading back and taking my chances with the alligators, but by that time the raft had pulled up next to us and Rodney was already on board. So off we sped, the bullets still speeding after us. God knows who was doing the shooting. Probably that fat geezer in the Honda.

And so our holiday ended on that very sour note. We were gonna go back and say goodbye to the lads,* but we were so knackered we decided to just go and have a kip at the airport.

As it turned out, things had gone a bit wonky back home too, as Raquel very quickly informed me. The lorries the reverend had been blessing and that had gone out delivering to all the churches and cathedrals were full of *white* wine! I don't know, you leave the country for a few days and all your hard work and planning goes to pot. That's another important business lesson for you, if you want something done properly, do it your bloody self!

---

* I'd just like to reiterate that the Italian-American lads we met and stayed with on holiday were a bunch of smashing, friendly, law-abiding blokes, and nothing like they're portrayed to be in the movies and on the telly. Also they were not gay.

CHAPTER 28

WALKING ON WATER

I'd been sailing the good ship Trotter through a patch of fiscal turbulence. No matter how hard I tried, nothing was shifting. On top of that Raquel had the right hump, Rodney was on 'edge' and Damien was chucking things at people's heads. I couldn't really blame Raquel though. She was overworked what with Damien and the housework. On top of that she was suffering from what they call post-natal depression. Poor girl was really bad with it'n all, whenever she made my breakfast she'd slam it down on the table like she was hammering in a nail. I tried to be supportive (taking my plate in to be washed up and leaving my dirty laundry in one convenient pile) but it made no difference. It was putting a bit of a strain on our relationship to be honest. She was always complaining about me going out at night drinking and gambling. And yeah, I was down the casino most nights, trying to win us a few bob, but if she'd only gone down there and seen how much I owed 'em she'd have understood how hard I'd been trying.

Just when I thought things couldn't get any worse some bastard broke into the lock-up and stole a load of our stock. So, the first rule of business being 'protect your investment', I got Rodney and Albert to move the rest up into Rodney's old room. There was a fair bit, but it was quality gear (an antique deep-sea diver's suit, some personalised ID bracelets, a load of 'Free Nelson Mandela' T-shirts, some Bros LPs, a couple of boxes of men's wigs, a few hundred litres of Romanian Riesling, a batch of Betamax copies of *The Poseidon Adventure*, that sort of thing). But no sooner than it was in the flat, Raquel starts on at me to clear it out again. I told her not to worry, but two months later and she was *still* going on about it! The thing is, she was looking on it as though it was a load of old rubbish. I tried to explain to her, one man's junk and all that, but she copped a deaf 'un.

'Hasn't it dawned on you yet that all you have here is what the thieves left behind?' she said.

'Yeah,' I said, 'but who's to say I won't flog all this stuff tomorrow?'

'Del,' she said, 'what are the chances of you bumping into a bald-headed, anti-apartheid, deep-sea diving Bros fan who owns a Betamax video recorder, drinks Romanian Riesling, and whose name is Gary?'

She always had a way of cutting straight to the crotch of the matter like that, so I got Rodney and Albert to move the lot into the shed down on Grandad's old allotment. Nobody had set foot on it for years, so I reckoned it'd be safe there, plus I'd received a summons giving us two weeks to clear it up 'cos people had been using it as a dump and it had become a health hazard, so we had to make the trip anyway.

But the cherry on the cake came when I received a letter from the council telling me they'd accepted my offer to buy the flat. It'd been so long since I'd sent the application I'd forgotten all about it. So that was it. The flat was mine, well, mine and Raquel's. Problem was the mortgage was two n'alf times the rent, and I couldn't afford the rent. You can imagine the news didn't go down well with Raquel and I got another earful. I kept telling myself something would turn up to shift the tide and get us earning again, but the strain was getting to me. I could feel myself going under… and then something turned up.

As you know, every so often I hit upon a genius idea, and the day I walked into Rodney's mate Myles's organic food shop was one of those times. I'd had plenty of urethra moments in the past, but this one took the digestive! Times had changed. It was the nineties. People had become a lot more health-conscious and were turning their backs on hearty, traditional English grub like hot dogs and pizza, and were after food so fresh it still had mud on it. I never understood it myself, I'd take a Whopper Meal over a bowl of beansprouts any day, but that was the way the wind was blowing. And that day in Myles's shop, I caught a whiff of that wind, and there, mixed in with the smell of 'orseshit, I detected the distinct aroma of bunce!

I hadn't realised just how trendy water had become. Yeah. Water. I know, it still amazes me now. All these people going out to spend their hard-earned dosh on bottles of water, when the stuff was being pumped into their homes twenty-four-seven. Madness! So, with this new-found appreciation of all things earthy, I thought I'd have a look around and see if Peckham didn't have its own ancient water source. And stone the crows, it did! The really amazing thing though was that it was slap bang in the middle of Grandad's allotment. Coincidences don't come more coincidental than that, do they? At first my heart was telling me to just leave it be. It was such a beautiful, natural wonder, I was tempted to keep it as my own little secret. But then I thought, *Sod it, there's a fortune to be made here*, so I set the ball in motion and got Myles down to the allotment to advise me. I kept Rodney out of the way as much as possible, not even telling him about the find to begin with 'cos, well, he'd always had this problem with honesty.* Not

---

* In that it'd always been important to him (See page 57). How can you trust a man as honest as that?

that I had anything to hide. Honesty has always been important to me too, but too much of it in business can really slow things down. It was for his own good anyway. He'd been looking very pale of late (and that's saying something as on a normal day he made an albino look flushed). It was just that he'd been under a lot of stress and it was beginning to take its toll on his overall 'performance'. And while I've most definitely *never* had any problems of that particular nature, I told him of some pills I'd heard about that could help perk him up a bit, but he didn't want to know. It was all very personal, so I'll leave it there before I say too much.

Anyway, Myles took a sample of the spring for testing, and just as my gut was telling me, it turned out to be pukka! After that there was no stopping us. We were flogging it quicker than we could bottle it, and not to just any old philistine, Peckham Spring was being sipped in some of the finest restaurants and hotels in the land. Even Myles started selling it in his shop. At the time Cassandra was in charge of small businesses investments at her bank, so, keeping it in the family, I decided to pop in and get some advice on how to take things to the next level.

It was a brilliant feeling. Finally, after all those years of grafting, we'd made it! Well, you know they say once you get to the top people can't wait to knock you off? It's true. It started with some malicious rumours. Apparently the estate was suffering from some unexplained drought. The thinking was that there was a major underground leak somewhere, but they looked and couldn't find one. Then the source of the problem was found to be coming from the vicinity of Nelson Mandela House. A team of council inspectors came sniffing around asking questions about some chemical drums that some git had dumped in a local pond. The final insult came when they started having a pop at Peckham Spring water itself, saying it weren't as pure as its label claimed it was, and apparently they had proof. Well, I was as shocked as anyone. I told them it had a certificate of purity signed by Myles himself, reminding them that he weren't just any old Tom Dick or Harry, he was a member of the SWANS committee! Then they started playing mind games by asking me what the SWANS committee was. I told them to hold on and gave Rodney a bell, but Cassandra said he'd locked himself in the bog and was refusing to come out.

What began as a blissful dream ended in a bloody nightmare! And once again it looked as though I'd be going up before a judge. Now, I'm not saying I didn't bend the rules a bit in what I done, and maybe I even deserved the slap on the wrist I eventually got, but what the press wrote about me was absolute cobblers! I mean, selling water from my own kitchen tap? What sort of a bloke do they think I am?! Still, it was touch and go for a while. My lawyer, Solly, reckoned I could even be facing porridge. On top of that it looked for a while like Myles, Rodney and even Cassandra were gonna be hauled up as accessories. I was prepared to fight tooth and nail to prove our innocence. I was confident too. The case Solly had put together was more airtight than Boycie's wallet. I got him to prepare a last-minute plea of 'temporary nervous breakdown' though, just to be safe.

I'll admit, as the weeks rolled on the whole thing did start to play on my mind, and I started to wish I'd never found that sodding spring. I went to the cemetery to have a chat with Mum. I always found comfort there, if not always the answers I needed. But dear old Mum must have pulled on some of the right strings for me this time, as a week later the case against me collapsed due to lack of evidence.

Relieved ain't the word! If I'd had any dosh on me I'd have gone out to celebrate, but after paying Solly's fees I was skint. It was all a very sad and stressful time for the Trotter family. We just wanted to give

give something back to the world, a legacy of wellbeing that would last for generations (and, according to that World Health Organization report, it still might).

Looking back now I realise it was little more than a storm in a teacup. I mean it weren't like anyone got hurt. Raquel's hair grew back. Cassandra's suspension at the bank was lifted, and Rodney gradually weaned himself off the tranquillisers. Even Myles eventually came out of hiding.

The spring itself is sadly no more. As it happened there was a cave-in at the allotment due to a freak earthquake that took place just days after the council's investigation began. You probably didn't hear about it, it was only a few minor tremors, but it was still enough for the Peckham Spring to be lost to eternity. It just goes to show you how fragile and precious nature is. Still, never mind, eh? Onwards and upwards. *Je suis le bouef*, as they say in Nantes!

❧

What happened with the spring was one of the major factors leading to Raquel and I going through a brief separation (that and the post-natal depression). We didn't separate far, she just took Damien over to Rodney and Cassandra's and kipped on their sofa bed for a bit. It was a bit awkward for Rodney and Cassandra 'cos they were trying for a baby and Cassandra had been given advice by the doctor about taking her temperature on the hour to figure out an 'optimum time for fertilisation'. Call me old-fashioned but optimum time for fertilisation in my book is bedtime (with maybe a quick go at it before breakfast if you wake up feeling sparky). Still, Cassandra always did love a chart.

I could understand Raquel's frustration. I'd been going out a lot again, but only 'cos I was lining up a deal with Ronnie Nelson, who owned the One-Eleven Club. There she was, tucked up nice and warm with a cup of tea and a packet of Hobnobs, listening to Horatio Trotter's tales of the sea, while I was having to slog it out over the roulette tables, forcing myself through a Scotch or three trying to bring a few quid in. It was worth it in the end 'cos I completed the deal with Ronnie and ended up bagging us a consignment of state of the art camcorders. Russian military grade they were, and fair enough, they were a bit on the bulky side, and they only took Russian video cassettes, but other than that they were a blinding bit of kit. I was also doing a lovely line in ski gear at the time, you know, puffy jackets, thermal hats, goggles, that kind of thing.

Trouble was, no matter how thick I laid the patter on, the punters weren't going for it. I even got Rodney to model the gear down the market, to give 'em a better idea of what they'd be getting, but that seemed to turn them off even more. It was Rodney's fault. I kept telling him he should be going for the laid-back, sophisticated, snowboarder vibe. He looked more like he was auditioning to become the new face of Imodium. Then again he was under a lot of pressure at the time, what with Cassandra and her 'temperature'. I don't know, I sometimes wondered what it was they were trying for, a baby or a barbecue. One day he told me about a nightmare he'd had where he was being chased down the Old Kent Road by a giant thermometer. Don't bear thinking about, does it?

Anyway, in some ways it was good Raquel and Damien were away from the estate for a bit as we were going through a period of riots at the time. There was old bill everywhere! But you know what it's like on these estates sometimes, people get bored and feel the need to do a bit of damage, and you can't blame the residents for fighting back. We finally patched things up (me and Raquel, not the rioters and the police, though they calmed down too after a bit) and, for a while, things settled back into the same old routine.

Damien seemed to be growing an inch a day. Not quite as fast as Rodney when he was a nipper, but fast enough. Business was up and down as often as Rodney on his fertilisation scheme.

Little did we know it then, but big things were waiting just around the corner.

CHAPTER 29

TIME FLIES

I'd been reading a book all about what it was to be a modern man (it was called *Modern Man*) and it offered advice on things like how to become less self-centred, more appreciative of, and respectful to, women, more positive and decisive, and how to get more in touch with your sensitive side (not *too* sensitive, you didn't have to wear a bra or nothing). I skipped the irrelevant bits (fortunately I've never had any problems with being self-centred), but the rest was really interesting, and reading it helped me to reach a very important decision: I was gonna get a vasectomy.

I was thinking of Raquel and what she'd been through giving birth to Damien. She didn't go a bundle on the idea, but I'd made my decision, and when Del Trotter makes a decision, the decision stays decided. Well, nine times out of ten it does. The thing is the more I thought about it the more I started to worry about... well, my tadpoles. I mean, once you'd had the procedure done they wouldn't be able to take their normal route, so where would they go? I'd already been told by a doctor that they were very strong swimmers,* and I

---

* 'The Michael Phelps of the tadpole world' were his exact words.

didn't wanna end up being too frightened to sneeze, so I knocked the idea on the head. Not that it really mattered anyway. I mean, Raquel weren't getting any younger, bless her.

I had more pressing concerns by that time anyway, like the fact that we were lumbered with one hundred and twenty-five Latvian alarm clocks that went off whenever they bloody well liked, two hundred 'aerodynamic cycling helmets' (horse-riding helmets some git had painted red) and a load of baseball caps that even East 17 fans were turning their noses up at. I'd also been knocked back by the council on an application for a home improvement grant. I'd only wanted to put some new kitchen units in, it weren't like I was after whacking an extension on the balcony or building a double garage.

It was a trying time for all of us, but especially Rodney and Cassandra who were still trying for a sprog. The hospital kept dragging them in for tests and showing them videos of ovums and things. Hats off to Rodney for his stamina, he was walking around looking like Dracula had pegged him as a regular suck.

Then one day we got a phone call. Raquel answered it and I knew immediately something was up. I was in the bedroom at the time but couldn't help but overhear (once I'd crept into the hallway).

'I haven't heard from you for years,' she was saying. 'No, I'll come to you this weekend. Del? I suppose I'll have to tell him the truth...'

Now, I'm not normally an insecure sort of bloke but I'll admit I was halfway towards packing a suitcase when I heard all this.

It was her parents.

Up till then I hadn't known she had any. Well, obviously she had some, what I mean is she never mentioned them. I thought they'd probably died or something.

Turns out they were just exstrained. When Raquel had told 'em years ago that she wanted to be an actress there'd been a bust-up.

Nobody wanted to be the first to break the silence, so on it went. Until now. She'd told them about Damien (and me of course) and they wanted to meet up. I could tell she was nervous about them meeting me (can't blame her, I do tend to dominate a room) so I told her she should go on her own for the first meeting and we'd take it from there. I was bound to meet them soon anyway, her old man was an antiques dealer and I couldn't wait to show him the Jacobean cine-camera I had in the lock-up.

As it happened, that weekend there was a party being organised by Harry Malcolm, the landlord of the Crown and Anchor. It was a fancy-dress bash being held at his house over Dulwich way. The costumes were being judged, and whoever had the best would win a hi-fi system worth a grand! As Cassandra was visiting Alan and Pam at their villa in Spain, Rodney was free too, so I told him we should let our hair down, get a couple of costumes and go and see if we couldn't net ourselves a new stereo.

Rodney wanted us to go as the Blues Brothers, but there was no way we'd win the prize if we just wore suits and bunged on a pair of sunglasses. So I popped down the fancy-dress shop and picked us up some Batman and Robin costumes (I was the caped crusader of course, you weren't getting me in a pair of green Speedos, not without booking me a holiday first) and we headed over in the van. Course, the sodding thing only breaks down on us, so we had to run the last mile or so, belting through the streets like a right pair of wallies.

When we got to the party it turned out poor old Harry had passed away the day before. Nobody had told us. Well, Rodney and I felt like a right pair of tits, bursting into the room singing the *Batman* theme tune, but it weren't our fault.

It weren't a bad night. I was a bit put out when I got some stains from the humid dip on my cape and then knocked one of my ears off on the bog door, but a bit of spit and Sellotape made sure I didn't lose my deposit.

And Raquel's weekend with her mum and dad went well. She didn't talk much about it, but she weren't crying or leaving me, so I took that to be a good sign.

───※───

We were down the market, doing our best to shift some of them caps, when we spotted a gang of muggers helping themselves to an old dear's purse. Rodney gave chase, hot on the leader's tail. I grabbed my suitcase and legged it after 'em, passing Rodney as he came running back in the opposite direction, the leader then hot on *his* tail. By following the sound of Rodney's begging I was able to get ahead and, leaping around a corner, I dropped the mugger with the suitcase. The old bill weren't far behind and before you could say 'What's all this then?' our mugging friend was cuffed and dragged off. Course, he soon grassed up his mates, so it was ASBOs all round!

To show his gratitude, the mayor very kindly bestowed upon me a medal for bravery. I was only too happy to have done my duty. Even happier when the council suddenly changed its mind and approved my home improvement grant. Lovely jubbly!

That night brought another piece of good news, but sadly, the celebration was short-lived. Cassandra and Rodney had been given the nod from the doctor, they were pregnant. We had all of a few days to celebrate then Rodney got a phone call from the bank. Cassandra had been rushed into hospital. She'd had a miscarriage.

Now, you may have noticed a few times in this book that I've taken the mick out of Rodney a bit, but that's what brothers do, innit? But the truth is, I love him. Of course I do. He's my brother. And watching him turning inward and going all quiet, I would have done anything to take it away from him. And I know I'm the sort of bloke that's always making promises, but that's just me. As soon as there's a problem I promise to fix it. Sometimes I do, 'cos I'm good at solving problems. But as much as I'd been there for him in the past, to feed him and clothe him and wipe his… tears away, and as much as I'd shielded him from the nutters and the villains and the old bill, this time, Rodney's problem wasn't something I could fix. Not even close. Course, Cassandra was hurting too, but she was stronger than Rodney. She could dig in and find the reserves to deal with it. Rodney had never been good at coping, tending to shut himself off and bottle it all up. And that's what he did. He wouldn't even say the words. I understood, they're 'orrible words: 'dead', 'miscarriage', 'gone'. Who'd wanna say any of them? But sometimes you have to make these things real, let 'em out into the air so you can size 'em up, accept 'em, then let 'em go.

It took a couple of weeks to get him to that point. Eventually, I'll admit, I cheated a bit. I got him in the lift, and halfway up, when he looked the other way, I flipped the little switch behind the control panel, making it stall. You know by now that those lifts break down more often than Ian Beale, so he didn't suspect nothing. We sat in there for a couple of hours, me pretending to have a panic attack, him, eventually, opening up and starting to talk. Every honest bit of sadness fell out of him until all I could do was put my arm round him and promise him that it would get better. Life usually does after all. You get your share of happiness, your share of sadness, and we're all just bouncing from one to the other, going up and down, just like that bloody lift wasn't.

Eventually I flipped the switch again and he went back home to Cassandra and they finally had a proper talk. It didn't mean it was over, but at least they'd started.

I was still crying over those poxy horse-riding helmets. Which leads me to another one of my brilliant innovations: Trotters Crash Turbans – for the Sikh who wants to get home safely. I'd never given it much thought before, but at the time I was being stalked by a Dr Singh, who was after me to sort out a decorating job I'd done on his surgery. As always, I'd done it in good faith, and I thought it looked pretty nice. The thing is a couple of months after, the surgery walls had started to peel a bit. According to Dr Singh – who was also known locally as the Turbanator, on account of his cruising around on his moped and telling people (well, mainly me) that he'd '*be back*' – his walls looked as though they had scabies. I just didn't realise that paint had a use-by date, it was an honest mistake.

Anyway, I'd seen Singh plenty of times on his bike (there came a point when I was seeing him everywhere. I couldn't even go down Sid's and eat a fry-up in peace without him popping up and peering in the window), but I'd never seen him wearing a crash helmet. Then Rodney told me that by law Sikhs don't have to wear crash helmets. Well, you know what I'm like with my health and safety, I was worried sick. All these Sikhs riding about without protection. So I borrowed one of Raquel's scarves and bandaged it up on top of one of the riding helmets and bingo! It was just a prototype of course, but I was certain we were onto a winner.

As it was though, TCT would have to sit on the back burner for a bit, as there was a more pressing concern on our minds, well Raquel's mainly: her mum and dad were coming for dinner.

She was beside herself, convinced that someone would show her up in some way. I understood and promised her I'd keep an eye on Rodney and Albert. And apart from Albert getting confused over what was the gravy granules and what was the coffee granules, it went very well. They were a nice pair, Audrey and James, and I like to think I knocked 'em bandy with the old patter. Audrey didn't always pick up on my jokes, bless 'er, but James was able to swap a few naval stories with Albert, as he'd been on the waves before packing it in to take up antiques.

Antiques. Yeah.

Having washed down the Kenco-enthused lamb noisettes with a nice cup of Bisto, Jim and Audrey agreed to stay over for the night. Wanting to make sure Jim's motor held on to its wheels, I stuck it in the lock-up.

The next morning I was reversing it out for him when something caught his eye: a pocket watch. Dirty old thing it was, picked up in a house clearance sixteen years earlier, about the time Rodney started working with me.

'This is marvellous!' Jim said, studying the watch. 'I've never been so excited.'

At the time, I couldn't help thinking of poor Audrey on their honeymoon, but once he'd explained, I understood why it was such a big deal.

See, Jim was a bit of an horologist, which I'd always thought was the technical term for kerb-crawler, but actually means someone who's really into watches and clocks, and he told us all about some bloke called Harrison.

Apparently, in the old days, sailors struggled to navigate their ships. You could always tell your latitude by keeping an eye on the sun or the pole star. Figuring out your longitude though was a right bark, until this bloke Harrison came up with a watch that did it for you. He made five of these things, but there had been talk of a sixth, what he called his 'Lesser Watch' (though why he thought so little of it I couldn't tell you, I thought it was a corker myself). When he died, nobody was sure whether he'd completed work on it or not. Well, he had, and now, two hundred years later, it was knocking about in my lock-up.

Couldn't write it, could you? Well, you could, obviously, I just did. Still, what a turn-up, eh?

So Jim took it away, checked it out and threw a dollop of Brasso at it, and Rodney dug out a receipt (I'm not a fan of receipts, they clutter up the place, and being the eco-friendly bloke I am, I don't like wasting all that paper).

Then, with Jim's help, the watch was booked into an auction at Sotheby's. We had no idea how much it was gonna fetch. A few grand maybe. Whatever it made would be an absolute gift.

On the day of the auction, me and Rodney went down and stood about at the back.

Finally, the watch was wafted around in front of the punters.

'This,' said the auctioneer, 'is quite simply the most significant discovery in horological terms of this century.' He had all the patter, this boy. 'The watch has been authenticated and accepted by the leading experts as being made in 1774 by John Harrison. It is the, until now, mythical "Lesser Watch". I'd like to start the bidding at one hundred and fifty thousand pounds.'

Well, you can imagine, I came over a bit funny then. The last time I'd felt something like it I'd just finished a bowl of Mike's beef burgundy. I went for a burton right there on the carpet and Rodney had to drag me out.

After a minute or two, my head cleared and Rodney told me that, last he'd heard, the bidding had reached three hundred grand! We legged it right back in.

The bidding was still going.

'Three and a quarter,' the auctioneer said, 'the bid is in the room, three and a half...'

'Three hundred and fifty grand!' I said, feeling a bit hot under the collar again.

'Three and three quarter,' he carried on. 'Four. The bid stands at four million pounds...'

And then it was Rodney's turn to go horizontal.

The final bid was six point two million pounds.

I'll type that again if you don't mind: six point two million pounds.

Actually, I think it needs capitals: SIX POINT TWO MILLION POUNDS.

How do you make this thing do the really bold letters? Hold on...
SIX POINT TWO MILLION POUNDS.

I'd promised myself, hadn't I? I'd promised myself and told any sod who would listen.

'This time next year we'll be millionaires.'

I said it, over and over and over again, I said we'd make it. And yeah, it had taken a few more years than I'd bargained for but who's arguing when you finally manage it, eh?

Six point two million pounds.

Just over three million each for me and Rodders (he got his payday in the end, see?).

We dashed home to tell the girls.

Actually, no we didn't, we stopped at Boycie's, where Rodney bought me a Rolls-Royce. The jewel in Mum's crown, that boy, I'd always said that too.

Raquel cried, bless her. Oh all right, I had a few tears myself, do you blame me?

All the time I was waiting for something to go wrong. For the phone to ring and someone to tell us it had all been a cock-up. The phone never rang. The money arrived.

We'd done it.

Course, as exciting as it all was, and as tempting as it was to go mad, I knew we had to be sensible and not just start throwing the dosh about like we didn't have a care in the world. But then I thought *balls to that* and we went out and bought a proper house, with no lifts, and no one above us and no one beneath us... and it was massive! It had a snooker table, khazis on suite, squirrels, everything! It had a bit of a garden too for Damien to play in (two acres' worth, but he was a little devil and needed the room). Rodney and Cassandra got themselves an apartment in the city, all steel and glass and a balcony you could stand on and not get half a brick chucked at you.

We even bought Albert one of those powered yachts. True to form he drove it into a bridge and sunk it, but he enjoyed every second it spent above water level.

We had a golden few weeks. Not a care in the world. And I finally got to experience Concorde! It weren't as fast as I imagined it to be. But the first thing I did, before any of that, was order Mum a brand-new headstone. Actually it's more of an obelisk. Huge it is, and very much the Ferrari of shrines (which is exactly what I told the designer I wanted).

Anyway, after a while I began to get twitchy. See, I'd always imagined I'd make my money by scheming, wheeling and dealing and playing the game. Now that it had all fallen into my lap I felt like... well, like I'd cheated. I knew what it was, the reason I started feeling the way I did. It was the thrill of the chase, and the fact that I weren't in it any more. I'd started the firm all those years ago, determined to make it to the end of that rainbow, and now it was as though I was there inside that warm shimmering glow, and I was looking back to where I'd started. I saw Mum there, coming out of the café to give me a little cake, a big smile on her face letting me know everything was all right. I saw Grandad there, sitting in front of his tellies, digging something out of his lughole. Little Rodney was there too, whizzing around on his Jacko roller-skates... and I felt, I don't know, that it was all over. Trotters Independent Traders had ceased trading. No longer would I wake up feeling that hunger to stock up the van and hunt for a pitch. No longer would I feel like Christopher Columbo sailing out to discover the New World. I used to feel like that, even when times were tough and the chips were down, actually *especially* when times were tough and the chips were down.

But then it hit me. Becoming a millionaire didn't mean the game was over. It just meant a new game was beginning. The deals were still there to be made, only the numbers had got bigger. It had been staring me in the face all along. I could play the stock market! I could invest!

'This time next year,' I told 'em all, 'we'll be billionaires!'

CHAPTER 30

THIS TIME LAST WEEK...

When David Bowie sang 'Five Years' it was a song about how long there was until the end of the world. It weren't quite as dramatic in our case but, for the length of one, high-speed run through the streets of Monte Carlo, it certainly felt like it.

We'd been riding high for so long by then it didn't occur to any of us it would ever end.

We'd made good use of our fortune, opening the new Trotter Wing at Peckham General Hospital (lovely day that, meeting the Queen and Prince Philip, or Liz and Phil, as I'm confident they would have insisted I call 'em had that bodyguard not stuck his oar in and rugby-tackled me to the ground). We'd donated to several worthy charity cases, including Albert, who settled on the south coast where he reunited with Elsie Partridge.

A stockbroker had suggested we invest in the Central American market, and for a while we were quids in, making more money than the London Mint. Then the market crashed, and we crashed right along with it. We'd been in Monte Carlo at the time, staying with my old pal Dominic at the Hotel De Paris. Lovely bloke Dominic, ran a blinding hotel. His one failing is that he wasn't very fit. Well, he couldn't keep up with me and the family when we legged it out of the hotel doors, suitcases in hand. I'd paid for our suite on a credit card you see and that had been frozen, along with all the rest of our assets.

Luckily our flights had already been paid for so we managed to get back home safely, just in time to receive a summons to appear in the bankruptcy court. I was a big man with broad shoulders, and I was willing to accept full responsibility for everything, even though it was probably Rodney's fault. I had nothing to hide anyway, and was determined to tell the truth, once I'd worked out what it was.

All my old mates came out in support, and come the day I had Boycie, Denzil, Trigger and Sid as character witnesses. Boycie took the stand and confused everybody as to whose side he was on, Sid was more worried about defending his *own* character, Denzil cried, and Trigger stood up and told the court he heard voices in his head, which didn't help me in any way, but it was a welcome distraction from the boredom of the case.

Trotters Independent Traders was declared bankrupt. They took our homes, our cars, everything connected to the business and worth a few quid, and then they gave us a year to pay off the debt: £48,754 – plus interest!!! I thought it was a bit harsh to be honest. We'd done our best and always played fair. The cheques to the Inland Revenue had always been sent on time. Fair dos, they bounced, but at least they always bounced on time.

Mike had been through the mill 'n all, as he'd followed my investment advice and ploughed everything he had into the venture. Trouble was the fraud squad reckoned he'd also ploughed quite a bit of what he *didn't* have into it, and they did him for embezzling the brewery. It was an absolute farce! Never was a man more innocent. Course, he confessed to it all, but it was still a farce. After he went inside, Sid took over as manager of the Nag's Head, so at least the quality of service didn't change.

Luckily for us, there was one bit of property the company didn't own, a safe place we could all rest our heads: the old flat.

So it was from the high life back to the high rise. Of course, it took its toll on everyone. Raquel was looking more and more like Anne Robinson by the day, and you know enough about Rodney by now to know he didn't take it well.

'Don't worry,' I told him. 'This time next year we'll be millionaires.'

'This time last *week* we were millionaires!' he said. Actually it was more of a scream.

Naturally, we were all worried that if we couldn't pay the debt we'd lose the flat and end up homeless.

'They'll never take the flat,' Rodney said.

'Why?' I said, feeling the tiniest glimmer of hope. 'Have you got an idea then?'

'No,' he said, 'I just mean it's been on the market for five years and nobody's even looked at it.' Dipstick!

A year to raise the best part of fifty grand and make Trotters Independent Traders rise again, like Felix from the flames. It was do-able. You know me, I love a challenge. But being a bankrupt, I was no longer allowed to run a company. Luckily Rodney had a brilliant idea (well, he did once I'd given it to him). He would take over as managing director of the company, with me stepping back into a smaller role, handling sales, purchasing and stock.

He loved the idea of being his own boss and immediately whacked an advert in the small ads of the *Peckham Echo*, offering our services to prospective customers. In no time at all we received our first call – from the Sultan of Brunei. Rodney, being a total moby, couldn't believe his luck, right up till 'the Sultan' asked for advice on 'how to start a crappy three-wheeled van on cold winter mornings'. It was Mickey bleedin' Pearce on the wind-up.

Then, just as we thought we'd seen the worst of it, we got a call from Elsie Partridge's son telling us that Uncle Albert had passed away.

He'd been happy down by the coast. Elsie had been in a care home for the last six months, but he'd seen her every day and her family had taken him in as one of their own. I'd felt guilty sometimes about all the travelling we'd done without him, but he hadn't minded. Anyway, it turned out that Albert Trotter, the globetrotting man of the sea, had never actually had a passport!

We went down to pay our last respects. Everyone from the manor was there and Elsie's son threw a good wake. The highlight was the twenty-one-gun salute. They used a shotgun, so there were a few burst eardrums (and Denzil took a pellet in the shoulder), but it was still bloody good!

In between trying to do a bit of business and avoiding Rodney and Cassandra as they indulged in a spot of sexual fancy-dress (you'd wanna avoid it too if you'd seen 'em!), I came up with a way of solving all our money worries in one night: I'd become a contestant on the TV quiz show *Goldrush*.

Some of you may remember the episode (I hear some of my bits are popular on YouTube). I've got mixed feelings about it. Obviously it was nice to meet Jonathan Ross (or J.R. as he insisted I call him). I pulled him to one side before we started filming and we got on like a house on fire. I regret not keeping in touch but the phone number he gave me turned out to have been for a hairdressers in Bromley. I've tried a few different combinations since 'cos I wanted him to do a foreword for the book (Alec Sugar was busy).

Once we were on air though, things started to go downhill. It was hard to think under the lights. I managed to get myself on the Rainbow Road which is where you get asked a series of questions with the prize money going up for each one you get right. I'd got as far as £25,000 when Jonathan asked:

'Which classical guitarist wrote the opera *The Child and the Enchantments*? Ravel, Segovia or Rodrigo?'

The only classical guitarist that came to mind was Brian May. Luckily I was able to use my 'S.O.S.', which meant I could phone up a mate for advice. I chose Rodney 'cos he loves a bit of classical and, after a tricky start where he told Jonathan to piss off (he thought it was Mickey Pearce), he told me to go for Ravel. Which surprised me 'cos I only knew them for making shoes.

I lost the £25,000 I'd already won and ended up leaving with a pound.

Obviously, at the time I was gutted, but I got a call later from the production office saying they'd made a mistake. Ravel *had* been the right answer and they offered to give me the fifty grand and let me come back on the show.

Thinking Mickey Pearce was trying to pull a fast one again, I told them to give the money to charity. It was only much later when I discovered it really had been the production office and that I'd nixed the chance of paying off my debts. Still, at least someone benefited from it.

For a while it seemed things couldn't get any worse. Uncle Albert had left us, we were in hock, Rodney was 'running' the firm, and as a final kick in the teeth, I resorted to working two days a week as Boycie's driver. What else could I do? We needed every penny we could get. Just to add salt to the wound, Boycie was eyeing up a deal with a Lebanese businessman that would see him earn a fortune to go with the fortune he already had. And Boycie being Boycie, he couldn't resist rubbing it in, ordering me about, getting me to clean his car and make the tea. Still, I squirted a load of onion puree into his hair gel and he went about smelling like a Big Mac for a month or two, so that evened things up a bit.

Then, finally, some good news: Cassandra was pregnant again.

I'd all but given up on Rodney in that department. He and Cassandra had started trying again a while back, doing the rounds at the fertility clinics when nothing was happening. You should've seen it round the flat; you couldn't get a bottle of milk in the fridge for all the samples Rodney had to store. I felt for him. They'd been at it like a pair of goats. Rodney became so pale he had to have his passport photo redone. I remember him saying that if it hadn't been for the free magazines he'd have packed it in a lot earlier.

Anyway, they then announced they were giving up on the idea. So, the news that Cassandra was up the duff came as a shock to us all.

'We changed our minds,' Rodney said. 'We decided to have this baby as a token of belief in our marriage, of Trotters Independent Traders, of the future of Britain, and most importantly of all, of our belief in this family.'

I'll admit I choked up a bit. 'If your dear mother could hear you now,' I said, 'she'd be so proud of you.'

He later admitted that it was also due to their belief that Damien wouldn't dream of hiding Cassandra's contraceptive pills, but there's no denying it was a good speech.

A letter arrived from The Seamen's Association. Naturally, I thought it was for Rodney, but it turned out to be for Uncle Albert. It was an invitation to attend a naval reunion in a little village in Normandy, France. Rodney and I decided it was only right that we should attend on his behalf. Raquel suspected we were just going so we could pick up a load of cheap booze at Calais. I don't know, you would've thought she knew me well enough by then to know better than that. Granted, we did stop off at the hypermarket, and it just so happened that Denzil showed up with his new van, but all we were after was a bit of cheese and a football shirt for Damien.

Representing Albert alongside the rest of his crew (which turned out to be a bloke called George Parker) was not only a duty, it was an honour. We took his ashes and scattered 'em at sea. He would've liked that.

⁕

The deadline for paying off the debt was looming ever closer. No matter what I tried I kept hitting a brick wall. I weren't the only one trying though.

Rodney was trying to push us into 'consultancy and party planning', which, as I told him, might have been all well and good up Sloane Square where people liked a bit of roasted pepper and a bucket of couscous, but round our way they were more of a kebab and tattoo crowd. Raquel suggested we should try feng shui, see if that brought us some good luck, but for the life of me I couldn't see how eating raw fish was gonna get us anywhere. Even Trigger was trying to help by inventing a brand-new state of the art backscratcher made out of chopsticks. Still, we weren't the only ones suffering at the time. Poor old Denzil had been under a lot of strain with his health. Actually, the doctor reckoned it was the straining that was the problem. He didn't 'alf make a fuss though. The way he went on you'd have thought he'd just been given two months to live, all he had was a touch of haemorrhoids.

'Haemorrhoids!' he said. 'They're more like bleedin' asteroids!'

Course, we all took the Michael a bit, and I told him to stop being a tart, but then again I've been fortunate enough never to have suffered with anything like that. I like my roughage too much. And give him his due, as piles go they were pretty bad by all accounts. Anyway, I don't want to embarrass a mate so I won't say any more.

The next nail in the coffin arrived when we got a letter from the official receiver. The flat was going up for auction. We had four weeks to come up with fifty grand! And that was when I went down the cemetery to see Mum. I gave the obelisk a spruce-up, collected the spent hypodermics and cans of Special Brew and told Mum all about our troubles. She'd come through for us in the past when the going got rough, so it was worth a shot. The truth is I was desperate. I was so uptight by then, Nigel Kennedy could have played a symphony on me.

Rodney brought out the big guns too, investing in a mail order creative writing course, and trying to knock out a screenplay. I felt like knocking *him* out when he first told me, but then at least he was trying. And there's a lot of money can be made in writing and coming up with stories. Look at that J.F.K Rowling bird, the one who wrote those books about the little posh git in the John Lennon glasses. Made an absolute fortune! Then there was that bloke who wrote about Hannibal the cannonball. I bet he weren't short of a few bob. As you know, Rodney had struggled a bit in this area in the past, so, warming to the idea, I decided to help him. And we came up with a belter of a synopcyst. It was like *Jurassic Park* meets *My Left Foot*, you know, an action-packed adventure but deep and moving at the same time. It was all about this team of scientists (led by Mel Gibson) who fly out to investigate some strange happenings on an uninhabited island, only to discover a forgotten tribe of killer cavemen. We called it *The Island of Death.** I wanted us to form our own film company: 'Trotter Brothers'. You already had Warner Brothers, and they were a huge

---

* Reading that back now, I realise it had a few snags, but we were pissed out of our heads at the time.

success. Rodney didn't reckon the name though, saying it sounded more like a scrap-metal yard than a film company.

Then, as if he didn't have enough on his plate, Sid, who'd been having a bit of a spring clean behind the bar, showed Rodney a photograph of the very first Jolly Boys Outing. All the old boys were in it, me, Boycie, Trigger, Denzil, Grandad, and one more face that stopped Rodney in his tracks: Freddie 'The Frog' Robdal. It was like he was looking at himself.

We'd wondered why Freddie had taken such an interest in our welfare, leaving all his money to Mum all those years ago. Now we knew. Rodney was his son. Course, Rodney had had his suspicions. I had too. I mean, when you reach your early twenties and your six-year-old brother is taller than you, you can't help but feel something's a bit off. But it was Uncle Albert who confirmed it for me one night when he'd had a few too many rums. Well, I couldn't tell Rodney, could I? It would have broken his heart. So that was it. I knew he knew, and he knew I knew. But we didn't talk about it. We'd have to at some point, but by then we only had a week to get ourselves out of the red and save the flat. We needed a miracle.

And we got one.

It weren't Mum this time, it was Uncle Albert.

A solicitor wanted to talk to us, so me and Rodney went down to his office and I gave it to him straight: 'Tell us how much you're suing us for, and I'll tell you why we can't pay.'

'I think you're labouring under a misapprehension,' he said. 'I wanted to talk to you as the executor of your uncle Albert Trotter's estate.'

Turns out that Albert hadn't spent all the money we gave him when we'd sold the watch, and he left me and Rodney £145,000 – each!!!

Good old boomerang Trotter. I still miss you now, you old sod, war stories 'n all.

❧

If there's one thing I've learned in life, it's never to chuck in the towel, 'cos you really don't know what's coming round the next bend, and if you can hold on long enough, you might just find it's something good. It's amazing how quickly fortunes can change, sometimes for the worse, sometimes for the better. And immediately after Uncle Albert had swooped in to save the day, Cassandra went into labour and gave birth to a healthy, beautiful baby girl. I remember seeing the look on Rodney's face when he first met his daughter, Joan, and at that moment, I understood. You can slow a Trotter down. You can knock a Trotter down. But you can't keep a Trotter down. 'Cos we're dreamers you see, and dreams, the best ones at least, never truly die.

CHAPTER 31

I KNEW IT MADE SENSE

Rodney was determined to play it safe. The way he looked at it, he'd been given a second chance to get back on his feet and give baby Joan a secure future. I told him and Cassandra they could stay on at the flat for as long as they liked, but within the week they'd found a new place and were moving their gear out. Nice drum it is too, two bedrooms, a stone's throw from their old flat and an even shorter throw from the pub. It's on the ground floor too so no more being ogled by passengers in passing planes either. Cassandra even managed to get a job back at her old bank, so they had at least one regular income.

Raquel and I discussed the matter and decided it was best to play it safe too, so after the debt was paid I put a chunk away for a rainy day and ploughed the rest into a shipment of state of the art Hungarian-made satnavs that Monkey Harris had got his hands on. They were quality machines that used only the best statelites to tell you exactly where you were anywhere in the world, and put you on route to anywhere else you fancied going at just a touch of a few buttons. And just as the feeling in my gut was telling me, they ended up selling like rock at the seaside. Well, people knew quality when they saw it, and at a tenner a pop, only a twonk of the highest order would've said no. Like Rodney for example. Right from the off he wanted nothing to do with them, and, fair dos, it turned out he may have had a point, but still, you'd have thought he'd have learned by now not to interfere with my gut when it's talking to me. The problem, and I swear I only discovered this *after* I'd sold them, was that they gave directions in every sodding language *but* sodding English! It was an honest mistake. I'd checked them before doing the deal, but all the user manuals were in foreign, so I weren't to know, was I? It weren't all bad though, as I tried to explain to Rodney. I mean, for the technologically savvy motorist well versed in Eastern European lingo and wanting to find the quickest route from London to Budapest, they were a dream come true.

It was around about this time that Raquel and I decided to spend a couple of weeks down on the Hampshire coast in Uncle Albert's caravan. He'd treated himself and Elsie to it after his windfall, and we had a sort of timeshare deal going with Elsie's son and his wife. They were trying to talk me into flogging it and splitting the profits, but I couldn't. It was our last connection to the old boy, and it just didn't seem right. Plus it came in handy when things got on top and I had to keep my head down for a bit. And while it weren't the most luxurious of mobile homes, it was a step up from the shed on Grandad's allotment. We left Damien behind to stay at Rodney's. Course, he moaned about being put out what with the baby and there not being enough room, but as I said to him, there are worse things in life than having to go and stay at your uncle and aunt's for a few days, so be a good a lad and shut up about it.

Having the time off school weren't a problem either, as he'd only recently got himself into a spot of bother with the board of governors. See, the school's lunch menu had come down with a sudden dose of the Jamie Olivers, and Damien, spotting an opportunity to earn a few quid in his lunch break, started flogging his own kebabs round the back of the science block. Someone grassed, and Raquel and I were called in to talk with the headmaster. Personally, I couldn't see what the big deal was. I mean, what right-minded teenager would choose a jacket spud and a dollop of crème fresh over a bit of good old-fashioned sheep in a bap? The headmaster copped a deaf'un and started going on about obesity academics and diabetes, before giving Damien a two-week suspension.

<hr />

Rodney seemed to be on top of the world for a while, what with being a dad, having his own place, and being the managing director of his own company. But when him and Cassandra told us all about some new, life-changing fad they'd gotten into, I knew he was already starting to get twitchy. It was called 'The Law of Attraction'. Apparently, the idea was that the more a person pushed positive thoughts out into the universe, the more they'd be rewarded. For example, if you concentrated really hard and positively, and often enough, on becoming a millionaire, you'd end up being one. Now, I'm no scientist, as you know, but since the very exact same thing had happened to me, I thought there might be something to it. Fair enough, it had taken my concentrating for the best part of forty years for it to finally happen, and I can't remember ever concentrating on making it go belly-up, but like I said, I ain't a scientist, so what do I know?

Anyway, they lent us a book and a couple of DVDs to help fill us in on the finer details of how it all worked, and I got Damien to get on the old Google and do a bit of research, and I must say I was positively blown away by just how big the whole thing was. So, when Rodney and Cassandra invited us to join them at one of their 'Positive Self-Visualisation' classes, Raquel and I jumped at the chance. There I'd been thinking this sort of thing was a load of old guff that only complete and utter dipsticks were taken in by, but it really opened my eyes. I'd visualised myself plenty of times in the past doing really positive things (scoring the World Cup winner against the Argies, owning my own private jet, saving a school bus from plummeting off the side of a bridge after an earthquake has left it teetering on the edge, that sort of thing), but it turns out I just weren't doing it positively enough. But thanks to the classes (actually, I only went to one) I discovered the well of positivity buried deep within, and, more importantly, a way to spread it to the rest of the world. And that was how the Trotters Transcendental Training programme came to be.

To be honest, I never thought it would catch on, but I concentrated so hard on it that it did, and we had a very successful twelve months. I got Mickey Pearce to help me knock up a DVD and it took the mail order world by storm. And thanks to Damien and his Internet I was able to spread the light to places I'd never even heard of before, like Abergavenny and Fiji (which must be where the cameras are made). One night Damien even set up a web-conference, you know, so I could see my followers and they could see me while I lectured 'em on how they should be visualising more positively. It was going all right for a minute or two and then some mush in Dubai did something really 'orrible all over his webcam, which left me no choice but to immediately cancel the conference and go and rinse my eyeballs out in a bucket of Optrex. Things went even more wrong when a week later a follower in the Philippines visualised himself getting a gun and walking into his local branch of Bank West Pacific and emptying their vaults. That was the problem, I couldn't help but be judged on the quality of my followers. And I reckon Rodney had something to do with it too, he was leaking negativity all over the place by that point. So, after ten minutes of visualising myself getting as far away from the whole thing as I possibly could, it happened. Course, I didn't want my followers thinking I'd gone back on my word and badmouthing me on Twitter, so I made out I'd died of a positivity overdose and handed the enterprise over to a worthy successor, a man who had taken the light into his heart like no other and who had adapted his entire life to the cause. And I'm pretty sure Trigger is still running it to this day. Course, the disciplehood has dwindled a bit over the years, but they both seem to enjoy themselves, so good on 'em, I say.

As much as you might think that dabble in the self-improvement game would have put me off, it didn't, and just a couple of months later I had another crack at it. Cassandra had been struggling to get rid of her gut after the pregnancy so she joined Weight Watchers, and it got me thinking (as so many things do), and I came to a realisation (as I so often do when I think). I'd always loved my grub and helping people, so what if I combined the two. What an opportunity! And I didn't mean it as in an opportunity to make some dosh (although that never hurts), I meant it as in an opportunity to help my fellow man and woman. Well, the chubby ones. And that's when I invented my very own diet: Trotter-Trim. It was, and still is, a groundbreaking combination of science, nutrition and basic common sense. The real beauty of Trotter-Trim, and what made it so appealing, is that no foods are off bounds. Right. You can eat *whatever* you want, *whenever* you want it – if you wake up in the middle of the night fancying a plate of chicken tikka masala and chips, you can *have* a plate of chicken tikka masala and chips, and still be guaranteed to shed the pounds. Course, I got Rodney to include a small-print clause warning very clearly that the diet might not actually work, but that weren't to say I didn't believe in it 110%. We spread the word about, plastered the town hall with fliers, and even took out an ad in the *Peckham Echo*. Trigger, of all people, tried to warn us off. 'You shouldn't mess around with what you put in your body,' he said, 'look what happened to Michael Jackson.' As is usually the case when Trig opens his mouth, I had to ask for a bit of clarification. 'Well, his face turned white, didn't it?' he said. 'So what d'you reckon happened, Trig?' I asked. 'Did he cop a genetically modified gherkin with his cod 'n chips and suddenly turn into Casper the friendly ghost?' But that's Trigger for you. He always has had a tendency to speak his mind, which of course has always limited the conversation somewhat. To be fair though, he is a lot smarter than he looks.

Anyway, the day we let Trotter-Trim loose on the masses, I could hardly contain my excitement. I could see myself becoming the next Jenny Craig. I was even considering launching my own ready-meal range. But as much as it did catch on, the results were too mixed to call it an outright success. What really naused it though was an old mate of mine, Teddy Cummings. See, Teddy's daughter, Kylie, who lives over in Robert Mugabe Crescent, did a bit of glamour modelling, and she had a big photoshoot coming up and was desperate to lose ten pounds in two months. I told Teddy all about Trotter-Trim, and said that if she stuck to it she'd lose the weight no worries. She didn't. She put on two and a half stone and ended up in hospital with her jaw wired shut. Teddy weren't best pleased, naturally. Things would have been fine, but he went and grassed me to the council and I ended up getting a visit from Lisa 'the Geezer', the mayor. I didn't mind Lisa. Big old girl she was. Only woman I've known who had a cleavage on her back. She was one of them feminist types, so you had to watch your 'p's and 'q's (and 'f's and 'b's and 's's and 't's and a few other letters too) around her. We had an understanding though. I explained to her that I must be the most anti-sexist bloke there is and that she'd always be a bloke in my eyes. I think she appreciated it. I didn't want to push it though, so, as with so many of my ideas, Trotter-Trim went the way of the emu.

<hr>

Despite the combined efforts of me, Raquel and Rodney in helping Damien with his GCSE studies (and getting him to school in the first place), he failed the bleedin' lot. I'd been hoping he'd get at least three and be a slight improvement on Rodney, but it weren't to be. It was hard to be angry with him though. To tell the truth I'd known for a while that his interests laid elsewhere, just like his old man's had before him. 'He's just like me,' I told Raquel, trying to make her see it weren't the end of the world, although the way she looked at me then you'd have thought that's exactly what I'd told her it was.

The time had come for Rodney and I to have a serious chat about the future of Trotters Independent Traders. 'Oh leave it out, Del,' he said, 'I've been in a really good mood today.' He could tell by the tone of my face that what I had to say was important.

'I ain't getting any younger, bruv,' I explained, 'and the time has come for me to step back a bit and hand over some of the responsibilities.' He obviously weren't expecting it, but he understood.

'If you're sure, Del,' he said. 'I mean, I have had quite a few ideas over the last few months on the direction the company could be taking—'

'I know, bruv,' I said, already sensing that he was becoming overcome by the emotion of such a momentous occasion, 'which is why I think it's time Damien became a fully fledged partner in the firm.' I was touched by how deeply affected he was by this. He cried. And as I went on to explain what Damien could bring to the business, he even swore a few times, he was that excited! I asked him to stay while

I broke the news to Damien, but he said he needed a drink and went down the pub. Well, it was only natural that he wanted to celebrate. Cassandra called the following afternoon in a panic 'cos he hadn't been home all night, so it must have been some celebration.

Course, Damien took to his new position like a squirrel to nuts, and it was a joy for Raquel and I to see what a good team him and his Uncle Rodney made. Damien didn't hold back either. Eager to make his mum and dad proud, he thrust himself in headfirst and by the end of his second day had even taken the lead, with Rodney carrying the suitcase and putting in the order for the bacon sandwiches. It was amazing to see the 'can-do' spirit it reawakened in Rodney, watching him hunched over, wiping the sweat from his brow, before picking up the suitcase and lugging it up the next flight of stairs (the lifts are still knackered). It was almost like watching the good old days, just with Damien in my place. It weren't all hard work though, and Damien would have us all in fits by chucking in the occasional 'Come on, old'un, get a bloody move on!' Rodney would play along, grinding his teeth and shouting things that I couldn't possibly put in print. Bless him.

CHAPTER 32

20,000 CENTIMETRES
UNDER THE SEA

As wonderful and fulfilling as being a renowned and respected guru/
dietician had been, a part of me was still pining for the thing I'd
always been best at, my *raisin fruit de mere*: buying and selling. And so
for a while I joined Damien and Rodney down the market. With the
extra pair of hands we were able to approach things differently than
we had in the past, and we adopted a sort of pincer movement with
Damien and Rodney pitching up at one end of the market and me at
the other. We'd have bets on who would do the most business in an
afternoon, and while I won most (I was stepping back, I weren't losing
my touch), Damien pipped me to the post a couple of times. Being
managing director, Rodney decided to let us lead while he focused on
loading and unloading the van, fetching the refreshments, keeping a
general watch over things, and having the odd kip.

To celebrate I arranged for us all to spend a few days down in
Uncle Albert's caravan, take in some sea air, maybe even stretch
our legs and see if we couldn't do a bit in the New Forest. It was a
squeeze but little Joan was fine on the camp bed next to Rodney and

Cassandra, and with a spot of contortion and a bit of force, Damien managed to make do with the sofa. Once you've lived in our flat, tight spaces don't bother you (remember that magician, the mopey git who spent a few weeks locked in a box hanging over the South Bank while all the people down below threw sausage rolls at him? Well, he originally planned to perform the feat in Rodney's old bedroom, but his medical team said it was too cramped). On our second morning there, I told Rodney and Damien that I had a surprise for 'em and we jumped in the Capri and headed up the coastline. I pulled over alongside the stretch of coast I was after and we got out. They were confused and moaning about the nip in the air, but I told them not to worry 'cos I had something in the boot of the car that would soon get the old blood racing again. Remember years back Raquel had been going on at me to clear all that old 'junk' out of the flat and we'd moved it down to Grandad's allotment? Remember I mentioned an antique deep-sea diving suit? Well, I'd forgotten all about it, but I was down the allotment one day (I try to make checks every now and then just to make sure nobody's using it as a rubbish tip), going through the shed, and there it was, in all its fishbowl-helmeted glory. The strange thing was that the more I looked at it, the more it seemed to be calling to me. It was as if I could almost hear it whispering, *'Use me, Del... use me.'* At the time I put it down to the fumes coming from a box of old paint that had leaked on the floor and, thinking nothing more of it, I locked up and went home. But over the next few days I started thinking about Freddie the Frog and the legacy he'd left Mum. Rodney hadn't talked about him much but I knew he still thought about him. Only natural. But then, just on the off chance, I bumped into this bloke down the pub who was talking about those people what track sunken treasure. He'd seen a documentary on the Discovery Channel all about it. Apparently, they plotted out the tides, did a bit of maths based on the weight of the object, and Bob's your uncle, they could narrow down the search to within spitting distance. I popped back down to the shed and had another look at that suit, and sure enough it started calling to me again, but the voice was louder this time. *'Use me, Del,'* it said, *'use me to get the gold…'*

But I can't even swim, I thought.

'Use Damien then,' the voice said.

But he can't swim either, I thought

'Get Rodney to do it then!' the voice shouted. Well, it was almost like I was being given a sign or something. I put it down to the paint fumes again, and I was about to lock up and go when it hit me: what if I got Rodney to put the suit on and go down and have a look for the gold? Course, I ain't daft, I knew the odds of finding it were slim, but with a few calculations and the right precautions, it couldn't hurt to at least give it a go, could it? Plus I knew Rodney would relish the challenge.

'What the bloody hell is that?' he said when he saw me dragging the suit out of the boot.

'It's a ham sandwich, Rodders,' I said, 'what d'you think it is?'

He looked out to sea, then at the suit, then at me.

'No, Derek!' he barked, and went and got back in the car.

'What do you mean "no"?' I asked him.

'I ain't doing it!'

'I haven't asked you to do anything, have I?'

'No, but you're going to,' he said, 'I know you.'

'Rodney,' I said, 'please be more pacific, 'cos you've lost me here.'

He just clammed up then.

'Don't look at me,' Damien said, 'I ain't putting that thing on, I dunno where it's been.'

'It's been in your great-grandad's shed.'

'That explains the eggy smell then,' he said.

I explained to Rodney about the treasure hunters I'd heard about and how accurate they could be with their calculations.

'And you did all those calculations, did you?'

'Not personally, no,' I admitted. 'I wouldn't mess about with something so important. I delegated the job to an expert at the Greenwich Maritime Museum.'

'You spoke to the Greenwich Maritime Museum?'

'Yeah. I'd popped in to take a butcher's at our old watch and got chatting with one of the top bods there. He was only too happy to help,'cos it was an interesting problem.* I didn't tell him exactly what we was hunting for,' I admitted, 'but we know where the coffin was dropped and I could figure out the weight and the size easy enough so he had all he needed. He narrowed it down to a two-hundred-yard radius, give or take, and it's there.' I pointed out to sea.

'Two hundred yards?'

'I know Rodders, brilliant, eh? So now all we need to do is pop down there and get it.'

'Why is it that whenever you say "we" what you really mean is *me*?' he said.

'I'd do it myself, Rodney, but I can't swim, and neither can Damien,' I told him. 'And I can't ask Raquel to do it, can I?'

'But even if I did go down, which I won't, there's no way I'll find it. What do you expect me to do? Just keep wandering around down there until I stub my toe on it?'

'Course not,' I said, 'I've given it a bit more thought than that! Wait there and I'll fetch the rest of the kit.' I came back with the

---

* This was true,'cos my mate, Kelvin, had had a nightmare of a cleaning shift after a schoolkid upchucked over an old propeller. A couple of drinks, a score in his pocket and the chance to get his teeth into something interesting had improved his mood no end.

wetsuit, the oxygen cylinders, the satnav, a length of rope and the *peace de resistence*, the underwater metal detector!

'It looks like a normal metal detector in a plastic bag,' he said.

'Which,' I admitted, 'is exactly what it is. But I watched a YouTube video all about it and you should be fine. All you've gotta do is wave it around, keep your eye on the little blinking light thing and, when it goes red, Bob's your uncle, next stop Fort Knox.'

'Oh this is bloody stupid—'

'Rodney,' I said, 'I wish you had as much faith in yourself as I have in you. You can do it, Rodders, you can.' I turned to Damien. 'You believe in your uncle, don't you, Damien?'

'No, I think he's right, it is bloody stupid.'

'You see, Rodney?' I said. 'We're all right here behind you, and we'd never let anything happen to you. Besides, what's the worst that can happen? If you don't find nothing you've been for a bit of a dip, but if you do find something – we're rich!'

I could see him starting to wane.

'You won't let anything happen to me?'

'Course not,' I said, holding up the rope. 'You'll be attached to this, if you get in any difficulty just give it a yank and we'll pull you straight back up.'

It was a very proud moment walking down to the motor dinghy. Rodney had opted for the wetsuit, it was a bit tight, and he fell over a couple of times, not used to walking in flippers, but apart from that he looked the dog's Jacob's. And as the three of us set sail for the spot I'd calculated, he said nothing, just mumbled to himself under his breath. We were like the three geezers in *Jaws* going out to kill Jaws, except we weren't killing Jaws, we were going out to find a coffin full of gold.

'This'll do, Damien,' I said, checking the map one last time. He cut the engine and we floated there for a few minutes while we tied the rope securely round Rodney's waist.

'Now just take it easy,' I told him, 'I'm not asking you to swim to France, all you've got to do is… well, sink. But do it at your own pace, and remember, pull on the rope the first sign of trouble.' He nodded.

'You know it makes sense,' I said, patting him on his cylinders. And with that Damien and I hoisted him over to the edge of the dinghy and he flopped over and under.

'I don't like this, Dad,' Damien said.

'Don't worry, son,' I told him. 'You don't know your uncle like I do. He can perform miracles when he sets his mind to it. Just make sure you hold on to that rope.'

Course, before I even finished the sentence there was a tug on the rope. Then another. And within a few seconds it was thrashing about all over the place. Bloody hell, he must've only gone down ten feet! Damien pulled the rope, but was struggling to get leverage so I helped him, and together we pulled till we were sweating and panting. But if we were panicking then, we were hyperventilating when a couple of minutes later the other end of the rope came shooting out of the water – minus Rodney.

'Do they have sharks out here, Dad?' Damien asked.

'*Champs-Elysées!*' was all I could manage. We hung on, and I shouted down to Rodney, wherever he was, to keep calm and not forget to visualise. But as distressing as it was, I also felt a quiet confidence that things would turn out fine, 'cos I meant what I'd said to Damien about Rodney performing miracles. He hid it well, but he'd always been full of determination. And after all, he was a good swimmer, and he had all the kit with him. I told the coastguard just that when we called them a few hours later. They seemed angrier than you'd expect about the whole thing. The rollicking I got from one of 'em left me with bruises. It didn't help that I was also getting an earful from the girls back at the caravan. Luckily, what with the noise of the helicopters and the speedboat engines outside I couldn't hear half of what Cassandra was calling me.

Rodney was eventually fished out a little further down the coast. Apparently things hadn't been going too badly, then, on reaching a depth of about five feet, he'd looked down, mistaken the rope we'd tied round his waist for a giant octopus leg, and it came undone in his struggle to break free. Luckily, his oxygen had lasted, and beyond being a bit shrivelled and suffering a minor case of the bends, he was fine.

'Look on the bright side,' I said, as we drove back home, 'all a bit of an adventure, weren't it? There's people that pay good money for that sort of extreme holiday experience.'

We nearly had another one then as the dipstick attempted to strangle me while I was driving. I deserved it, but he could have at least let me stop the car first. It's lucky for all of us that I'm such a skilled driver.

CHAPTER 33

LONG LIVE THE KING

Back in London, things soon got back to normal for a while, then Boycie, Marlene and Tyler vanished off the face of the earth. Trigger, who'd always been soppy for an *X-Files* video, reckoned it was a classic case of alien abduction, but I weren't sure. I mean, alien or not, one look at Marlene when she wakes up in the morning is enough to make anybody run a mile.* I was more concerned that the satnav I'd flogged Boycie had taken them on a scenic route off a cliff.

But then a nasty rumour went round that Boycie had had to do a bunk 'cos the Driscoll brothers had got it into their heads that he'd turned informer and had played a big hand in securing their most recent stretch. Now, as you know, I've known Boycie pretty much all my life, I grew up with him, did business with him, I was best man at his wedding, and I can say without a shadow of a doubt that this rumour had a definite ring of truth to it. Course, I knew Danny and Tony would come knocking. They'd already paid a visit to Denzil and Trigger. Sure enough the knock came. Fortunately I had Rodney with me for back up if things got out of hand (I say 'with me', he was

---

* Their milkman told me.

actually hiding in the airing cupboard. I found him in there an hour or so after Danny and Tony had left, wedged between the wall and the immersion heater). They asked me where Boycie was and I told them I hadn't a clue, which was the truth. And they accepted it. I knew then they were slowing down, and, unless they were just saving it all for Boycie, they'd lost that psychopathic edge that had made them so deadly.

So it didn't come as too much of a surprise when they themselves then vanished. Word spread that they'd tried to put one over on a Russian connection. The Russian connection, not taking too kindly to this, decided to settle the matter with the aid of a Kalashnikov, and ever since Danny and Tony Driscoll have been spending their hard-earned days of retirement somewhere at the bottom of the Solent. For all that they believed they were 'respected', I can't think of a single person who shed a tear at the news of their demise. On the other hand, I can think of quite a few people who shed quite a few tears when a couple of months later the prodigal tight-arse himself turned up back on the manor. Apparently the Boyces had been living in Shropshire – on a farm! It had obviously gone to his head, he was all done up like a ploughman's lunch. Still, it was good to see him and know they were all all right.

What with the recession, Trotters Independent Traders got a bit of a shot in the arm as people started shopping round looking for quality goods at knock-down prices. Damien managed to get his hands on a consignment of flat-screen TVs from a Lithuanian contact who'd been earning a living on the front line of the home entertainment industry for years (he was a clown at children's parties). We could barely keep up supply, they were flying out of our hands. And on the subject of telly, the Trotters once again made an appearance on the small screen. Well, *nearly*. Rodney and I signed up for that

Dragon's Den. Well, they give out cash for any old cobblers, and I had no doubt that I could present a business plan that would knock 'em bandy. But I had such a huge back catalogue of brilliant ideas by this point, it was difficult to know which one to go with. I'd initially thought of presenting the panel with the Trotter Groom Master. The busy man's one-stop gadget for looking his best, it was a handy, brick-sized, automated device for dispensing the various grooming products your hard-working bloke needs, all at the click of a button. Having knocked up a couple of prototypes I gave one to Denzil as a birthday present, and he'd loved it, right up till it squirted half a bottle of Brut into his eyes while he'd been plucking his nostrils. Realising it needed a bit more work, I decided to play it safe and dug out the old Trotters Crash Turban. Sadly the dragons weren't impressed, despite Rodney modelling the prototype in a series of potentially hazardous test situations we'd rigged up in the studio. I'd known in my guts that it hadn't gone down well, but that said, some of their comments were bang out of order. I deeply regret what happened, but it was a complete accident. As I explained to the police, the punch I'd thrown was intended for Duncan Valentine, but I tripped on one of the sandbags we'd been using to test the crash turban's resilience to sudden impact, and Deborah Meaden just happened to get in the way. The interview wasn't broadcast, which was no great surprise. I was just glad that I was able to patch things up with Meaden without the need to go to court. Thank God I had that box of top-end lingerie in the back of the van.*

It was shortly after that abortive strike for fame that I ended up becoming mates with David Beckham (I say mates, a real mate would have given you a quote for the cover of his book. You'd think he'd have

---

* I was also quite proud to see her wearing some of it during her later appearance on *Strictly Come Dancing*.

had a spare five minutes now he's jacked in the footy). It was one of those typical bits of business good luck. Becks was after a bouncy castle for his son's birthday bash and had been let down something chronic at the last minute. A mate of mine was working on the catering team and gave me a bell. It was a frantic twenty minutes on the phone but I managed to get hold of one and the deal was struck. Becks was over the moon (apparently his missus loves a bouncy castle and had given him a right earful when it looked like he'd drawn a blank). To show his appreciation he invited me and the family along to the do, which pleased Raquel and Cassandra and put me firmly in the good books for a bit. We nearly had an embarrassing moment when Damien was caught behind the ghost train with one of the girls out of Little Mix, but he made himself scarce sharpish and nobody made a big deal out of it. As usual, Rodney was a bit on edge, but after a few Bacardi Breezers he loosened up a bit and got chatting with Elton John, telling him all about his Bunch of Wallies days. Never one to miss an opportunity, and remembering that we still had a few of those men's syrups knocking about, I offered Elton his pick, you know, just in case the transplant started playing up. He passed on the offer but I gave him my card, and if you're reading this, Elt, I'm still here if you need me.

❧

This year I hit seventy and I decided that maybe, just maybe, it was time to retire. Not 'cos I can't do it any more, I'll never be too old to buy and sell, but 'cos, well, I've had a decent innings, and it's time for Damien to step up to bat. The truth is you really start to feel it when you hit seventy. All the little twinges suddenly don't feel so little any more, the occasional afternoon catnaps turn into deep, five-hour-long oblivions and, I never thought I'd say it, but even Hobnobs take on new appeal. It's not just me though. Trigger finally hung up his broom, and when he's not watching *The X-Files* or managing the Trotters Transcendental Training programme, you'll often find him in the Nag's Head or chatting with the pigeons in the park. The last time I spoke to Boycie he was considering getting a nip 'n tuck. I told him he might as well go the full hog and have his whole face done, and he took it on board. God knows what they'll do with the moustache, give it back to him after they've finished so he can frame it, I s'pose. And that's not to mention Denzil. Yeah, I'm sorry to say the asteroids returned, with a vengeance. The poor old sod was hobbling around like he had rickets, a permanent grimace on his face. I don't know if I'd read it somewhere or if Damien had told me, but apparently fluoride is good for reducing swelling. I mentioned this to Denzil, you know, just in passing, and the next thing I knew I got a phone call at one o'clock in the bleedin' morning. It was all sobs and wails and the word 'why' repeated over and over. Course, no phone call at one o'clock in the morning is going to be good, but this one nearly gave me a connery! Turns out it was Denzil. He'd taken my fluoride tip to heart and, in a fit of desperation, had coated the asteroids with an entire tube of Oral-B Pro-Expert. Well, when I'd said fluoride was good for reducing swelling, I was talking about pimples. I didn't know he was gonna go and do something like that, did I? Anyway, feeling partly to blame, I shot over to his flat and rushed him down to A & E. God knows what they did to him behind that curtain, but those screams will haunt me till my dying day. On the upside though, the ward had never smelled so fresh and minty. I don't want to embarrass a mate, so I'll leave it there.

You're probably wondering about Mike, or maybe you forgot all about him, either way, I'll tell you what happened. His sentence was reduced and he finally got out. He turned his back on the pub game and emigrated to the Isle of Wight where he went down the Jeffrey Archer route and started writing a memoir of his time inside. I keep leaving messages for him but he ain't got back yet. Then again he always did struggle with electronics. I might hop on the ferry and pop over to surprise him. Both of us being authors now, we could swap notes and chat about narrative arcs and juxtapositions and what 'ave you.

As for the family, Rodney and Damien are doing fine. Cassandra's had another couple of promotions at the bank so she's happy. Joan is twelve (where does the time go?) and already the most adored child in Peckham. The poor girl can't fart without her mum and dad posting a bulletin to the world and his neighbour about it. Raquel's happy, she's started doing the whole amateur dramatics thing, it's not my cup of tea, but, you know, it scratches the itch.

Which leaves me.

I'll be honest, the transition to retired life ain't been easy. I tried to give the old amateur dramatics a go, you know, to spend more time with Raquel, but she wouldn't let me. Rodney suggested I make a bucket list, but, as I said to him, what's the point? I've only got two and one of them don't work. Then Boycie got me into that ancestry dot com, you know, that website that allows you to trace your family tree. He reckoned he'd traced his all the way back to Julius Caesar, but I couldn't even find Grandad. Then I got into a row with an administrator on the forum and they banned me. Last summer I was knocking about the flat, trying to find things to do (Raquel suggested hoovering, but I can't stand the noise), so Damien suggested we join the Peckham Rye Golf Club. I thought the fresh air would do me good, so we did. But whacking a ball around a field lost its appeal after about an hour, so I decided to liven things up a bit by challenging Damien to a buggy race.

Damien won, but only 'cos a kamikaze fox forced me to swerve into some bushes. I say bushes, it was actually the chairman and his missus nipping out of the nineteenth green for a crafty fag in the rough. I apologised confusely and offered to pay for the dent in the buggy *and* take them both out for a slap-up meal, but they wouldn't have it, and before I could shout 'fore' I was slapped with a lifetime ban. Unbelievable. I'd only been doing 10mph, max, and nobody was seriously injured. Political correctness gone mad, that's what it was. Anyway, it was a few days later that I borrowed a leaf from Rodney's book and took up a spot of painting. And it turned out I'm a dab hand. I set the easel up on the balcony (Raquel made me after the fumes in the front room caused her to have a funny turn) and in no time I was knocking out portraits, landscapes, seascapes, muriels, still lifes, there was no stopping me! I also tried a bit of that apstraction, you know, like what that Jackson Bullock geezer used to do, but it weren't for me. I've always preferred realism in my art. Last Christmas I wanted to do something really special for Rodney, so I knocked him up a portrait. You should have seen his face when he unwrapped it on Christmas morning. He thought I was getting him a watch. He was so surprised by it he said he felt nauseous, which, for an artist, is the highest form of praise you can get. Probably. I could just see it hanging in pride of place above the fireplace in his living room, the perfect conversation piece for when Cassandra had her work colleagues over for dinner. Sadly it wasn't to be, as the painting fell out the back of their car on the way home and got mangled by a council gritter. That's Rodney for you though, always had trouble closing boots properly. But as I said to him, it don't matter, I can always paint another one.

Still, when I started writing this book I made myself a little promise that this would be the full stop at the end of this part of my life. And I think it was just what the doctor ordered. I needed to pour it all out onto the page, seventy years of taking knocks and getting right back up again, making money, losing money, making money again, going from rags to riches, back to rags, back to rich(ish). It's the perfect way to wrap up a working life, and leaves me free to walk away from it all.

But Ronnie Nelson gave me a bell last week. He's out of the game these days too, but one of his old contacts had turned up with a load of those touchscreen tablet things. Blinding bit of kit they are, built in video cameras, Internet, games and all that. The only drawback is that they get a bit hot after you've been using them for a while (he mentioned blisters). The thing is, I just know I've still got a job lot of genuine vinyl gloves somewhere so, if you paired them up… I know, I know, but it ain't easy getting out of a game when you've been playing it as long as I have. It don't matter anyway, I've passed the mantle on to Damien now. This King is cream crackered. Long live the King. And d'you know what? I reckon this time next year he might just be a millionaire. After all, he who dares wins, eh?

The End